THE NEW AMERICAN WORKPLACE

THE NEW AMERICAN WORKPLACE

Transforming Work Systems

in the United States

ELEEN APPELBAUM AND ROSEMARY BATT

ILR Press

an imprint of

Cornell University Press

Ithaca and London

First published 1994 by ILR Press.
Second printing 1995 by ILR Press/Cornell University Press.

Text design by Kat Dalton.

Printed in the United States of America

Library of Congress Cataloging-in-Publication Data

Applebaum, Eileen, 1940–
The new American workplace: transforming work systems in the
United States / Eileen Applebaum and Rosemary Batt.
p.   cm.
Includes bibliographical references and index.
ISBN 0-87546-318-5 (acid-free-paper).—ISBN 0-87546-319-3 (pbk.)
1. Work—United States.   2. Work environment—United States.
3. Industrial organization—United States.   4. United States—
Manufactures.   I. Batt, Rosemary L.   II. Title.
HD8072.5.A66   1994
331.25′0973—dc20   93-31201

To Gene and Ron

The research for this book was conducted under the auspices of the Economic Policy Institute.

CONTENTS

ACKNOWLEDGMENTS

W e would like to thank the Sloan Foundation, which provided generous financial support for the research, writing, and publication of this book. We are grateful for the encouragement of Arthur Singer of the Sloan Foundation and to Jared Bernstein, Terrel Hale, and Stephanie Scott of the Economic Policy Institute for technical assistance. Peter Auer provided us with timely information. Michael Piore, Thomas Bailey, Paul Osterman, and David I. Levine gave us detailed comments on an earlier version of the manuscript, and Thomas Kochan and Kirsten Wever provided us with helpful suggestions and advice. We are, of course, responsible for any errors that remain.

PART I.

THE CHALLENGE

1.

INTRODUCTION

S harply rising competition in world and domestic markets during the past two decades has put increasing pressure on U.S. firms to undertake innovations in their work systems. Management practices in some countries whose firms compete successfully against American producers differ markedly from the post–World War II organization of production in the United States. Among the alternative approaches to organizing and managing work, several are being used with apparent success (Dertouzos, Lester, and Solow 1988): quality circles and continuous improvement in Japanese firms; worker participation in plant-level and strategic management decision making in German companies; autonomous teams of workers who are responsible for decision making in Swedish operations; and interfirm networks, which are responsive to changing market conditions, in Italian and German industrial districts.

There are many reasons business as usual no longer works, but two in particular are salient. First, firms in newly industrializing countries are competing in price-conscious markets for standardized goods by paying wages that are a fraction of those in the United States. Second, the increased capacity for diversity and customization inherent in microprocessor-based technologies has cut the cost advantages of mass production and increased competition in quality-conscious markets. U.S. companies must now compete on the basis of cost, quality, and customization.

Although U.S. manufacturing firms were the first to feel the economic pressure to change, the service sector has also started experimenting with organizational restructuring. Service providers are responding to attempts by manufacturing firms to reduce the costs of service inputs and thereby compete more effectively in export markets. Changes in technology and deregulation in such industries as telecommunications, airlines, trucking, and financial services have recently accelerated domestic competition among service providers. Further, the mobility of information technologies coupled with international deregulation has enhanced international competition in such areas as telecommunications, information, and financial services markets.

Similarly, the dramatic growth of the federal debt coupled with the fiscal crises of state and local governments has spurred broad interest in "reinventing government." Recognizing that privatization often fails to ensure efficiency, many public sector agencies are seeking to improve the quality and efficiency of public services by introducing workplace innovations as an alternative to privatization.

In work settings across the country, employees are also becoming increasingly interested in innovations to improve performance. Persistent high unemployment and declines in real wages are strong incentives for workers to want to participate in organizational change. Between 1979 and 1991, the entry-level real wage for high school graduates fell by 26.5 percent for men and 15.5 percent for women. And although entry-level real wages for college graduates increased modestly in the 1980s, those gains have been wiped out since 1987 (Mishel and Bernstein 1993). For many workers, the desire for more productive and fulfilling work is also a strong incentive to participate.

Finally, U.S. labor unions are motivated to participate in organizational change because of their need to develop new strategies for representing the interests of workers and preserving their own institutional integrity. As the emphasis has shifted from wage bargaining to job saving, unions find they need to be proactive and participate at an early stage in decisions that affect the viability of the employer.

For all of these reasons, a broad constituency for workplace change has emerged in the United States during the last two decades. Employers seek to provide better-quality goods and services at lower costs, employees to save jobs and recover income loss, unions to rebuild their institutional strength, and governments to rebuild faith in public institutions. The central question is whether these diverse groups can collaborate in the creation of new systems of work that meet the needs of the various parties involved.

The 1970s and 1980s were an important period of experimentation with new work systems. In this book we document numerous examples of experiments spanning these decades—innovations in management methods, work organization, human resource practices, and industrial relations.[1] Both the management literature and the popular press have noted the apparent success of these innovations in improving quality and reducing cost. In the 1990s, a new *vision* of what constitutes an effective production system appears to dominate management's views, if not yet its actions.

The new vision of "transformed" or "high-performance" work systems, developed during the past decade, incorporates an eclectic mix of principles drawn from past eras in the United States and from production models adopted in other countries. Some strategies, such as total quality management (TQM) via statistical control processes, originated in the United States in the 1920s at Bell Labs and became a central feature of war production in U.S. companies during World War II (Walton 1986: 8; Eidt 1992). Others, such as self-managed teams, emerged in Britain but spread to other countries as early as the 1950s (Trist 1981).

Self-conscious efforts to improve work systems—to reduce the alienation, increase the commitment, and make better use of the intelligence and skills of the work force—have occurred with some regularity since Elton Mayo's experiments at Western Electric's Hawthorne plant in the 1920s. Thomas Bailey (1992:9) observes that "since the 1930s, there have been at least two depressingly similar cycles of enthusiasm and disillusionment, of earnest rhetoric and minimal action, of high profile plans and evaporating practice." These occurred during the human relations movement in the 1930s and the social relations or sociotechnical systems movement, starting in the 1950s (see Bailey 1992 for a review).

It is reasonable, therefore, to inquire first whether the new practices undertaken by U.S. employers are transitory or long-term responses to the challenges of increased international competition and economic stagnation. Are the changes superficial, or do they represent structural changes that will permanently transform the internal organization of work, realign the relationship between labor and capital, and interact with national institutions external to the firm to alter the way in which capital markets, labor markets, and economic policies function? This question has several parts. First, is fundamental change required? Can the challenges that face the U.S. economy be met through reforms at the margins of mass production—reforms that achieve one-time improvements or that use programmable automation technologies to make mass production somewhat more flexible while leaving the production system essentially unchanged? Or are more profound changes in firms and institutions required?

Another distinct question is which changes matter: which organizational strategies result in continuous improvements in performance as opposed to one-time cost savings? Which favor the steady accumulation of incremental changes?

Finally, we need to consider what changes are actually occurring. Are U.S. firms simply modifying the mass-production system in order to preserve it? It was, after all, the basis of the unparalleled success of the United States between 1945 and 1970 as measured both by the competitiveness of U.S. firms in domestic and world markets and by the growth in income and improvements in the living standards of workers. Are firms transforming their work systems in fundamental ways? Or is it possible that intentions and outcomes are diverging: that firms intent on making modifications to preserve the old system may find themselves backing into a transformed production system, or that firms attempting to make fundamental changes may encounter obstacles to success?

We address the first two questions in parts I and II of this book, where we develop our conceptual framework. We consider the third question in parts III and IV, where we analyze evidence from surveys and case materials on organizational change in a wide variety of U.S. firms and industries and propose public policies that can help diffuse high-performance work systems more broadly.

Our central argument is that two features distinguish the current period of experimentation from the past. First, a broad and diverse constituency has emerged in support of workplace change, composed of employees, companies, unions, and government agencies at the local, state, and national levels. As a result, the extent of experimentation with one or another innovative practice is more widely dispersed than in earlier periods, affecting a substantial majority of large U.S. companies. The question is no longer whether change in work organization will occur, but what changes will occur and who among the various stakeholders will benefit most. The answer depends on who the critical actors are in the process of organizational change and what their relative balance of power is.

Second, a growing minority of companies have already made a commitment to transform their work systems into high-performance organizations. These examples provide cause for guarded optimism about the ability of

U.S. firms to compete successfully in world markets and the possibility that U.S. workers will be employed in jobs that provide opportunities to acquire skills and that pay middle-class wages. Best-practice American companies have distilled and selectively adopted techniques and features of production models developed abroad, but they have combined them with distinctly American practices—including applications of the principles of organizational psychology and American experiences with collective bargaining.

No *one best way* is emerging—there are various routes to improving performance, each of which has its strengths and weaknesses and each of which may have distinct implications for different stakeholders. In our review of the evidence, we have identified two distinct and coherent models of high-performance work systems in the United States—what we refer to as an American version of lean production and an American version of team production. There is considerable overlap between the two models, for they rely on similar applications of information technology and similar quality tools to improve performance. The models differ, however, in their mobilization of the work force and the relative weight they give to the strategic value of human resource and industrial relations practices. The lean production model, perhaps best characterized by the influential Baldrige criteria,[2] relies most significantly on managerial and technical expertise and centralized coordination and decision making. By contrast, the team-based model combines the principles of Swedish sociotechnical systems with those of quality engineering and locates the source of competitive advantage and continuous improvement in the front-line, or production-level, work force. It therefore more thoroughly decentralizes discretionary decision making. In addition, it incorporates structures for the representation of workers' interests at several levels of the organization: the work unit or shop floor; intermediate levels, such as the department or establishment level; and the strategic or corporate level. Although both lean and team production systems may exist in either union or nonunion settings, the fully developed American team production model, in which workers are represented on high-level corporate committees that plan and implement strategic goals, is more likely to be found in unionized firms.

The evidence suggests that both models yield dramatic improvements in firm performance on a variety of measures, including productivity, defect rates, customer satisfaction, market share, profitability, and employee relations. The outcomes *for firms* using the two models appear to be quite similar, but the outcomes *for employees* may be different. The case study evidence discussed in this book suggests that the American version of team production provides employees with greater discretion or autonomy, more employment security, and a greater guarantee of a share in any performance gains.

Our caution that one's optimism should be guarded comes from our review of survey and case evidence showing that only a few organizations have achieved major transformations and the accompanying performance improvements, and these have done so under unique circumstances. The most successful cases involve companies that experienced economic crises or substantial loss in market share but also had both a risk-taking leadership and sufficient resources to support extensive investments in training and work reorganization and sustain possible short-term profitability losses in order to achieve deeper and longer-term gains. This combination of circumstances is rare, and consequently few American companies have undertaken substantial changes. Furthermore, the U.S. institutional environment provides virtually no support for transforming work systems. If anything it is hostile to such attempts. In sum, the efforts by most companies to change end up being piecemeal and marginal, not necessarily intentionally.

We develop our argument as follows. In chapter 2, we argue that fundamental change is necessary because firms can no longer capture the cumulative gains in productivity they traditionally experienced under mass production by "moving down the learning curve." As a result, firms in advanced industrial economies must develop new sources of organizational learning to compete effectively in quality-conscious markets. The challenge for U.S. companies is to overcome the obstacles to organizational change that exist in the context of the American institutional framework. By institutional framework, we mean both the private and public institutions that reduce or socialize the costs of transformation. These include employers' associations, unions, research and development institutions, education and training institutions, institutions for disseminating information about best-practice techniques, as well as other public policies governing labor, product, financial, and technology markets.

Also in chapter 2, we discuss two strategies that companies developed in the 1970s to try to "reform" mass production or make it more flexible. The first one was the American human resource model (Kochan, Katz, and McKersie 1986), which is associated with firms such as IBM and Hewlett Packard. Drawing on principles of organizational behavior, these companies believed that improved performance rested on improved employee job satisfaction. They focused on changing corporate culture and management-employee communications and on providing incentives such as recognition and merit pay. They did not, however, fundamentally challenge the logic of mass production. Alternatively, other companies chose to try to make mass production more efficient via a low-cost route—by cutting labor costs, outsourcing work, and relying increasingly on high turnover and a contingent work force of part-time, temporary, and leased workers. U.S. companies continue to draw on these ideas and traditions, and we return to them in part III.

In part II, we diverge from the U.S. story to consider the alternative production systems that emerged in other countries in the 1970s and early 1980s. During the last decade or so, U.S. firms and unions have increasingly borrowed ideas and techniques from successful competitors abroad as well as from the American past. This extensive borrowing from a variety of sources has contributed to a rather confusing use of terms and concepts.

The importance of part II for our argument is twofold. First, chapter 3 summarizes the features of foreign work systems that have inspired innovations in U.S. companies. By discussing such concepts as self-managed teams, quality circles, training, worker participation, codetermination, works councils, and other practices in their original context, we hope to clarify their meaning. Our focus in describing these alternative systems is on their sources of continuous improvement and their basis for competitive advantage. Second, by describing and comparing these systems in the context of the institutions that support them, we hope to clarify why transferring isolated practices to the U.S. context is unlikely to produce the advantages companies often anticipate and why the United States needs to develop supportive public policies and institutions. Because this part is intended to serve these two purposes, it is schematic, designed to highlight the distinct sources of performance improvement and competitive advantage of each model. It does not provide a comprehensive analysis of each system, and we do not do justice to the extent of variation that exists within each country. For purposes of this discussion, we are considering best-practice models.

We examine four work sytems or models: the Swedish sociotechnical systems (STS) approach; Japanese lean production; flexible specialization, as exemplified by the Italian industrial districts; and German diversified quality production. From this review, we argue that no one successor to mass

production is emerging. Rather, different countries have developed alternative production models with different strengths and weaknesses.

For conceptual clarity and consistency, we define each system in terms of
four components: its management methods, work organization, human resource practices, and industrial relations. Under management methods, we
include market strategy, organizational structure, and overall process approaches, such as the use of total quality or just-in-time inventory systems.
Work organization refers to the design of shop-floor or front-line jobs and
the deployment of workers, including such practices as job rotation and
teamwork. Human resource practices include training, compensation, and
strategies to induce worker effort and commitment, such as employee involvement and employment security. Industrial relations refer to the power
relationships between managers and workers and the role of the union in
the production process. Table 4.1 summarizes each of the models (in addition to the American human resource model) along these four dimensions
and provides the basis for a comparative discussion of the strengths and
weaknesses of each model in chapter 4.

In part III, we assess the evidence of workplace innovation in U.S. organizations. Chapter 5 summarizes the evidence from a variety of surveys undertaken since 1980 in an effort to evaluate the extent of workplace change
over time. The evidence generally shows that the majority of large firms
have adopted some innovative practices and that the number of firms and
employees undertaking such practices has grown significantly since 1980,
although the innovations still affect only a minority of employees. This evidence supports our contention that there is broad and growing interest in
organizational change.

The surveys do not provide a very clear picture of how these workplace
changes fit together, however, so in chapter 6 we turn to the case materials
to consider the actual changes that are occurring. Our review of 185 consultants' reports and academic case studies of workplace change enable us
to examine the practices borrowed from the models outlined in part II. We
find that U.S. companies have largely implemented innovations on a piecemeal basis and that most experiments do not add up to a coherent alternative to mass production. In addition, the cases offer insights into how and
why firms make decisions to implement new policies, how these have
changed over time, and the dilemmas for firms, managers, front-line employees, and unions that slow the implementation and diffusion of such
practices. The latter theme is developed in part IV.

A separate chapter is devoted to organizational change in service activities because so much of the current literature focuses only on manufacturing or attempts to generalize from it to all workplaces. In fact, there are many similarities between manufacturing and service activities, and some of these similarities have occurred because goods producers recognized the need to adopt a customer-service orientation. Most of the observations and arguments developed in chapters 5 and 6, therefore, arise from data from service industries as well as manufacturing.

One of the challenges of this book has been to develop a language to discuss changes that affect all employees—a language that does not rely on images of the "shop floor" and "production," which also carry a male gender bias. Instead, we try to refer to the work site or unit, front-line rather than shop-floor workers, and work systems rather than production systems.

There are differences, however, between manufacturing and services, based in part on the nature of the work and the rapidity of change in service markets. Chapter 7 examines how service providers are applying general theories of organizational change to a variety of activities, including banking, insurance, telecommunications, sales and marketing, and public sector work.

Part IV discusses solutions, at the level of the firm or organization (chapter 8) and at the level of public policy (chapter 10). Though most firms have adopted changes on a piecemeal basis, some have accumulated a decade or more of experience and have developed a coherent set of practices from a "menu" of organizational tools designed to improve performance. In chapter 8, we develop our argument concerning the emergence of alternative lean and team-based work systems in the United States.

In chapter 9, we examine why so few U.S. organizations have developed new coherent work systems. We analyze the obstacles to diffusing such systems across firms and industries from the perspective of the various stakeholders involved—including employers, managers, front-line workers, and unions. Employers face the high costs of transformation and the potential for short-term losses in profitability. Moreover, companies that increase their retained earnings so as to invest in workers are likely to become targets for corporate takeovers. A market failure occurs in these cases. In addition, managers and front-line employees alike often resist change because most employers have been and continue to be unable to provide the employment security that constitutes a quid pro quo for employee commitment to improving firm competitiveness. Downsizing and restructuring also shift employees to new departments and locations, thereby destabilizing fragile experiments in collaborative work systems. Similarly, unions face dilemmas in entering partnerships with management, arising from their lack of institutional security, the lack of resources needed to participate in joint structures and business decision making, and anachronistic labor laws.

In chapter 10, we develop five categories of public policies to address these obstacles and support the shift to high performance. These are increasing job training, promoting employee and union participation, increasing the firm's commitment to its stakeholders, building interfirm collaboration and quality standards, and ruling out the low-wage path.

Earlier rounds of work restructuring in the 1930s and 1950s were largely ideological: work reform was viewed as a tactical tool for improving workers' attitudes and job satisfaction. The emphasis was on motivation, and workers rarely had the discretion or authority to alter the production process or to have a say in how the gains were to be distributed. The link between job satisfaction and productivity proved to be fuzzy at best. Workplace innovations were discretionary actions initiated by management to pacify workers and could be cut back in times of crisis to reduce costs.

Much of what is happening in U.S. firms today still fits that description. In the name of trendy theories—from total quality management and process reengineering to skill-based pay, quality improvement teams, and worker empowerment—many companies are trying to motivate employees while downsizing their work forces and driving down wages and benefits. Fortunately, this is not the whole story.

A small but growing number of American producers have recognized that organizational transformation is essential to achieving continuous improvements in cost and quality, especially now that production based on long runs of standardized products that compete on the basis of price is on its way to countries from Mexico to Malaysia. Organizational transformation is at the heart of the competitive strategy adopted by these U.S. companies.

Although there is accumulating evidence that this strategy for making U.S. companies competitive works, change has been slow and uneven. Good information about how to implement change is scarce, the up-front costs of training and upgrading workers' skills are sometimes prohibitive, the stock market penalizes companies that use earnings for these purposes, and managers are often reluctant to grant front-line workers autonomy or to share authority and decision-making responsibility with them. Likewise, employees are wary of changes that, in other contexts, are associated with eliminating jobs and speeding up work.

Finally, the institutional framework in the United States makes fundamental reorganization of the work system in American companies more difficult than it needs to be and provides perverse inducements to firms to compete on the basis of low wages rather than high skills. A more diffuse transformation of the American workplace in which there is increased autonomy, authority, capabilities, and employment security of front-line workers may require fundamental changes in labor and capital markets.

Despite the obstacles, some firms have succeeded in becoming high-performance workplaces. As this book documents, these new American workplaces have emerged in firms that have successfully combined the best of lean production and sociotechnical systems with distinctly American human resource and industrial relations practices. Managers in these companies report that quality ratings and productivity have soared. Equally important, these companies are the best hope American workers have for middle-class opportunities—good wages, employment security, and interesting work.

WHY CHANGE? THE BREAKDOWN OF
MASS PRODUCTION

Academic researchers have attributed the rapid growth of the industrialized economies in the period from (approximately) 1945 to 1970 to the cumulative gains in productivity and growth in output inherent in a socioeconomic system based on mass production. That system relied on a set of interrelated characteristics. dedicated technology; Taylorist work organization;[1] the sharing of performance gains between workers and firms; consumption growth based on the rise of real wages; and investment dynamics based on the accelerator principle, which relates expansion of capital stock to the rate of growth of consumption demand and to internal cash flow, whereby improvements in technology are embodied in later vintages of capital. The conditions for this "virtuous circle" of growth are captured in the Kaldor-Verdoorn law (Kaldor 1966, 1972; Michl 1985; Boyer and Petit 1989), which is summarized in the following two statements:

1. Mass production based on the application of Taylorist work organization yielded economies of scale and a reduction in unit labor costs, allowing productivity to increase when output increased and plants operated at close to full-capacity utilization. Thus, *strong demand growth favored growth in productivity.*

2. Unions in these mass-production industries bargained for real wage increases in line with average gains in productivity in the economy as a whole. At the same time, oligopolistic price behavior (mark-up pricing by firms largely insulated from international competition) meant that profits

grew in line with productivity while the relative price of standardized, mass-produced products fell. The result was that rising real wages and falling relative prices supported the growth of consumption. These increases in consumption demand (via the accelerator), coupled with the stable share of profit in output, fueled investment in newer vintages of capital (yielding higher labor productivity). This sharing of productivity gains between workers, firms, and consumers meant that *productivity growth favored demand growth.*

Many workers outside primary manufacturing firms and labor markets did not share fully in the benefits of growth. The application of Taylorist principles in service industries such as insurance, for example, allowed firms to cut costs and increase volume and profits, but low unionization rates meant that firms were not compelled to share these gains with front-line workers. Nevertheless, wages grew outside the unionized sector as well. This occurred for a number of reasons, including the increase in the number of college-educated workers and the expansion of managerial and professional jobs; the decision by nonunion employers to match union wage scales in order to make union membership less attractive to workers; and regular increases in the minimum wage, which effectively pegged the entry-level wage in the secondary labor market at half the average wage. A rising standard of living for workers and a growing middle class contributed to the growth in mass consumption that justified mass production and made it profitable. If private sources of demand growth faltered, monetary and fiscal policies to jump-start the domestic economy and stimulate demand growth would soon restore the virtuous circle of growth.

This framework for cumulative growth in productivity has now broken down almost completely. Academic researchers have advanced many explanations for the slowdown in productivity in the industrialized economies. Here we simply note two important contributing factors: (1) the ability of the newly industrialized countries (NICs) and even the less developed countries (LDCs), with their much lower wages, to compete successfully in price-conscious markets for standardized products has undermined both the rise in real wages that drove the consumption dynamic in the industrialized countries and the high-capacity utilization that supported investment; and (2) the increased capacity for customization and diversity inherent in microprocessor-based process technologies has reduced the cost advantages of mass production and increased competition in quality-conscious markets.

LEARNING CURVE PERSPECTIVE

Some of the insights into productivity improvement and manufacturing cost dynamics identified by economists have been explained in the operations management literature through the concept of the learning or experience curve (Andress 1954; Boston Consulting Group 1972; Abernathy and Wayne 1974; Hayes and Wheelwright 1984, chap. 8). Focusing on production at the firm level—on what might be termed the internal organizational logic of the mass-production system—operations researchers have conducted numerous studies of particular products. The earliest study, appropriately enough, analyzed the Ford Model T between 1908 and 1926 and found that the direct labor per unit (the learning curve) or value added per unit (the experience curve) was a decreasing function of the cumulative number of units produced.

In contrast to the economists' definition of improvements in labor productivity, in which a gain in productivity is defined as a reduction in labor hours per unit over a particular time period, the learning curve identifies the reduction in labor hours in relation to the cumulative units produced. In the learning curve framework, hours per unit decrease systematically with each doubling of the cumulative volume of production. Thus, the growth of productivity in the economists' framework depends on how quickly firms are able to increase the cumulative volume of production.

The productivity gains realized by moving down the learning curve derive from two sources. Static economies of scale come about as the result of spreading fixed costs over an ever larger volume of output. Scale economies can be obtained through "higher utilization of existing facilities, using higher volume facilities which have lower capital cost per unit of capacity and permit increased throughput without a proportional increase in manpower, and reducing changeover costs by dedicating specific production facilities to certain high-volume products" (Hayes and Wheelwright 1984: 250).

Dynamic gains in productivity and reductions in costs are related to "learning." The learning that contributes to a steady reduction in manufacturing costs as cumulative volume increases is of a very special type, however: "practice makes perfect." It refers to the accumulation of knowledge by the company as a result of repetitively making a larger volume of the same product in a dedicated production line or facility.

The elements of organizational learning as firms move down the learning curve can be grouped into six categories (Abernathy and Wayne 1974:117–18; Hayes and Wheelwright 1984:257). First, as products become more standardized and less diverse, models change less frequently. Second, specialization of process equipment and facilities increases, as does vertical integration and investment. Third, as management rationalizes the production process, throughput time improves, the division of labor increases, direct labor input falls, and the amount of direct supervision decreases. Fourth, firms further segment the production process to take advantage of economies of scale (e.g., engine plants, which offer economies of scale, are centralized as volume increases). Fifth, material input costs come under control either through vertical integration or by exercising increased control over suppliers. Sixth, and finally, rationalization of the production process leads to greater specialization in labor skills and shifts the demand for skill from the flexibility of the craftsperson to the dexterity of the operative.

Thus, what firms learn in moving down the learning curve is the most efficient method for mass producing a standardized item. Deviating from this approach, either by increasing product variety or by improving product quality, *brings an end to the cumulative gains in productivity and increases costs.*

As William J. Abernathy and Kenneth Wayne point out (1974:109), the practical limits to the learning curve come from the fact that firms "cannot expect to receive the benefits of cost reduction . . . and at the same time expect to accomplish rapid rates of product innovation and improvement in product performance." A further implication is that "product innovation is the enemy of cost efficiency, and vice versa." The limit to cost reduction and productivity improvement is "determined by the market's demand for product change, the rate of technological innovation in the industry, and competitors' ability to use product performance as the basis for competing" (118).

According to Abernathy and Wayne (1974:118), the risks associated with a strategy of achieving competitive advantage by moving down the learning curve come from the fact that the "conditions stimulating innovation are different from those favoring efficient, high-volume, established operations." The risks are greatest for firms that are most successful in reducing price and capturing market share. The successful company must capture a larger and larger market share to continue to double cumulative output. As the market expands, it becomes easier for competitors to segment it and, by employing "more flexible production process structures," to win over the top end of the market with a product that offers superior performance or customized features. The company on the learning curve becomes increasingly vulnerable to competition on the basis of quality and diversity. At the same time, the changes it has undergone in perfecting the production of a standardized product at ever-lower costs reduce its ability to respond to competition on this basis.

ATTEMPTS TO REFORM MASS PRODUCTION

Whether viewed from the perspective of economics or that of operations management, the argument for organizational transformation in U.S. firms is now quite widely accepted. Cumulative gains in productivity and reductions in cost *on the basis of high-volume mass production of standardized products* is no longer a sufficient basis of competitive advantage for most firms in the advanced industrialized countries. This technology is now widely available to firms in the NICs and in the LDCs, including overseas branches of multinational firms, whereas wages in these countries are a fraction of their levels in the industrialized economies. Increasingly, firms in low-wage countries have captured market share in the production of standardized products that compete on the basis of price. Further investments in mass-production facilities by companies in the United States and the other industrialized countries add to worldwide excess capacity and undermine, rather than increase, the firms' profits.

Although this argument has gained acceptance during the last decade, it was not so clear or broadly accepted in the 1970s and early 1980s as U.S. companies wrestled with declining market shares and a serious profit squeeze. Two strategies for reforming mass production emerged. One was the American human resource (HR) model, often considered the basis for enlightened management. The other involved making mass production more efficient through cost-cutting and squeezing labor. In many ways, these alternatives continue to inform managerial thinking, and for that reason we describe them in some detail below.

American Human Resource Model

The American human resource model evolved in U.S. firms in the 1950s and 1960s in response to industrial psychology theories of motivation, behavioral science theories of job enlargement and enrichment, and organizational behavior theories of better communication and employee involvement. Psychological theories of individual behavior in the workplace developed in the 1960s suggested that employee job satisfaction, if maintained over time, should translate into improved job performance. Behavioral science theories developed in the same time period stated that introducing greater variety, challenge, and opportunities for developing new skills into the design of jobs increases workers' interest in and motivation to perform their jobs (Herzberg 1968). Sociotechnical systems theory also developed at this time and influenced some firms that adopted the American HR model to experiment with teams.

The American HR model originally emerged as an alternative to workplaces governed by collective bargaining rules. Unlike the industrial relations (IR) model, the HR model paid attention to the psychological aspects of the relationship between managers and employees. As one authoritative account of the HR model that contrasts it with the IR model points out, "While the traditional union system stresses contractual rules and uniformity, the new nonunion model stresses individual motivation and differences in abilities and work performance" (Kochan, Katz, and McKersie 1986: 93). The HR model does not fundamentally challenge the logic of mass production, however, although it does give management more flexibility to deploy workers as needed.

Similarly, the contribution of organizational behavior theory to the HR model is the so-called unitary view of the firm. This view emphasizes the commonality of goals between the organization and the individual and treats conflict as an aberration caused by a lack of managerial competence, which should be overcome by improving human relations. The unitary view is consistent both with the theory that organizations are cooperative and with the theory that organizations are systems of hierarchical control. The first perspective emphasizes a paternalistic approach by management to employees: executives make key decisions and educate employees to gain agreement; conflict represents a failure of leadership; corporations should have familial relations. The second perspective emphasizes that the organization controls the efforts of individuals to achieve common goals. By contrast, the IR view holds that the interests of management and workers are inherently different and that organizational control translates into the manipulation of employee interests.

Whatever the underlying rationale, according to the unitary view, unions have no legitimate role and exist to the extent that management is incompetent. Unions introduce distortions into the price mechanism and create inefficiencies.

Advocates of the American HR model argue that it offers several advantages over collectively bargained human resource policies in organized plants and that these advantages translate into superior performance. The sources of competitive advantage come from lower labor costs, from the savings realized by reducing the resources devoted to conflict management, and from the greater flexibility available to management in the deployment of workers. The attention to individual motivation in the American HR model, however, is its distinguishing characteristic and assumed source of competitive advantage. By designing compensation schemes that recognize individual differences and reward employees accordingly and by designing jobs to provide task variety, challenge, and the opportunity to learn new skills, firms expect to reap the rewards of greater worker motivation and improved job performance.

Empirical research has not confirmed these advantages. Although fewer grievances and a lower rate of absenteeism are associated with the American HR model (Kochan, Katz, and McKersie 1986), studies do not shed light on whether this is due to fewer conflicts or to the suppression of worker voice. Work rules that have developed over time presumably become outmoded and need to be changed, which is more difficult if the employment relationship is longstanding. This explains why major changes in work organization or human resource practices—including American HR model practices—are frequently initiated in new or "greenfield" plants. Researchers have not yet determined, however, whether productivity is higher in new sites because the technology is newer or because the management approach is based on the American HR model.

The biggest difficulty with the American HR model is that empirical research has failed to find strong relationships between work design and satisfaction or between job satisfaction and subsequent productivity (for a review of these studies, see Bailey 1992). As Thomas Kochan, Harry Katz, and Robert McKersie note, "There is little empirical support to demonstrate that improving individual attitudes and/or motivation produces lasting economic benefits to organizations" (1986:87). They attribute this paradox to the tendency for new workplace practices to occur within an "experimental" work unit and to the failure of improved attitudes and motivation to be diffused across the organization. Bailey (1992) suggests another explanation. He argues that for the greater motivation of workers to translate into improved performance for the organization, workers must have *the necessary skills* and *participatory organizational structures* to apply their creativity, imagination, and intimate knowledge of the work process effectively. Reviewing the econometric evidence on the effect of participation on performance, David I. Levine and Laura D'Andrea Tyson (1990) found that the size and strength of the effect is contingent on the form and content of the participation. Guaranteed individual rights for workers, an independent role for worker voice, and substantive rather than consultative participatory arrangements (all of which are less common in nonunion than in union settings) and profit sharing (which is more common in nonunion settings) were found to be important in influencing performance.

Thus, the performance effects of the HR model are modest at best and have not provided a basis for a significant or accelerated improvement in firm performance. Adopting this model is not a substitute for the participatory organizational transformation that high-performance workplaces require. Indeed, the case materials reviewed in chapter 6 suggest that the lasting contribution of the HR model may be the experiments with teamwork that a small number of firms adopted in the 1960s and 1970s based on the sociotechnical systems approach. Additionally, to the extent that these firms experimented with new workplace practices during those two decades, they were more willing to experiment along more fundamental lines in the 1980s.

Flexible Mass Production

Alternatively, many U.S. firms have responded to the pressures for change resulting from the increased competition by cutting their costs, reducing their permanent full-time work forces, and making greater use of microprocessor-based information and process technologies. This has occurred both in small and medium-sized companies engaged in such operations as metal stamping, the injection of molded plastic parts, and high-volume machining and in large firms producing at high volumes for mass-consumption markets. This approach, sometimes labeled flexible mass production, retains hierarchical management structures, old-style power relations between supervisors and workers, the separation between conception and execution, the relatively high use of low-skilled workers, and the routinization of work. It also includes, however, the use of less dedicated, more flexible technology (programmable machine tools, management information systems for scheduling the delivery of raw materials); cross-training of skilled workers in the context of a general deskilling of front-line or production workers; and subcontracting, outsourcing, and contingent employment contracts to achieve flexibility in responding to market turbulence and variations in demand. In the last two decades, many U.S. firms have sought to increase their flexibility through increased reliance on part-time, temporary, and other contingent workers (Appelbaum 1989, 1992; Golden and Appelbaum 1992; Tilly 1992; Carre 1992).

Examples also exist of firms that have "backed into" team production as a cost-containment measure in the context of downsizing, thereby requiring workers to perform administrative tasks (scheduling holidays, tracking punctuality and attendance, communicating announcements from management) in order to reduce the number of supervisors or to form "teams" whose main purpose seems to be to motivate the workers to work harder (rather than smarter) by setting up competition among the teams for rewards.

What these measures have in common is that they do not change the fundamental nature of the production system or threaten the basic organization or power structure of the firms. They are reforms at the margins of the mass-production system. The new sources of competitive advantage that these reforms produce appear to be a somewhat better use of technology and of the narrow layer of skilled workers and a cheapening of front-line workers through the use of lower-paid part-time, temporary, or leased workers who generally receive neither company benefits nor training.

This strategy does not appear to lead to success at increasing the competitiveness of domestic enterprises in the long run, particularly if competitors in other advanced industrial economies have adopted more fundamental changes in the use of technology and the organization and management of work. A flexible production system, whether in mass or low-volume industry segments, still competes primarily on the basis of price. Yet the lower limits to which wages can be pushed in industrialized countries are considerably higher than the wages paid in other parts of the world. In addition, gains in productivity achieved by shrinking the company and closing the least efficient facilities may give the firm an immediate boost, but they do not set the stage for continuous improvement and further gains in performance. Nor do they improve the firm's ability to respond quickly to changes in market demand or to compete in quality-conscious markets.

Several recent studies of the productivity effects of downsizing, for example, have shown that this strategy is usually *not* successful. The American Management Association's (AMA) 1992 survey of nearly nine hundred member companies (which in total employ 25 percent of the American work force) found that although an attempt to realize gains in productivity is the most commonly cited reason for downsizing, the results are usually disappointing: "Companies that make cuts tend to do it again, and the results are quite likely to be negative—lower profits and declining worker productivity" (AMA 1992:1). A similar result emerged from the Wyatt Company's 1991 study of restructuring in one thousand large firms during the preceding five years (Wyatt Data Services 1991). Firms in this study overwhelmingly cited a desire to reduce expenses, increase profits, and increase productivity as the reasons for restructuring, but surprisingly few accomplished these goals: "Less than half the companies achieved their expense reduction goals; less than one-third increased profitability; and less than one in four [increased productivity or achieved] other restructuring goals" (6–7). Both the AMA and Wyatt studies attribute the lack of success of downsizing or restructuring in raising productivity and increasing profits to declines in employee morale and motivation.

IMPETUS FOR CHANGE

The limited gains arising from adopting the American HR model, on the one hand, or flexible mass production, on the other, have led a growing number of firms to experiment with other forms of organizational change during the last decade. U.S. companies and organizations have little guidance, however, as they seek to transform themselves in response to the new competitive realities. As we discuss in more detail in chapter 9, neither technology nor the institutional framework dictates the nature of the change to higher-performing production systems. As a result, we observe different paths to change and a diversity of outcomes (see also Turner and Auer 1992). If anything, the legal institutions governing capital and labor markets in the United States provide incentives to firms and managers to pursue short-term goals and investments with a quick payoff—exactly the opposite of what is required for high-performance work systems. U.S. labor law further inhibits organizational transformation by making wages and working conditions the only subjects of mandatory bargaining and treating business decisions as management prerogatives.

As a result, many U.S. organizations seeking guidance as they undertake

major changes in work organization and decision making have looked to
the approaches developed by their competitors in different national contexts. We examine these approaches in the next two chapters. Though they
vary dramatically in content and in the relationship between firm and state-
level policies, a common thread is that firms gain a strategic advantage from
training front-line workers and utilizing their full participation and that of
their representatives at various levels of the organization.

Though still fragmentary, empirical research suggests that more participatory structures may translate into improved performance. Researchers
have conducted dozens of studies on the impact of participation or work
redesign on productivity. Many, though not all, have found that work redesign has positive effects on productivity (reviewed in Kopelman 1985).
Levine and Tyson reviewed empirical studies of the relationship between
participation and productivity and concluded that the nature of the participation determines the strength of the effect on productivity and that substantive arrangements have greater effects than those that are merely consultative (Levine and Tyson 1990).[2] The conclusion that emerges from
numerous empirical studies of work reorganization and participation is that
piecemeal adoption of one or another participatory practice is likely to
have, at best, a small effect on firm performance (see Bailey 1992 for a
wide-ranging review of these studies). The challenge for American firms,
therefore, is (1) to identify and master the new sources of competitive advantage that yield a significant acceleration in the improvement of performance; and (2) to replace mass production based on the logic of the learning
curve with a coherent production system that draws on new sources of continuous improvement and that uses new forms of organizational learning to
mobilize the knowledge and problem-solving abilities of employees.

For employees, the challenge is twofold: to recognize that education and
training must become an ongoing prerequisite for participation in the labor
market; and to accept the need to participate more fully in problem solving
and decision making at work as a strategy for improving employment and
income security.

For unions, the challenge is to define a new role for themselves in representing the interests of workers in production systems in which workers'
skills and participation in decision making are the basis of competitive advantage. Unions must expand their role from one of safeguarding workers'
rights to participating in the critical business decisions that ultimately determine the working conditions, employment security, and economic welfare

of workers. Thus, unions have a new role to play in assuring that firms achieve performance gains; at the same time, they must continue to represent the interests of their members and ensure that workers share in those gains.

Finally, for the country as a whole, the challenge is to replace an institutional framework that successfully supported the mass-production system—and continues to favor short-term strategies for keeping that system viable—with a new framework that favors the adoption of one or several transformed systems.

PART II.

THE ALTERNATIVES

3.

ALTERNATIVE MODELS OF PRODUCTION

Although the obstacles to change are great, so are the imperatives for change: the breakdown of the mass-production model in the advanced industrial economies means that firms cannot remain competitive. To some extent, U.S. firms are changing in order to "catch up" with changes already adopted by foreign competitors. In this respect, they have one of the same advantages as the late adopters: they can learn from the experiences of other countries. In this chapter, we discuss these alternatives and the possibilities they offer U.S. firms.

U.S. firms are often exhorted to draw lessons from abroad so as to become more flexible and efficient, but the advice usually focuses on isolated practices and fails to note that these practices are elements of distinct and coherent production systems, each with its own internal logic and dependent on broader institutions for success. This chapter describes the main alternatives to mass production adopted by other industrialized economies: the Swedish sociotechnical systems, Japanese lean production, Italian flexible specialization, and German diversified quality production. The focus is on each system's sources of continuous improvement and the basis of its competitive advantage.

SWEDISH SOCIOTECHNICAL SYSTEMS

The sociotechnical systems approach grew out of the work of the Tavistock Institute in Britain in the 1950s and was elaborated on thereafter by Scandinavian researchers. Swedish attempts at work reorganization in the early 1970s focused on the use of autonomous work groups to humanize work. The initiative to undertake these efforts occurred in response to demands from workers for more humane and democratic workplaces. Managers adopted this approach in order to solve recruitment and retention problems in a tight labor market and to increase job satisfaction and reduce turnover and absenteeism. Swedish unions objected, however, to the lack of employee and union participation in management decision making and management reluctance to accept work-group autonomy, thereby slowing these early attempts at reform. Not until the mid-1980s, following passage of a codetermination law and negotiation of a framework for implementing that law, did a new period of work reorganization in Sweden begin.[1]

This time, the change was driven as much by efficiency concerns as by the desire to humanize work. Swedish firms now seek a more decentralized and flexible organization of production in order to be more responsive to the new competitive conditions that have affected even the low-volume, niche markets in which firms such as Volvo and Saab compete.

The teams to which Swedish workers belong are formal, functional work groups rather than quality circles or groups formed on an ad hoc basis to address particular problems. To achieve flexibility, work groups have far-reaching, high degrees of competence, and team members engage in a variety of tasks, although individuals may have different levels of qualification and each team member is not expected to develop competence in every group task. Wage premiums provide incentives for workers to engage in continuous training, and firm-sponsored training for new employees has been increased from a few days to several weeks. Swedish firms also use gainsharing to reward workers, so that groups of two or three teams receive some of their pay based on group performance. The state regulates layoffs and plant closings, and tight labor markets and full-employment policies, rather than no-layoff clauses in union contracts, successfully provided employment security until the recession of the early 1990s.

The degree of autonomy of Swedish work groups varies considerably. At Volvo's Uddevalla plant, completely autonomous teams assembled whole cars. At the Stockholm post office, decentralization and delegation of responsibility have transformed work groups into quality improvement teams. Teams that regulate themselves internally and that are responsible for pacing, coordination, sequencing, and quality control have been the linchpin of the efforts of Swedish organizations to improve performance.

Production teams are responsible not only for direct production tasks but also for routine maintenance and housekeeping and administrative tasks such as distributing work assignments among group members and scheduling vacation time. Like quality control circles, Swedish production teams are responsible for process improvement and problem solving. Autonomous teams in auto plants, which assemble entire vehicles and operate without an assembly line, are not suited to high-volume production but, rather, to low-volume, high-quality production for niche or luxury markets.

In comparison with Taylorist work organization and assembly-line techniques, use of the teams is expected to increase the efficiency of Swedish firms in several ways. The increased variety and customization of products mean that some versions take longer to assemble than others. In team production, these models can be assembled alternately with standard models and do not require a separate assembly line. Integrating preventive maintenance and repair functions into the work group reduces downtime and allows for quick intervention in the case of machine failure. Integrating quality control into the work groups improves quality and reduces the amount of rework. Further, short absences can be covered by the group without finding a substitute. Group work is also thought to be more attractive to new labor force entrants than assembly-line production and to enable manufacturing firms to overcome severe difficulties in hiring qualified young workers in a tight labor market. Finally, managers of large corporations look to work groups to facilitate organizational decentralization and the flattening of hierarchies. At the Uddevalla plant, for example, the span of control was 50:1 or better, comparable to General Motors' Saturn plant, usually considered the best in the world among auto assembly plants. There were two layers of managers—a central plant manager and a manager for each of six production shops. In all, there were sixteen managers in a plant with nine hundred to one thousand workers (Hancke 1993).

The main advantages of the Swedish system are its ability to achieve high levels of design quality, and Swedish firms did perform well in luxury, niche markets during the 1980s. Sweden did not distinguish itself in its ability to achieve high levels of productivity during this decade and it is generally believed that relatively low productivity is the price that was paid for good jobs. But the productivity performance of the Uddevalla plant—the most advanced sociotechnical plant in Sweden—exceeded the best-performing luxury car assembly plants in North America and equaled or slightly exceeded the average for luxury car assembly plants in Japan and Europe.

Moreover, gains in productivity in the Uddevalla plant, which only started operation in 1989, were remarkably rapid, averaging about 50 percent a year. It took about 120 hours to assemble a car in 1990, 50 hours in 1991, and 32 hours in 1992, and the plant had not yet achieved peak efficiency. This was supposed to happen in 1993, when assembly time was expected to drop to 25 hours, equal to the most productive luxury plant in the world. (The material on Swedish work organization is from Auer and Riegler 1990; Turner and Auer 1992; Naschold 1992; Levine and Tyson 1990; Cole 1989.)

In response to the challenge of increased competition in quality-conscious markets, Swedish companies began to implement the total quality techniques propounded by W. Edwards Deming and others and to adapt them to the Swedish team production system. The success of this effort at Uddevalla may never be known. As a result of the decline in total car sales from more than 400,000 at the end of the 1980s to 300,000 in 1992 (correspondence from Peter Auer, Dec. 22, 1992) and in sales of large cars from 200,000 to 130,000, Volvo management announced that it would close the Uddevalla plant in the spring of 1993 and the Kalmar plant in mid-1994. The company has attributed the closing of these two plants, which were the most advanced in their use of new production methods and multiskilled teams, entirely to market factors and not to deficiencies in the new techniques (Brown-Humes 1992). Thus, Uddevalla appears to have been closed for reasons unrelated to work organization. Nevertheless, some observers have seen in this the end of the Swedish model. It is worthwhile, therefore, to review this case.

According to Peter Auer (correspondence, Dec. 22, 1992), the main reason behind the closings appears to be overcapacity. With a total capacity of 70,000 to 80,000 cars per year, the plants that are to be closed are smaller than the main Torslanda/Göteborg plant, which produces 200,000 cars a year. Nor is there any reason to close the Belgian plant, which has a capacity of about 130,000 cars, is the most productive of all Volvo plants, and is located in the EEC's domestic market. In addition, as Auer points out, given the vested interests in the older plants, it may have been easier to close the new, or greenfield, plant at Uddevalla, whose work force is less than 10 percent that of the more traditional plant at Torslanda. The union prefers to keep open the older plants and those that employ more workers; and the strength of both the union and the local management is greater at the larger plants. Traditionalists in the Torslanda local of the union joined forces with the traditionalists in management in favoring the closing of Uddevalla. Further, the Uddevalla and Kalmar plants are both simply assembly plants and thus lack the body shop, paint department, and other production departments with technical equipment and large financial commitments that make it more difficult for management to discontinue operations (see also Berggren 1993). Finally, what Auer calls a "conservative reflex" may be at work—in times of crisis, management prefers to stick with what is old and familiar, rather than with what is new. This tendency is reinforced, following the Renault-Volvo alliance in the mid-1980s, by Renault's management, which is ideologically opposed to the Uddevalla concept and has committed itself to Japanese lean production in its plants (Hancke 1993).

The decision to close the Kalmar plant may be delayed or rescinded if the economies of the United States and United Kingdom improve in 1993 and exports pick up. According to Auer, however, Uddevalla appears to be condemned to find a place "in 'the cemetery of failed models' without ever having had the chance to demonstrate that human-centered work organization might strike the balance between productivity and welfare at work" (correspondence, Dec. 22, 1992).

JAPANESE LEAN PRODUCTION

The starting point for the new approach to manufacturing management in Japan is the recognition that impediments to the smooth flow of materials—whether as a result of long changeover times, bottlenecks, machine downtime, or quality defects—cause delays and imbalances in production against which firms must hold inventory buffers or work in progress. In lean production, engineers use a variety of techniques to reduce these impediments, including techniques to facilitate changeovers, rationalize plant layout, train workers in quality control practices, improve equipment maintenance, simplify product design for easier manufacturability, and involve workers in problem-solving activities to simplify the production process or reduce defect rates. Applying these techniques leads to continuous incremental improvements in the production process as small gains in conformance quality (i.e., the degree to which the product conforms to the design for that product) and productivity accumulate over time. Production and innovation are linked in a lean production system, and engineers work closely with production workers.

Japanese engineers developed lean production by applying quality management concepts developed by Deming (1984), J. M. Juran (Juran and Gyrna 1988), and Kaoru Ishikawa (1985). Deming's approach to management was as "scientific" and as "engineered" as Frederick Taylor's but used statistical methods and relied on educated workers to improve quality and productivity simultaneously, rather than focusing only on productivity improvements derived from the detailed division of labor and the separation of conception and execution. The Japanese adaptation of Deming's approach was to teach statistical process control and problem-solving techniques to hourly workers and to use quality control circles as an important management tool to improve quality. Quality control circles (QC circles) are small groups of hourly workers, led by a foreman, that meet voluntarily to solve job-related quality problems (e.g., defects, scrap, rework, downtime). The use of QC circles leads to reduced costs, improved productivity, and the improvement of morale, motivation, and self-development among workers. QC circles are a way of recognizing that the information and knowledge that hourly workers have can contribute to process improvement and are an important form of employee involvement, but they are not work teams nor are the QC circles empowered to make managerial decisions as are self-managed teams. They are parallel structures that co-exist with the "normal bureaucratic organization and hierarchical authority, but leave these arrangements untouched" (Hill 1991:549).

Insofar as lean production reduces impediments to the production flow, buffers of inventories to smooth this flow are also reduced. Reduced inventory buffers expose problem areas and focus the efforts of the QC circles on these areas. In addition, direct cost savings accrue from these reductions in inventories as well as from the reductions in rework as defect rates are reduced. The minimization of buffers via just-in-time inventory policies means that Japanese work systems are fragile as well as lean—there is the potential for problems to disrupt production throughout the plant.

To overcome this fragility, Japanese firms have instituted human resource practices designed to develop the commitment and capability of workers to respond quickly and flexibly to problems as they arise. Pay policies, training practices, and employment security in large manufacturing enterprises provide the support and incentives that attract a multiskilled work force with a high level of commitment to the firm and the ability to solve problems.

The organization of work on a team basis also supports the firm's goals. Teams assume responsibility for a variety of everyday functions—maintenance, safety, and quality control—and most observers report that workers rotate through the various jobs performed by the team, increasing their skills and their understanding of the production process. (Clair Brown, Michael Reich, David Stern, and Lloyd Ulman [1993] report, however, that, contrary to their expectations, job rotation was not common within a shift or week in the Japanese plants they visited.)

Japanese teams are not autonomous, however. Foremen still play an important role in performing administrative tasks, supervising workers, and applying standardized work procedures, although these procedures are usually developed by the workers themselves in conjunction with engineers and are subject to subsequent improvements by quality circles. And, although there are fewer levels of hierarchy than in traditional mass production, hierarchical relations are important in Japanese firms. Japanese workers have significant involvement in decision making, but upper-level managers generally make the decisions. Japanese lean production increases the participation of front-line workers, but not their power (Marsh 1992).

Static economies of scale continue to be important in the high-flow Japanese auto assembly plants, and at least some of the advantages of the Japanese production system are attributable to capacity utilization rates in excess of 90 percent. It is with respect to the dynamic gains in productivity and reductions in cost due to organizational learning, however, that the advantages of lean production over mass production manifest themselves. Lean production replaces the "learning" associated with the routinization of repetitive tasks performed on dedicated machinery producing a standardized product with a new type of learning that results in continuous improvements in performance. In lean production, management employs a number of techniques to turn organizational learning from a passive into an active process, in which learning depends on conscious efforts to improve the efficiency of the production process. These include the use of statistical process control to identify nonconformance to standards; just-in-time inventory systems to ensure, among other goals, that problems surface quickly; rapid feedback about quality to workers; cycle-time analysis to reduce the total time a process takes and to increase throughput or reduce changeover times; and process simplification to examine each step in the production process in order to remove those steps that do not add value to the final output and to eliminate any wasted time or motion in those that remain. The resulting improvements take place continuously, but in small steps.

In the mass-production system, high-volume producers faced the dilemma that, beyond some level of defects, efforts to improve conformance quality raise costs. Improvements in quality halt the movement down the learning curve and thereby increase costs. As markets for even relatively standardized products have become more quality conscious, companies that continue to rely on a mass-production system and use traditional means to improve quality—increasing the number of inspections, relying on improved sensors to detect deviations—have had difficulty remaining competitive. Lean production directly addresses this dilemma. In contrast to mass production, in which an improvement in conformance quality beyond some point entails increased cost, lean production leads to simultaneous improvements in quality and reductions in cost. (The material on lean production is from Cole 1980, 1989; MacDuffie and Krafcik 1990; MacDuffie 1991; Zipkin 1991.)

Compared with mass production, lean production supports an increase in variety because smaller lot sizes of various models can be produced on a single assembly line, thereby sharply reducing the time required for change-overs and eliminating the need for large buffers of work in process for each model. Nevertheless, the reductions in labor hours and increases in inventory turns associated with lean production require a marketing strategy that "emphasizes low cost and high quality, while putting less weight on variety and availability" (Zipkin 1991:50). In Japanese auto assembly plants, for example, average employee hours to build a vehicle fell from 279 per vehicle in 1969 to 132 in 1988 (compared with an unchanged 186 in U.S. plants during the same time period). Almost all of the reduction in labor input in the Japanese plants occurred between 1969 and 1981, however. In the 1980s, as Japanese producers increased variety, extended the range of vehicles, and entered luxury markets, the labor hours stabilized. Build hours fell only from 138 in 1981 to 132 in 1988 (Williams et al. 1992). Thus, there appear to be limits to the lean production system. In addition to second-order questions about whether the just-in-time (JIT) system shifts the burden to suppliers or increases transportation costs by requiring the frequent delivery of parts in small quantities (*Japan Labor Bulletin* 1991:4), there is the more fundamental question Paul H. Zipkin raises about the general applicability of the lean production model (1991:50):

> JIT, at least in its pure form, assumes or implies a specific marketing strategy. This strategy emphasizes low cost and high quality, while putting less weight on variety and availability. This is precisely the strategy used so successfully by

the Japanese automakers in the 1970s and early 1980s. It has also worked well in other consumer durables markets. . . . It is clear that this particular marketing strategy will not work in all markets. . . . Even the big Japanese exporters, as they aim more towards luxury markets, are adopting alternative [production] strategies.

ITALIAN FLEXIBLE SPECIALIZATION

The impetus for flexible specialization came from the increased economic fluctuations and increased variability in demand that began in the 1970s. An increasingly turbulent market environment required greater flexibility and adaptability than was typically achieved by the combination of large, centralized, hierarchical corporations, dedicated equipment, and an unskilled or semiskilled work force performing repetitive and fragmented tasks. Many firms responded to increased uncertainty in demand by trying to make mass production more flexible through the use of more flexible technology, combined with the undermining of labor unions, greater use of contingent employment contracts, and the relaxation of labor standards governing minimum wages and protections against arbitrary dismissal. But, as discussed above, this approach has several weaknesses. As in mass production, increasing the variety of products increases costs, and flexible mass production does not improve the ability of firms to deliver customized products to quality-conscious customers.

In contrast to flexible mass production, flexible specialization emphasizes (1) small-scale production of a large variety of goods, a strategy whose viability has been increased in recent decades by the introduction of information technologies that improve the cost competitiveness of small-batch production; (2) strong networks of small producers that achieve efficiency through specialization, and achieve flexibility through collaboration; (3) representation of worker interests through strong unions that bargain over wage norms at the national level and seek cooperative solutions to work organization and the flexible deployment of labor at the local level; and (4) municipal governments that provide collective goods and services, thereby reducing costs and encouraging cooperation. Firms in these networks cooperate with each other on the basis of trust, sharing information as necessary regarding technology and product markets while still competing with each other for customers. As a result, firms in industrial districts or interfirm networks can achieve economies of scope—an enhanced ability to respond to market-driven changes in product characteristics and marketing requirements. Their competitive advantage lies in their ability to produce and deliver quickly to market high-quality products with a wide range of characteristics or innovative designs.

Academic researchers originally applied the term *flexible specialization* to the fluid but stable networks of specialized enterprises typical of industrial districts. Interest in such networks grew as a result of the success of the industrial districts of Italy and Germany in the 1970s and 1980s in enabling small firms to compete successfully in international markets for traditional manufactured goods. Today, firm size is no longer viewed as a defining characteristic. Large companies may also be viewed as flexibly specialized if they have adopted a decentralized corporate structure, have developed stable, nonpredatory relationships with subcontractors, and are agile in forming and reforming strategic alliances with other firms in their network to develop innovative products in response to market turbulence and variable demand. Whether composed of large or small enterprises, networks achieve competitiveness by employing a highly skilled labor force and establishing fluid collaborative relationships so that they can respond quickly to fluctuations in the composition of demand for products and to demands by customers for variety and customized options, not by reducing direct labor input or deliberately driving down cost. The emphasis is on innovation in product design.

Technology has generally been an important facilitator in the development of the networks. Flexible manufacturing networks have been described as a "whole class of network-based adaptations taking advantage of the possibilities opened by the new technological environment" (Holley and Wilkens, n.d.:4). Moreover, technology supplements agglomeration economies as an alternative to corporate structure. Economies of scale remain important in training, research and development, international marketing, and follow-up and support services for customers. In industrial districts such as those in Italy and Germany, local governments provide many of these services, but it is unclear whether this entirely offsets the advantages of higher-volume producers.

In small firms, the adoption of flexible specialization usually dictates the use of work groups; and the dependence of firm owners on the skills of their workers suggests a fair degree of autonomy. Learning takes place as temporary links among firms are dissolved and new links are forged to produce new products. Finally, the mobility of workers among firms contributes to their accumulation of a variety of skills. Interenterprise institutions that facilitate the reemployment of workers contribute to both employment security and the preservation of these skills.

An important problem of mass production that flexible specialization overcomes is that of excess capacity. Collaborative relationships among firms enable individual firms to respond to increases in demand for output without adding equipment that might soon be redundant. Networks are also conducive to product innovation and to extensive customization, and networks generally serve niche markets. The main source of competitive advantage in flexible specialization is that smaller firms engaged in joint ventures and other collaborative relationships may require shorter development times for new products than large bureaucratically organized firms. This confers an advantage on networks in markets where the competition is based less on price and more on quality and variety—for example, fashion-conscious apparel markets, machine tools, and electronics.

The performance gains from flexible specialization are realized mainly under conditions of turbulence in product markets and rapid variations in demand. The greater economic stability of the 1980s compared with the 1970s raised questions about the presumed advantages of flexible specialization. Rapid innovation in new product markets is also a strength of flexible specialization. Variations in demand may decrease, however, as product markets mature. A U.S. computer company recently announced a shift from a flexible production strategy geared to variable demand for customized products to a high-volume strategy geared to competition on the basis of price (*Washington Post*, Nov. 6, 1992). Again, this suggests that the gains of flexible specialization, while important in some industrial sectors, may not be applicable in general. (The material on flexible specialization is from Piore and Sabel 1984; Piore 1990; Trigilia 1990; Nagel and Dove 1991; Sengenberger and Pyke 1992; Sabel 1992.)

GERMAN DIVERSIFIED QUALITY PRODUCTION

In diversified quality production, high-volume producers combine the craft skills of a highly trained labor force with the technological options for diversifying products made possible by microelectronics in order to segment mass markets and gain market share in the high end of the market, where superior performance and customized design are able to command higher prices. Since workers' wages are paid out of value added, this high–value added strategy allows firms in a high-wage economy to remain competitive.

The success of the German auto industry in the 1970s and 1980s in domestic and foreign markets, despite strong unions and rising real wages, is attributed to the decision by German producers to pursue quality-conscious markets in which competition was based on the quality of design, the customization of product options, and the differentiation of products, rather than on price. In autos and other industries, organizational flexibility in meeting customer requirements is achieved through the development and flexible deployment of a skilled labor force. The broad skills gained in apprenticeship programs completed by most German front-line workers enables managers to assign workers to various tasks, as needed, and workers to master new skills more easily. The ability of German companies to adapt to changing demand requirements is increased by works councils and other joint labor-management institutions that facilitate "negotiated adjustment" to new technology and changing market conditions. Microelectronic technology improves the cost effectiveness of producing at volumes that, though high, are below the scale of mass production, for markets in which design and variety are important. Microelectronic technology also enhances the ability of large firms to make both design and production processes more flexible.

An important characteristic of firms that are diversified quality producers is their reliance on redundant capacities. These capacities, which the firm calls on only occasionally, include investments in broad worker skills, flexible work roles and organizational units, duplication and overlap in organ ization al structures as functional boundaries are blurred, decentralized competence, and mutual trust and loyalty. Redundant capacities enable firms to reduce their reliance on buffers of stocks of materials and work in process but still to avoid bottlenecks by averting crises before they occur. In this sense, an investment in redundant capacities replaces an investment in buffers (Streeck 1991).

Diversified quality production can emerge as small, specialized producers increase their volume without sacrificing quality and customization or, alternatively, as mass producers move up market by upgrading their quality and design and increasing their variety. Having high volumes allows firms to take advantage of economies of scale, which continue to be important, whereas the use of labor skills and technology to achieve product variation allows them to realize the new economies of scope. Diversified quality production is a strategy that in the 1970s and 1980s allow highly unionized German manufacturing firms to remain competitive in world markets while paying high wages.

Microelectronic technology has facilitated the adoption of diversified quality production systems in two ways. First, it has altered economies of scale so that manufacturers are able to reach the break-even point with smaller volumes than in the past—though "smaller" should not be confused with "small-scale" production. German automobile and durable goods producers remain large enough to realize economies of scale. Second, it makes it possible for automated equipment to be far less dedicated to given products, and hence reduces the rigidity of production equipment.

It is not flexible technology that accounts for the flexibility of diversified quality production systems, however. Arndt Sorge and Wolfgang Streeck attribute organizational flexibility to the fact that workers' skills are broad enough to allow extensive internal retraining and redeployment. In these circumstances workers "can afford to accept a flexible allocation of work tasks. This, in turn, makes it possible for management to make concessions on employment security, and for workers to define their interests in terms of imposing external instead of internal rigidities on management" (Sorge and Streeck 1987:25). A flexible internal labor market also favors some form of shared responsibility by unions and management—that is, codetermination—in managing the implementation of technology and the retraining and redeployment of workers. Thus we have the paradox of the German system—the coincidence of extensive legal regulation and external rigidities with a high degree of flexibility on the shop floor. Kirsten Wever and Christopher S. Allen (1992) argue that what often look like rigidities in German firms turn out to be powerful sources of flexibility.

The advantages of diversified quality production over mass production can be seen by recalling the limits to the learning curve described above. As the mass-production system expands, opportunities increase for companies that are differently organized and managed to segment and capture the high end of the market. In this end of the market, customers are willing to pay for quality, meaning in this case design quality—features, styling, superior performance, and other attributes that enhance fitness for use (Fine 1991). The organizational strengths and workers' skills present in a diversified quality production system are well suited to capturing market share in such high-end market segments. Capitalizing on these features has been a deliberate market strategy in German manufacturing. Sorge and Streeck (1987:10) argue that

> the economic and employment success of the German car industry in the 1970s and 1980s, when compared to the car industries of other countries, was strongly related to the pursuit of more qualitatively differentiated and quality-conscious markets. Success in such markets was conditional on the production of craft skills and their utilization for organizational flexibility. For this, German firms with the comparatively high skill level of their workforces were particularly well placed. Moreover and at the same time, they were constrained by their works councils to increase their vocational training efforts in response to youth unemployment; improve the quality of working life through task enlargement and task enrichment; avoid redundancies through retraining and redeployment in a co-determined internal labour market, etc.

Given these pressures, German firms probably had little choice but to enter high-end markets. Two other sources of flexibility in the diversified quality production system are the stable interfirm networks of large producers and their subcontractors and the nature of the investment by German companies (Soskice 1991, cited in Wever and Allen 1992).

The measured gains in productivity in German companies during the 1970s and 1980s were predicated on the direct effects of automation in reducing labor inputs and on product strategies aimed at increasing value added through quality design. Further incremental decreases in labor inputs via quality management techniques for continuous improvement are virtually unused in Germany (Ernst and Young and American Quality Foundation 1991), although this is changing as German firms are challenged by the entry of Japanese manufacturers into high-end markets. Some German auto plants find themselves in the 1990s at a serious cost disadvantage relative to Ford (Europe) and, potentially, to Japanese producers. Joint activities between labor representatives and management under codetermination do not involve the work force directly in participation in process improvement and quality assurance. The initiative for change in Germany is coming from the unions, which are taking a strong proactive role in advocating the decentralization of decision-making structures and the reorganization of work using self-directed teams to improve cost competitiveness, even in quality-conscious markets. (The material on diversified quality production is from Sorge and Streeck 1987; Turner 1991; Thelen 1991; Streeck 1991.)

4.

A COMPARISON OF THE MODELS

One of our goals in analyzing the American HR model in chapter 2 and the four alternatives to mass production that evolved in other countries in chapter 3 was to develop an appreciation of the internal logic of each system in order to enhance understanding of the source of competitive advantage in each case. This we have now done. A second goal, however, was to examine where the elements of these systems, which currently are being borrowed piecemeal and recombined into what U.S. firms hope will be a new high-performance model, fit into the original system from which they come and what these elements may contribute to new American models of production. We conclude our discussion of these alternatives in this chapter, therefore, by schematically laying out the elements of the five models in tabular form (see table 4.1).

We have arranged the elements in the models along four dimensions, which we found useful as we tried to interpret and analyze the case materials on U.S. firms. They are management methods, work organization, human resource practices, and industrial relations. One of the contributions of this approach is that it makes clear the very different functions and purposes of a variety of employee-involvement practices that, until now, have usually been grouped together. We have considered quality circles and problem-solving teams methods for quality management. They are parallel structures oriented toward the goals of improving quality and reducing costs, but they leave unchanged within the firm *both* the work organization and hierarchical power relations. Autonomous or semi-autonomous teams

43

Table 4.1 *Alternatives to the Mass-Production Model of Work Organization and Industrial Relations*

	AMERICAN HR MODEL (traditional)	SOCIOTECHNICAL SYSTEMS (Swedish)
Management methods		
Structure	Centralized Hierarchical	Centralized Flatter, but still hierarchical
Conformance quality		
Process improvement	No	Informal, by work teams
Process standardized	Yes, industrial engineers	No
Employee involvement in quality improvement?	No	Informal, by work teams
Design for mfg.	No	No
Design quality	Standardized products Cosmetic variations	Luxury
Market segment	Mass consumption	Niche
Volume	High	Low
Work organization		
Work reform driven by	Management	Workers
Shop-floor Teams Autonomous	No	Self-directed
Pace	No	Yes
Methods	No	Yes
Problem diagnosis	No	Yes
Jobs rotate/enlarge	Some	Yes
Cycle time per job	Short	Long
Quality assurance	No	By workers
Routine maintenance	No	By workers
Administrative tasks	Individual consultation	By workers
Skills		
Vertical tasks	No	Yes
Integration of horizontal tasks	Some	Yes
Depth of knowledge	Limited	Team characteristic, not individual

LEAN PRODUCTION (Japanese)	FLEXIBLE SPECIALIZATION (Italian)	DIVERSIFIED QUALITY PRODUCTION (German)
Centralized Flat	Decentralized Collaborative Small-firm network	Centralized Hierarchical
TQM (SPC statistical process control, process simplification, cycle-time reduction), JIT, QCs	No	No
Yes, by workers in QCs	No	Yes, negotiated with works councils
Yes, QCs	No	No
Concurrent engineering Cross-functional teams	No	No
Style, options	Nonstandard goods in old manufacturing industries Rapid product innovation	Superior performance Style, options
Mass consumption Very high	Niche Low	High end High
Management	Small-firms	Union
Supervised	Small work groups	No
No No, standardized No Yes Short By workers By workers No	Yes Yes No Yes Long By workers By workers By owner	No, but negotiated No, but negotiated No No Short By highly skilled No No
No, except for process improvement in QCs		No
Yes, substantial	High	Some, but within a particular craft
Trade off depth for greater breadth	Craft know-how widespread, but many unskilled workers	In-depth operational and analytical craft know-how

Table 4.1   (*continued*)

	AMERICAN HR MODEL (traditional)	SOCIOTECHNICAL SYSTEMS (Swedish)
Flexibility in deploying workers	Some	High
Human resource practices		
Training		
Job skills	Yes	Public education/training
Cross-training	Some	High, though not every worker can do every job
Group decision making/ problem solving	No	Yes
Leadership	No	Yes
Quality/statistical processes	No	No
Team building	No	Yes
Compensation		
All salaried	No	No
Seniority-based	No	Somewhat
Job-based	Yes	Mainly
Knowledge/skill-based	Rarely	Somewhat
Individual incentives		
Merit raises	Yes	No
Group incentives		
Profit sharing	No	No
Gainsharing	No	Yes
Stock ownership	Some	No
Employment security	Merit-based Avoid layoffs	Layoffs, plant closings regulated; government-subsidized in-plant training Full-employment policy
Trust	Medium	Maximal
Industrial relations		
Unions	Nonexistent Management anti-union	Strong, national unions represent 90 percent of blue- and eighty percent of white-collar workers, employers' association Centralized wage bargaining
Labor relations	Unitary, based on belief there is no conflict of interest between management and workers	Adversarial

LEAN PRODUCTION (Japanese)	FLEXIBLE SPECIALIZATION (Italian)	DIVERSIFIED QUALITY PRODUCTION (German)
High	Distinguishing feature of system; voluntary mobility among firms	Negotiated adjustment
Yes, on the job	Yes, formal and on the job	Yes, apprenticeship
High, every worker can do every job in work group	Relatively high, acquired through movement among firms	Yes, but only within particular craft
Yes, through QCs	No	No
For foremen through QCs	No	No
Yes	No	No
Yes	No	No
No	No	No
Mainly	No	Somewhat
Somewhat	Yes	Mainly
Somewhat	No	No
No	No	No
Bonus (= 2 months pay)	No	No
No	Local wages tied to territorial productivity	No
No	No	No
Lifetime employment	Voluntary mobility of workers among firms	Layoffs, plant closings regulated
No layoffs		
Reassignment of workers		Early retirement
Early retirement		
Maximal	Maximal, but in system not employer	Maximal
Enterprise unions	High rate of unionization (higher than in factories) National bargaining sets minimum wage; local wages and labor standards negotiated at local level	Strong, industry unions
Cooperative	Cooperative, localist, territorial	Adversarial

Table 4.1   (*continued*)

	AMERICAN HR MODEL *(traditional)*	SOCIOTECHNICAL SYSTEMS *(Swedish)*
Guaranteed individual rights for employees	No	Yes
Workers' and managers' status	Sharp status distinctions	Egalitarian; status differences muted (education, pay, perks)
Power sharing	Communication and consultation through employee suggestion surveys	Codetermination Joint labor-management committees
Source of performance improvement	Worker satisfaction; motivation assumed to increase labor productivity	Autonomous teams mobilize worker knowledge and initiative; teams do own inspection, maintenance, supervision—reduces defects, indirect labor Employee participation on shop floor increases motivation to contribute knowledge, effort Employee participation in decisions re training, technology improves firm decision making
Source of competitive advantage	Price	Design quality Customization

LEAN PRODUCTION (Japanese)	FLEXIBLE SPECIALIZATION (Italian)	DIVERSIFIED QUALITY PRODUCTION (German)
Yes	Yes	Yes
Egalitarian; status differences muted (education, pay, perks)	High rates of firm formation, dissolution: mobility between worker, owner roles	Status differences
Joint consultation committees Ringi system for communication/consensus building	Works councils Unions typically negotiate right of information on firm's activities and investments	Works councils Codetermination
Total quality management, including QCs, directs worker knowledge toward continuous improvement in production processes, conformance quality; steady accumulation of small gains in quality and productivity Employee involvement in QCs, teamwork increases motivation to contribute knowledge, effort High-capacity utilization and economies of scale	Respond quickly to customer requirements for nonstandard products Agglomeration economies Specialization by industrial sector	Highly developed craft skills of workers facilitate negotiated deployment of new technology, production of high–value added products Employee participation in decisions via works councils improves firm decisions re technology, training, and so on Scale economies
Price Conformance quality	Innovation Nonstandard products	Design quality Superior performance Customization

constitute a new form of work organization. If the teams are autonomous or have some independent decision-making authority, they also affect the power relationships on the shop floor. Finally, works councils and joint labor-management teams are part of the industrial relations system and alter the power relations at the level of the overall establishment—affecting the design and implementation of training programs, for example. These very different approaches to employee participation are supported by different human resource practices. Works councils, for example, do not require compensation schemes that include group incentives or training in leadership or team-building skills, as shop-floor teams do, but do require workers with in-depth job skills as well as assurances of employment security and income maintenance in order to facilitate negotiated adjustments. In general, we can distinguish among employee participation schemes based on whether the participation takes place in parallel structures or affects the work organization or power relations between employees and managers; the level at which the participation takes place—shop-floor, establishment, or strategic firm decisions (implementation of new technology, investment plans, marketing strategies); and whether it is consultative (as most QCs are) or substantive.

RELATIVE STRENGTHS OF THE ALTERNATIVE PRODUCTION SYSTEMS

Each of the alternative production systems has a distinct competitive advantage over mass production under current competitive conditions in world markets. Sociotechnical systems use production teams to combine high levels of design quality with steady improvements in conformance quality in goods produced for luxury or other specialized niche markets. Lean production enables high-volume producers to achieve simultaneous improvements in conformance quality and simplifications in production processes, so as to deliver higher quality and variety at lower prices in mass-consumption markets. Flexible specialization confers on small or decentralized firms the ability to innovate rapidly and to respond quickly to customer demand for product variation. Diversified quality production enables producers to supply high-performance, customized products to the high end of the market that do not compete on the basis of price.

The various production systems also have strengths and weaknesses vis-à-vis each other. The advantages of flexible specialization are most evident during periods of market turbulence or in niche markets and industry segments where rapid innovation is important. These advantages may be much less apparent in less turbulent times or in markets where variety is less important. Thus, the Italian and German machine tool industries have been successful in gaining world market share by relying on networks of small producers that take advantage of economies of scope to respond to customer requirements with customized machines produced in relatively low volumes. In contrast, lean production has resulted in some increase in variety but has had a major impact on conformance quality and labor productivity and, ultimately, on costs. Lean production has limitations as firms begin to move into markets in which design and customization are the main bases of competitiveness. The Japanese machine tool industry has succeeded by using economies of scale and continuous improvement to produce high volumes of relatively standardized machines in which defects and prices are low.

Diversified quality production excels when the goal is to produce customized goods that meet exacting performance standards at relatively high volumes for high-quality markets. In contrast to the lean production model, however, achieving high levels of design quality and conformance quality is costly under the German model. This is because there are no opportunities for organizational learning or the sharing of skills through worker participation in production teams and quality circles at the shop-floor level, even though labor is represented on committees that review work methods, negotiate adjustments to change, and participate in strategic decisions.

Finally, the new Swedish sociotechnical systems approach uses production teams to produce luxury goods. This provides opportunities for organizational learning and for the sharing of skills, but production costs have remained relatively high and production is not very flexible. Recent evidence suggests this is because of the relative newness of the model rather than the insufficient attention given to the TQM techniques, which have proven so advantageous in the lean production model (Hancke 1993; Berggren 1993).

All of the alternative production systems provide enhanced opportunities for worker participation, though the precise form this participation takes varies widely. The Japanese and Swedish models provide new opportunities for organizational learning through the involvement of small groups of shop-floor workers in production decisions and problem-solving activities—via parallel structures and consultative participation in firms operating under Japanese lean production and substantive participation through autonomous shop-floor teams in firms based on Swedish sociotechnical systems approach. The small firms of the Italian industrial districts are characterized by informal participation by workers in decisions regarding production methods and work flow. In German diversified quality production, participation occurs through elected representatives who take part in plant-level and strategic decisions.

Only the Japanese have systematically applied scientific total quality management techniques to production, and, as a result, they have benefited most in the market from having achieved simultaneous improvements in conformance quality and productivity. In Japanese lean production, workers participate in TQM through parallel structures such as problem-solving teams and quality control circles. Firms in other countries are now adapting total quality management techniques to their own production systems. Whether this can be done in the context of diversified quality production, which lacks both production teams and problem-solving teams, or whether the Swedes can combine these techniques with sociotechnical teams has not yet been resolved. Clearly, James P. Womack, Daniel T. Jones, and Daniel Roos (1990) anticipate that transformed production systems will have to converge to the Japanese lean production model to enjoy the advantages of TQM techniques, a view that is disputed by Lowell Turner and Peter Auer (1992). This raises the following issue. Are unrelenting process simplification and cycle-time reduction, which occur in lean production but are inconsistent with self-directed teams, essential elements of TQM and continuous improvement? Or, does moving these functions into production teams, rather than carrying them out in QC circles, open up new means of achieving organizational learning and continuous improvement in conformance quality, design quality, and efficiency.

LESSONS FROM ABROAD

Each of the main foreign alternatives—sociotechnical systems, lean production, flexible specialization, and diversified quality production—provides a means of addressing one or another of the weaknesses of the mass-production model. It is understandable, therefore, that U.S. firms have engaged in piecemeal borrowing of management methods, work organization, and human resource practices from abroad. In trying to understand the competitive strengths of these models, it may be a mistake, however, to take the company as the unit of analysis. As Wever and Allen point out, "In the global economy, competition isn't just between companies; it is between entire socioeconomic systems. These systems set the all-important social context that shapes the actions and the fortunes of individual companies" (1992: 37). The success of lean production in Japan in raising labor productivity in manufacturing, for example, depends in part on the high levels of capacity utilization in Japanese companies, and so far this has been achieved through a combination of trade and industrial policies not available in the United States. The success of the German and Swedish systems depends in part on worker representation on joint committees that negotiate change, an option largely unavailable in the United States, and on the development of a highly skilled labor force through apprenticeships in one case and public education and training in the other. The small firms in the industrial districts of Italy and Germany may produce short runs of highly differentiated products, but they are able to avail themselves of economies of scale in production, research, and marketing abroad through interfirm networks and service facilities estblished by municipal governments and business associations that provide these services in common to member firms.

The socioeconomic system also provides a more general framework in which to assess labor market adjustments to improvements in labor productivity. To the extent that gains in productivity lead to reductions in price and an extension of the market for goods and services, the labor-displacing effects of improvements in productivity do not necessarily materialize. Under the conditions of intensified competition facing industrialized economies today, however, no country has been able to rely entirely on growth of the market to provide good private sector jobs in transformed enterprises for all workers. The adjustment mechanisms vary. In Japan, they include lifetime employment for men in the core industries and a commitment to full employment achieved, in part, through an early retirement age and an extensive secondary labor market that employs young women, older men, and ethnic minorities to absorb the slack. The German "social market economy" relies on fewer hours of work per week and fewer weeks of work per year, a low female labor force participation rate, and generous social insurance schemes; Sweden depends on extensive retraining programs and other active labor market policies, part-time employment by women, and a large public sector that provides a large number of jobs.

In the United States, resistance to change on the part of workers and managers is fueled by the fear that jobs lost in high-paying industries will be replaced by jobs with wages that are too low to support a middle-class standard of living. The concern, which broader policies must address, is that although the United States may develop a corps of high-performance firms able to compete in world markets and to provide some workers with high-paying jobs, many firms will fail to make the change. These firms will continue to compete on the basis of low wages, dragging down U.S. living standards.

The preceding analysis has examined the strengths and limitations of the main alternatives to flexible mass production by focusing on their distinctive features as production systems, ignoring, for purposes of exposition, that, since the mid-1980s, there has been some borrowing across these systems. The analysis points up the internal logic or coherence of each of these production systems and the sources of comparative advantage of each compared with mass production. It should be evident from this discussion that simply improving the quality of the elements of production—providing increased training for workers, adopting more flexible computerized equipment—will not be sufficient to improve the competitiveness of U.S. companies or to raise the rate of productivity growth. Instead, these alternative systems point to the need to combine these elements of production in new ways so as to achieve continuous improvements in efficiency and quality and improve the responsiveness to changes in market demand. If the view that the new international competition is between economic systems—and not just between individual firms—is correct, then America's success rests on several interrelated developments: U.S. firms will have to develop new, coherent production systems that promote more employee participation and a greater role for worker voice in the American context. Unions will have to develop new capabilities that enable them to play a partnership role in managing the company while continuing to represent workers' interests. New institutions that provide representation and a voice in decision making for workers not represented by unions will have to be developed. And the American socioeconomic system will have to evolve and develop new institutions that support joint collaborations among labor, management, and representatives of the public interest on issues ranging from the training of workers and the diffusion of process technologies to employment security and the accounting rules governing the measurement of quality and firms' investments in human capital. We return to these issues in greater detail in chapters 9 and 10, after we examine recent experiments with workplace change and the efforts U.S. firms have made to develop high-performance work systems.

PART III.

ALTERNATIVE STRATEGIES IN THE UNITED STATES

THE EXTENT OF THE CHANGE: EVIDENCE

FROM SURVEYS, 1982–93

As is evident from our analysis of alternative production models, each model has a particular internal logic but all share some common features: the use of flexible technologies; some form of worker participation or teamwork; substantial worker education and training; the flexible deployment of workers; a commitment to employment security; a narrowing of the gap between workers and managers, as evidenced by education levels and worker involvement in managerial decision making; quality consciousness; and an active role for unions and representative employee committees in achieving performance gains in the production process.

These features have led theorists to develop the idea of a transformed or high-performance work system that represents a composite of several models that are all alternatives to mass production (Kochan, Katz, and McKersie 1986; Osterman 1988). The advantage of this approach is that it allows policy makers, trade unions, and firms to target a limited set of critical features that move the production process beyond mass production—the need for more diversified and quality products, flexible technology, broader jobs, flatter or smaller organizations, teamwork as opposed to individual work, training, employment security, performance-linked compensation.

From the perspective of practitioners implementing change, however, the range of possibilities is much greater, particularly given the lack of institutional supports or constraints in the U.S. context. A "transformed work system" has many meanings and may take very different forms, depending on whether companies borrow ideas from Japan, Sweden, Germany, Italy, or such nonunion American firms as IBM and Hewlett Packard. The meaning of such concepts as teams, skills and training, and the role of management vary substantially in the models we have reviewed and depend on the social institutions in which they are embedded. We should therefore expect variation not only in the way these concepts are applied in the U.S. context but also in the performance that results.

METHODOLOGY AND SOURCES OF DATA

Despite the widespread interest in work reorganization, our understanding of what has taken place in American workplaces still is poor. Evidence of an increase in the adoption of new practices comes from a few national-level surveys (New York Stock Exchange 1982; U.S. General Accounting Office [GAO] 1987; Lawler, Mohrman, and Ledford 1992; Osterman 1992).[1] Other evidence comes from nonrepresentative surveys conducted by membership organizations, consulting firms, and other private industry sources (Development Dimensions International [DDI] 1990; Grant Thornton 1991; Towers Perrin 1992; and Arthur D. Little 1992). Case studies provide further insights, but vary widely in quality, from academic studies to accounts in the popular press and unpublished consultants' reports. Overwhelmingly, the information in both the surveys and case studies comes from managers or consultants responsible for implementing changes, not from the employees experiencing them. The picture that emerges is necessarily one-sided and probably overstates the degree of innovation and change actually taking place. Managers rarely report failed efforts, and consultants rarely examine them in their reports, but undoubtedly there have been many.

Part III draws on each of these sources to reach conclusions about the extent and patterns of workplace change during the last two decades. In chapter 5 we summarize the major findings from survey research. Then, in chapter 6, we focus on a meta-analysis of case studies drawn from published and unpublished sources.

The surveys and case materials are complementary and answer different questions. The survey evidence provides point-in-time snapshots of the extent of adoption of a menu of particular practices, such as the use of teams, pay for performance or profit sharing, and training. It also identifies pat-

terns of adoption by industry, firm size, and other organizational characteristics, as well as changes in dominant practices over time.[2]

Case studies of firms or industries, by contrast, shed light on a series of
questions that surveys do not handle well. Are firms applying a set of practices that have an internal logic, along the lines suggested by the theoretical
models outlined in the previous section? Or are firms taking a more eclectic
or piecemeal approach? Do firms implement changes as pilot projects, as
time-limited experiments, or with the idea that they will be permanent?
What process of adoption and diffusion of practices occurs within and
across firms? Which changes are initiated from the bottom up, and which
from the top down? Is technological change a driver or an essential part of
organizational change? Is downsizing an inevitable part of the shift to
higher-performance work systems? If so, what happens to the displaced
workers? And, finally, what effects do workplace innovations have on performance? Although the cases cannot provide definitive or representative
answers, they suggest alternative theories and interpretations of change and
raise fruitful questions for further research. Our review of the cases is sug-
gestive in this vein.[3]

The academic and econometric studies of workplace change have tended
to focus on best-practice cases in an effort to understand the limits of organizational change and to measure the impact of workplace innovations
on performance. A handful of carefully done studies have documented the
quality and gains in productivity resulting from organizational change
(Katz, Kochan, and Gobeille 1983; Kochan, Katz, and Mower 1984; Katz
1985; Wall et al. 1986; Cooke 1990; Keefe and Katz 1990; Cohen and
Ledford 1991; Cutcher-Gershenfeld 1991; MacDuffie 1991; see Miller and
Monge 1986, Levine and Tyson 1990, and Bailey 1992 for a review of such
studies). The popular and business press also reports routinely on best-practice firms—Saturn, Xerox, NUMMI, Motorola, Corning, IBM, Hewlett
Packard, Federal Express. The frequent invocation of these examples, however, gives a distorted impression of what is actually taking place in the
United States, creating the sense that those firms undertaking changes are
adopting a fairly coherent and complete set of practices that are transforming their entire organizations.

Our review of 185 cases of workplace change gives us a new perspective
on the great diversity in adoption and implementation of practices and have
led us to conclude that the practices are considerably more piecemeal and
eclectic than the best cases suggest. In addition to the academic literature,

we draw on a number of published and unpublished sources: the American Productivity and Quality Center in Houston, Texas; the U.S. Department of Labor Bureau of Labor-Management Cooperation; the U.S. Department of Commerce, National Institute of Standards and Technology (NIST), administrator of the Malcolm Baldrige Awards; the Work in America Institute; the American Society of Quality Control (ASQC); and various trade journals and periodicals, such as *Industry Week, National Productivity Review,* and *Quality Progress.*

OVERVIEW OF THE SURVEY EVIDENCE

This section draws on a number of surveys carried out between 1982 and 1992 to summarize what is known about how widespread organizational changes are and how deeply they have penetrated the companies in which they have been undertaken. (Appendix A summarizes the findings of these surveys.)

The general conclusion that emerges from the surveys is that the proportion of firms with at least one employee-involvement practice somewhere in the company is large and growing and that a significant number of firms have begun to make more extensive use of these practices. Among the large Fortune 1000 companies, for example, the proportion of firms with at least one employee-involvement practice increased from about 70 percent in 1987 to about 85 percent in 1990 (Lawler, Ledford, and Mohrman 1989, 1992). By 1990, 66 percent of large firms reported having at least one quality circle, and 47 percent reported having at least one self directed team. Thirty-two percent of these large firms reported that more than 20 percent of their workers participated in quality circles, whereas 10 percent of these large firms reported this level of participation in self-directed teams. In a 1992 survey of a random sample of all U.S. establishments, drawn from the Dun and Bradstreet establishment file, 41 percent of firms reported having quality circles and 55 percent reported having teams (Osterman 1993). Twenty-seven percent of firms in this survey reported that 50 percent or more of their workers in core occupations participated in quality circles. These findings appear broadly consistent with those of the earlier studies. Paul Osterman found, however, that 41 percent of the firms in his sample reported that 50 percent or more of the workers in core occupations participated in self-directed teams, a much higher figure than in other studies.

It is more difficult to estimate the proportion of firms making significant changes in how work is organized and managed and the proportion of workers affected by these practices. The 1987 GAO survey, in which 476 Fortune 1000 firms participated, reported that one-quarter of U.S. firms had made significant changes in the organization and management of work and in the human resource practices that support these developments. But even in these firms, the changes usually affected no more than 20 percent of employees (Lawler, Ledford, and Mohrman 1989). This has led some observers to conclude that between 5 and 10 percent of the work force in large firms is affected by major organizational changes.

Osterman (1993:14) estimates that 37 percent of his sample can reasonably be characterized as transformed—a designation he applies to firms in which 50 percent or more of the workers are involved in any two of the following practices: self-directed teams, job rotation, quality circles, or total quality management. His results suggest that smaller firms (50–499 employees) are more likely to be transformed than larger ones, a finding at odds with most other studies. His results appear to suggest that between 20 and 25 percent of workers are affected by these changes, a much higher proportion than previously thought.

Results reported in nonrepresentative surveys by consulting firms or membership organizations have typically reported that a much smaller percentage of the work force is affected by high-performance work systems. The Towers Perrin survey, in which 287 firms participated, reported an increase in the use of at least one self-managed team, from 12 percent of firms in March 1990 to 36 percent in October 1991. The DDI survey of executives found that 27 percent of the 862 manufacturing firms that participated in their 1990 study used self-directed (self-managed) teams. Based on a review of practices at member firms of the American Society for Training and Development (ASTD), Anthony Carnevale estimates that "only 13 percent of American employers have organized employees in high performance work systems that deemphasize hierarchy and emphasize collaboration and teamwork. Those systems encompass a meager 2 percent of U.S. workers" (1992:53).

Firms also report widespread use of quality practices, although this appears to refer at times to the use of only one practice somewhere in the firm. Major companywide changes—total quality control or total quality management—are much less prevalent. Perhaps one-third of firms have implemented a major quality program. One survey found that almost half of U.S. firms involve more than 25 percent of their workers in quality-related teams, but only 16 percent report that 75 percent or more of their workers participate in regular meetings about quality.

It is difficult to use these surveys to estimate how many American workers are affected by employee involvement, work reorganization, or total quality programs because the surveys share three sources of bias. First, firms that have introduced new practices are the most likely to respond to surveys, so that response bias leads to an overstatement of the extent of change. Second, with the exception of the Osterman survey, which is representative of all U.S. establishments with more than fifty workers, and the Grant Thornton survey of mid-sized manufacturing firms, the surveys focus disproportionately on large firms, which are generally believed to be more likely than small companies to have made workplace changes. (We may know more about this when the Osterman survey is fully analyzed.) Thus, conclusions about the incidence of organizational change drawn from surveys may *overstate* the extent to which U.S. firms are involved in such changes. Changes made at large firms, however, may affect more workers than similar changes made at smaller firms, and conclusions drawn from the surveys may therefore *understate* the proportion of American workers who are affected by the changes.

Third, with the exception of one of the two DDI surveys, only managers and executives were interviewed, and only the Osterman survey included line managers. It is possible that assessments would differ if employees at other levels of the organization—mid-level managers, supervisors, and front-line workers—were interviewed about the nature and extent of efficiency- or quality-enhancing practices. Often, and this is especially true of the surveys on quality programs or human resource practices, the manager interviewed for the survey was responsible for implementing the program or practice. Such individuals are not disinterested observers of how widespread or how successful such programs and practices have been and may be overly optimistic in assessing the incidence and results at their companies.

PROGRAMS AND PRACTICES TO IMPROVE PRODUCTIVITY AND WORK LIFE

The New York Stock Exchange 1982 survey, in which 1,158 firms participated (a response rate of 26.5 percent) found that only 14 percent of the firms had at least one human resource practice in place to stimulate productivity. These practices affected 32 percent of workers. This is surprisingly low in that formal training and employee stock ownership programs were among the practices included in the survey. Among firms with programs or practices in place, 76 percent had formal training programs, 44 percent had quality circles, 35 percent had task forces, 25 percent had labor-management committees, and 16 percent had production teams. New compensation systems were not widespread—only 6 percent of firms salaried their blue-collar workers, 7 percent rewarded group productivity, and 25 percent had some form of stock ownership program.

The 1986 survey of human resource practices by John Thomas Delaney, David Lewin, and Casey Ichniowski for the Department of Labor, in which 495 business units participated (a response rate of only 6.5 percent) had similar findings (Delaney, Lewin, and Ichniowski 1989).[4] Training programs, team-building programs, and profit sharing were the most common practices in place at the time of the survey, scoring 3.0, 2.6, and 2.7 respectively on a scale of 1 (= not at all) to 5 (= a great deal). By comparison, quality circles, semi-autonomous work groups, and gainsharing all scored 1.9. In terms of future plans, however, the latter practices scored 2.3 to 2.4, suggesting that the incidence of these practices might be expected to increase.

The U.S. GAO 1987 survey of employee involvement at Fortune 1000 companies (actually 934 firms because of mergers), in which 476 firms participated (a response rate of 51 percent), found that many firms had one employee practice in place (Lawler, Ledford, and Mohrman 1989). For example, 61 percent had quality circles, 70 percent had other employee-involvement groups, 60 percent had job enrichment or redesign, and 65 percent had profit sharing. Most employees, however, did not participate in these programs. Thus, in 71 percent of the firms, less than 20 percent of the employees were involved in quality circles; in 63 percent, less than 20 percent were in other employee-involvement groups; in 78 percent, less than 20 percent were involved in job enrichment or redesign; and in 55 percent, less than 20 percent were covered by profit sharing.

By 1990, the use of these practices at Fortune 1000 firms had increased. The survey by Edward E. Lawler III, Susan A. Mohrman, and Gerald Ledford (1992), in which 313 organizations participated (an effective response rate of 32 percent), found that the proportion of firms using quality circles had risen to 66 percent and the proportion with some other employee-involvement program was 86 percent.

Work reorganization—especially the use of self-managed teams—increased rapidly during the three-year period, from 28 percent to 47 percent of firms. As already pointed out, however, the proportion of firms in which more than a small fraction of the workers were involved in such production techniques was virtually unchanged. The proportion of companies with a union-management quality of work life (QWL) committee also increased, from 30 to 40 percent of firms, between 1987 and 1990.

The use of compensation practices that encourage teamwork or skill acquisition also increased in the three-year period. The proportion of firms reporting the use of gainsharing increased from 26 to 39 percent of those surveyed, whereas the proportion reporting the use of knowledge or skill-based pay increased from 40 to 51 percent. These practices remain confined to a minority of employees, however. Only 3 percent of firms reported that more than 40 percent of their employees were covered by gainsharing in 1990, the same as in 1987. The proportion extending pay for knowledge or skills to 40 percent or more of their employees rose from 5 percent to 8 percent.

Most of the training provided by Fortune 1000 firms is in job skills. In 1990, 35 percent of the firms surveyed reported that they had provided job skills training to more than 60 percent of their workers in the previous three years, and 84 percent had provided it to more than 20 percent. Other training was much less likely to involve large numbers of workers. In 1990, less than 10 percent of the firms had provided training in the previous three years to more than 60 percent of their workers in group decision-making or problem-solving skills, leadership skills, business skills, quality or statistical analysis skills, or team-building skills; between 40 and 60 percent provided such training to more than 20 percent of their workers. Training for quality, team-building, and decision-making or problem-solving skills increased compared with 1987, while training in leadership and business skills decreased.

The DDI 1990 surveys of 862 executives (response rate of 23 percent) and of 272 individuals known to be involved with teams (response rate of 25 percent) focused on self-directed teams (SDTs), viewed as one of the most advanced forms of employee involvement. Like the GAO survey, this study found that only 27 percent of the firms had at least one self-directed team. Of these, 59 percent of the firms had 10 percent or fewer of their workers on teams; only 10 percent had at least half working in teams. Many more firms planned to be making widespread use of self-directed teams five years after the survey. Only 10 percent expected to have less than 10 percent of their work force involved in teams, and 47 percent expected to have more than half involved.

The teams were not as self-directed as expected. Fully 52 percent of teams reported to a team leader or supervisor in their daily activities. Many tasks were shared with supervisors or were still management functions. In more than half the firms, teams had sole responsibility for their interactions with internal customers and suppliers, for assigning daily tasks, and for safety and housekeeping. In 40 to 50 percent of the firms, teams had responsibility for scheduling vacations, process improvement, routine maintenance, and stopping the production line when necessary. Other production tasks such as preparing budgets, setting goals, selecting work methods, and dealing with external customers and suppliers were usually shared responsibilities or performed by management. The same was true of a variety of personnel practices having to do with compensation, performance appraisals, and training decisions.

Clearly, firms are experimenting wtih many models of SDTs. Most teams (54 percent) select their own team leader, but 32 percent have no input into the selection process. Only 21 percent use job rotation to a great extent, and 12 percent do not rotate jobs at all. The modal team size is six to ten members, but 31 percent have one to twenty members, and 8 percent have more than twenty members. Executives report wider use of gainsharing, productivity bonuses, and pay for skills than do those directly involved with teams. Pay for skills is the most common of these pay systems, affecting about two-fifths of team members.

The Towers Perrin surveys in March 1990 and October 1991 looked at practices at 287 firms (response rate of 44.5 percent) related to the changing character of the work force. Some of the practices examined related to quality, employee involvement, and training. What makes the report of these surveys interesting is that it compared the answers of the same individual at both points in time. It sheds some light, therefore, on the extent to which planned changes are actually carried out.

In March 1990, 12 percent of the firms were using self-managed work teams, and 4 percent planned to begin using them; 12 percent used gainsharing, and 6 percent planned to begin using such a pay system; 25 percent had retraining programs for employees, whereas 8 percent planned to initiate such programs. Nearly two years later, 36 percent had at least one self-managed work team, 21 percent were using gainsharing, and 47 percent had a retraining program. Thus, the use of these practices had increased much faster than anticipated—in spite of the recession and even though a small proportion of the firms reported cutting back on programs because of economic conditions.

The Osterman 1992 survey of a random sample of establishments drawn from the Dun and Bradstreet establishment file is the first representative survey on work organization and human resource practices[5] (Osterman 1993). The response rate was 65.5 percent, and 875 establishments participated, although the final number of usable cases was 694. The overall finding was that 37 percent of firms can be characterized as transformed—that is, as having 50 percent or more of their core employees involved in two of the following practices: self-directed teams, job rotation, quality circles, or total quality management. In contrast to the other surveys reviewed here, this study found that self-directed teams were more prevalent and used more extensively than quality circles. Fifty-five percent of establishments had at least one team, and 41 percent had at least one quality circle; 41 percent of establishments made extensive use of teams, whereas 27 percent made extensive use of quality circles. One-third of firms made some use of total quality management, and one-quarter made extensive use of this practice. There does not appear to be a dominant cluster of work organization practices—the firms in this survey used a variety of combinations—but the study was able to identify a set of HR practices that support the adoption of workplace transformation. These include innovative pay schemes, extensive training, and efforts to induce greater worker commitment. Unions and employment security do not appear to affect the diffusion of high-performance work practices either positively or negatively, whereas competing internationally, having high-skill technology, and having worker-oriented values all appear to have a positive effect.

PROGRAMS AND PRACTICES TO IMPROVE QUALITY

Two surveys of U.S. firms focused on quality rather than productivity, employee involvement, and work reorganization. The Grant Thornton survey in December 1990 examined practices in mid-sized manufacturing firms, whereas the Arthur D. Little survey in the fall of 1991 was of the largest manufacturing and nonmanufacturing firms. Both surveys found the reported incidence of quality programs quite high, although it appears that firms may be implementing isolated practices, including increasing the number of inspections (not usually considered a plus since the goal presumably is to build quality in rather than catch defects afterward).

The Grant Thornton survey, in which 250 firms participated (response rate not available), found that 79 percent of these firms use statistical control and increased maintenance to improve quality and 67 percent have stop-line inspection programs. But although 70 percent of the firms reported that they have total quality control or total quality management programs in place, only 31 percent actually calculate the total cost of quality and only 18 percent may enter the Baldrige Award competition in the next three years. This suggests that, like the productivity and work life programs, the incidence of quality practices is high but that the practices are not yet widely diffused within firms. Another interesting finding of this survey is that only 29 percent of the firms reported that price is the most important competitive factor for their products. Other firms reported that the most important factors are quality (35 percent), speed (6 percent), and service (24 percent).

The Arthur D. Little survey, in which five hundred firms participated (response rate not available), found that 93 percent have a quality program in place. Thirty-five percent of these programs consist of task forces working on improvements; 58 percent are intended to change companywide processes. Despite the high incidence of these programs, however, respondents at only a little more than a third of the companies (36 percent) thought that the quality program had a significant impact on the competitive position of the firm. More respondents were optimistic about the future, and 62 percent of firms expect their quality programs to have a significant effect in the next three years.

The final survey reviewed is the International Quality Study, a 1992 survey launched by Ernst and Young and the American Quality Foundation as part of an ongoing effort to examine quality practices in the United States, Canada, Germany, and Japan, in which 580 organizations (response rate of 84 percent) participated. The survey found that 49 percent of U.S. firms involve more than one-fourth of their workers in quality-related teams. In 60 percent of these firms, however, the proportion of employees participating in regular meetings about quality is less than 25 percent; in only 16 percent do at least 75 percent of employees participate regularly in such meetings.

This survey makes clear the difficulties of evaluating the extent to which employees are involved in quality efforts. It found that 39 percent of Japanese firms report that 75 percent or more of their employees regularly participate in meetings about quality improvement efforts. But it also reports that in two-thirds of Japanese firms, less than 25 percent of the workers are involved specifically in quality-related teams. Thus, although Japanese firms regularly involve more workers in quality efforts than do U.S. firms in Japan, workers are much less likely to be involved in quality-related teams specifically. As the authors of the survey point out, this finding raises questions of interpretation. It may be, for example, that cross-functional activity is so commonplace in Japan that special teams for improving quality are not necessary.

Summing up these diverse surveys is difficult, but it seems reasonable to conclude that between one-quarter and one-third of U.S. firms have made significant changes in how workers are managed and about one-third of large firms have serious quality programs in place or have experienced significant gains from their quality programs. Many more firms plan to implement or expand programs in these two areas, and there is evidence that change has accelerated and is occurring even faster than firms anticipated. This is true despite the recession and slow growth of the U.S. economy since 1990. The practices being adopted are quite varied—no one pattern has emerged. And even with respect to a single practice—self-directed teams—the DDI survey, which looked at SDTs in detail, found many different models. Linear movement from mass production to a unique successor is not evident from these surveys.

6.

EXPERIMENTS WITH WORKPLACE
INNOVATION: EVIDENCE FROM CASE
STUDIES, 1970–92

Our review of the case studies of firms implementing organizational change supports several of the findings from the surveys: the preponderance of firms are experimenting with parallel structures such as quality circles or problem-solving teams, but significant changes are affecting only a relatively small group of employees in any one firm. The cases also offer other insights into how and why firms make decisions to implement new policies, the alternative strategies being used and how these have changed over time, and obstacles to the implementation and diffusion of such practices.[1]

The following patterns emerge from the meta-analysis and may be taken as hypotheses to be examined more rigorously as better quantitative data become available. First, work reform efforts in the United States are characterized by their borrowing of *particular practices or pieces of* the models outlined in chapter 3—teams from sociotechnical models in the 1960s and 1970s, quality circles in the late 1970s and early 1980s, total quality management in the mid to late 1980s, and the idea of networks from the flexible specialization model from the mid-1980s on. We found no instances in which firms borrowed the union-led German model per se, even in unionized firms. Interest in this alternative has existed only among a few trade unionists and industrial relations scholars. Rather, U.S. policy makers have looked to Germany primarily for guidance in developing a U.S. infrastructure for technical training based on the apprenticeship model.

Consistent with this history, early programs tended to be "bottom up"—

69

originating in a particular unit and focusing on the production level. Advocates of sociotechnical systems and quality circles, for example, viewed gains in productivity as emerging primarily as a result of the performance of individuals. Participation in programs, therefore, was explicitly voluntary and tended to involve a minority of employees. More recent programs have tended to be more top down—for example, in those TQM programs that are heavily influenced by scientific management engineering, top management attempts to mandate change and participation throughout the organization.

Similarly, the goal of change efforts at the workplace has shifted over time—from the humanization of work in the 1960s, to job satisfaction and productivity in the 1970s, to quality and competitiveness in the 1980s. This shift is evident in the way the performance measures used to evaluate the programs have changed over time: from employee-oriented measures, such as job satisfaction and morale (including measures of working conditions and health and safety, as well as absenteeism and grievances), to measures of firm performance, including one-time cost savings and productivity improvements (output/unit labor time), to, more recently, quality and customer satisfaction measures, including defect or error rates as well as other costs of quality.

Second, although it is possible to trace the history of the introduction of various work reforms and organizational changes, these alternative strategies have not succeeded one another but currently exist side by side. Thus, although quality circles and other parallel structures were a "fad" in the early 1980s and have since been discredited in most U.S. applications as either not sustainable or providing limited results (Kochan, Katz, and Mower 1984; Lawler and Mohrman 1987), they continue to be employed in firms that have not used employee-involvement techniques in the past, as well as in firms that have moved on to other employee-participation programs.

Third, most of the changes are marginal. The overwhelming majority of cases in this study show that firms have introduced modest changes in work organization, human resource practices, or industrial relations—parallel structures such as quality circles involving only a few employees, a training program, or a new compensation system. We consider these to be marginal changes because they do not change the work system or power structure in a fundamental way.

Fourth, the work reforms and organizational changes have been piecemeal and varied, and strategies are often undertaken separately: (1) human resource strategies (motivational incentives, including employee involvement, compensation strategies, education and training programs); (2) work reorganization and team strategies; (3) scientific management strategies, involving the reengineering of work, the introduction of new performance measurement systems, and total quality efforts; and (4) industrial relations strategies (QWL, joint labor-management committees). Given the complexity and wide range of "innovations" to choose from, firms usually use outside management consultants to facilitate change, but consultants also vary widely in their approaches and probably contribute to shaping the diversity in approaches and outcomes.

Fifth, in some cases these strategies make up a whole—an eclectic model of a transformed system. A handful of firms, the best-practice cases such as Xerox or Federal Express, have accumulated knowledge and organizational learning by experimenting with a series of programs over time, such as quality of work life programs in the 1970s, quality circles and other forms of employee involvement in the early 1980s, and autonomous teams or total quality methods thereafter. Other firms, such as Saturn and Corning, have sent representatives to plants around the world and have developed an eclectic approach that incorporates elements from the various models. Some firms use these experiences to develop a menu of practices to choose from; others attempt to develop a set of internally consistent practices. The best-practice cases provide evidence of a more serious commitment to developing strategies for continuous improvement and provide the basis for theorizing about eclectic American models of high-performance production.

Sixth, although the majority of workplace experiments have taken place in manufacturing firms, service industries and the public sector became increasingly open to change in the 1980s as they experienced deregulation and cost containment on the one hand and a fiscal crisis and privatization on the other.

Similarly, as firms have learned the limitations of focusing their reform efforts on front-line workers only, they have expanded their attention to reorganizing the jobs and responsibilities of professional and managerial workers. Restructuring efforts at these occupational levels have included measures to eliminate management layers, to cut costs, and to improve productivity by establishing measurable performance objectives, as well as to redesign jobs and introduce employee involvement and team techniques.

Seventh, the implementation and diffusion of workplace change are poorly understood. The cases reviewed here often point to special circumstances—a serious economic crisis, a charismatic leader, a greenfield site, a new product line—as the impetus for change. Even the best-practice cases tend to be at the level of one plant or one work site and are not diffused throughout entire organizations.

Eighth, and finally, the case studies raise several important questions concerning interpretation and meaning. The cases make it clear that practitioners use similar terms to mean very different things. Teams, empowerment, and employee involvement in decision making are commonly abused terms. Teams often refer to anything from quality circles to autonomous production teams. Empowerment can mean the act of soliciting employee suggestions, imposing supervisory tasks on front-line workers, or giving workers full autonomy in making technical, work-related decisions. Involvement in decision making can refer to any number of domains of decision making: technical, social, personnel-related, managerial/administrative. This diversity of meaning makes it difficult to interpret the results of surveys that report increases in the use of practices such as "employee involvement."

In addition, certain information is not routinely provided in the surveys or case materials. Frequently, variables are omitted. We usually cannot tell from surveys or cases whether we are viewing the whole or a part. Surveys and cases, for example, rarely include information on the types of capital investment or reductions in force that firms undertake in conjunction with other "innovative" practices. They rarely report the impact of organizational change on employee wages or employment security. In only a few of the cases we reviewed was a commitment to employment security an explicit part of work reform—for example, a McDonnell Douglas union plant (McDonnell Douglas, 1987) and a Maxwell House union plant in Houston, Texas (Maxwell House, General Foods, 1989).[2] Moreover, few firms told about failed efforts, from which we could, in fact, learn a great deal.

In the following parts of this chapter we draw on the case materials to discuss these general developments. In the section that follows, we review a series of ideas and management fads that have gained popularity in the last two decades and provided companies and unions with a menu of strategies for improving performance along a variety of dimensions. Human resource strategies have been of three major types: consultative structures, such as quality circles, employee-involvement programs, and other forums outside of normal work channels designed to improve labor-management communication and employee effort; compensation strategies, designed to shape employee effort or other behavior; and training strategies, designed to increase skill and flexibility in the deployment of workers. Substantive changes have occurred in the organization of work through the enlargement and/or enhancement of job responsibilities for front-line workers and the shift to team-based production with, depending on the case in question, more or less supervision or autonomy for workers. Management methods have centered on incorporating total quality into scientific management through the reengineering of work processes, the development of new performance measurement and cost accounting systems, and the application of statistical process control and just-in-time inventory systems. Industrial relations strategies began with quality of work life programs and have expanded into various forms of representative structures for union involvement in decision making at various levels of the firm and in a number of areas previously reserved for management only. Together, these strategies provide the menu of alternatives U.S. firms have used in various combinations to develop coherent American models and that we elaborate on more fully in part IV.

PIECEMEAL BORROWING

Given the wide range of ideas about what leads to higher productivity and performance and the lack of institutional constraints on decision making, it is understandable that wide variation exists in management practices. Firms often rely on consultants to provide direction, but they also vary widely in what they recommend—some emphasize compensation, others training, others cost reductions through automation and the reengineering of work processes.

Some of the variation also comes from the lack of clear evidence regarding what does and does not work. In the cases we reviewed, virtually all of the firms, regardless of the interventions, reported an increase in employee satisfaction, productivity, and cost savings (often measured in dollar savings or the ratio of savings to bonuses paid out) and a decline in grievances or absenteeism and turnover rates, or defect rates. Academic studies, as well as some surveys, report similar effects (e.g., Lawler, Mohrman, and Ledford 1992). Many of these improvements probably did occur; what is unclear is the cause of the improvements—for example, a Hawthorne effect, a particular "innovative" work practice, a change in internal practices not identified in the study (e.g., technology, reductions in force), or external labor or product market conditions.

Some consultants and managers we talked with simply advocated change for change's sake. Their argument was that if managers periodically introduce changes in work or human resource practices, employees will be regularly challenged with something "new," or feel that management is paying special attention to them (a Hawthorne effect), and therefore remain interested and productive at work. They assume that "innovative work practices," which by definition are simply "new" practices, represent something "positive," "good," an "improvement." Their assumption is problematic, given the rather weak academic evidence and the problems of attribution. It also begs the question of good for whom: employees, employers, customers, shareholders?

Similarly, many practices termed "innovative" are, in fact, old ideas— autonomous teams, gainsharing, profit sharing. Many experts consider performance-based pay systems to be a central part of "high-performance work systems," yet piece rates and merit pay are traditional forms of pay for performance that employees and unions often oppose and that would hardly be considered innovative today. Thus, although we have survey and case evidence that employers are introducing many workplace changes, it is unclear what these changes mean overall and whether they should all be considered innovative or beneficial to the various stakeholders involved.

Moreover, in firms that report improvements in performance, it is often unclear whether the benefits represent one-time savings or ongoing improvement. The methodological difficulties of measuring the impact of workplace innovations is well documented in the organizational behavior literature, in which three generations of psychologists have developed quasi-experimental designs to test the results of narrowly defined interventions on worker effort (see for example, Katzell and Yankelovich 1975; Locke and Schweiger 1979; Miller and Monge 1986). Measuring the impact of a particular incentive program on workers is difficult even when it is possible to control for changes in other organizational variables. Measuring the impact of a particular change is virtually impossible when markets are turbulent and firms are simultaneously introducing changes in a number of areas—from product market strategy, to organizational size and structure, to work process and human resource strategies.

As a result, some of the best and most careful studies that document performance effects do so by measuring the effect of a group of changes. Using "cluster analytic methodology," for example, researchers have found that adopting a cluster of organizational changes makes a difference (MacDuffie 1991; Ichniowski, Shaw, and Prennushi 1993). Frequently, however, firms do not have the incentive or the resources to transform their entire production system, in which case they may implement one or another strategy that they find interesting or acceptable to the parties involved.

EMPLOYEE INVOLVEMENT IN PARALLEL STRUCTURES

The majority of cases we reviewed involved the introduction of parallel structures designed to elicit employees' ideas about ways to cut costs or make work processes more efficient. These represent consultative structures in that they enable management to draw on employees' ideas while retaining control over decision making.[3] Consultative efforts range from the use of simple employee suggestion systems to periodic group meetings that include supervisors and employees, such as quality circles, problem-solving groups, and task forces.[4]

Suggestion systems date to the human relations movement of the 1930s when companies implemented them as a way to enable employees to voice their suggestions or complaints (anonymously) about working conditions. Most employees became cynical about such programs, and they fell into disuse because management failed to take suggestions seriously or to respond promptly to suggestions. In the 1960s and 1970s, companies such as Honeywell (1980) and Phillips Petroleum (1981) restructured their programs to make them more personal, to focus them more on cost reductions, and to increase participation by offering small monetary rewards for the best ideas. The purpose of these programs is to improve morale (by showing employees that management listens to their ideas) and to cut costs.

These programs involve the most minimal level of participation, as reflected in both the costs and the results. Yet they are taken seriously enough by the National Association of Suggestion Systems that it issues annual awards to firms judged to have the best systems based on criteria such as the percentage of employees who submit suggestions, the total number of suggestions received, the percentage adopted and rewarded, the total tangible savings to the company, and the savings-to-cost ratio. Suggestion systems continue to be a common element of employee-involvement efforts in American firms, which use quantitative measures to judge the success of such programs.

For many firms such as Honeywell, suggestion systems were a precursor to the adoption of quality circles, borrowed from the Japanese model, which build on the logic of suggestion systems but give management more control over the process. Whereas employees on their own often make suggestions about cosmetic changes, weekly quality circle meetings facilitated by a supervisor provide a structure and focus for making suggestions directly related to the work unit.

Based on the cases reviewed in this study, quality circles and other problem-solving programs have the following characteristics: they are focused on the work unit but exist parallel to the production process, are voluntary in nature, do not provide monetary rewards for participation, and involve limited training (ten to twenty hours) for supervisors and sometimes employees in such "soft skills" as communication, group facilitation, or group problem solving. There is some incentive to participate insofar as workers get to leave work for regular QC meetings on company time and, in this sense, receive pay for their ideas at their regular hourly rate. The other incentives involve primarily nonmonetary recognition, for example, a certificate or articles about the program in the company newspaper.

Firms often describe problem-solving groups as "participative task teams" (Babcock and Wilcox, 1980), as examples of "team building" (TRW Semiconductors, 1980), or as "involvement teams" (Champion International, 1980). They are teams in a very limited sense, however, since the groups are organized for motivational or problem-solving purposes. The team concept, for example, is often used to spur competition between work groups, with the awards being pens, coffee cups, hats, and jackets for the winners.

As a low-cost strategy for eliciting employees' ideas, quality circles generate cost savings and claims of improved morale and communication between supervisors and workers. They have limited impact because of their focus on the work unit as well as their lack of integration into the work process itself. A number of studies document the limited nature of quality circles on these grounds, their tendency to produce one-time savings, the decline of employee interest over time, and, hence, their short half-lives (Bradley and Hill 1983; Kochan, Katz, and McKersie 1986; Lawler and Mohrman 1987; Drago 1988; Hill 1991). Quality circles organized on Japanese production principles, in which a group of front-line workers led by a foreman has access to engineering, accounting, and other professional and managerial resources, have proven inordinately expensive in the U.S. and

British contexts and are rarely employed. This is because of the large pay differential between blue-collar and professional or managerial employees in these countries (Hill 1991). Detailing such employees to a QC in a Japanese firm does not pose the same cost problems.

Quality circles and other parallel structures, however, have provided the basis for organizational learning along two dimensions. On the one hand, recognizing the limits of the work unit focus, some firms during the 1980s experimented with the concept and expanded it to include a wide variety of other problem-solving groups, task forces, "study action" groups, and employee-involvement teams that cut across departments, functional areas, and different levels of the organization. These experiments gave people experience in collaborative and cooperative modes of work, particularly in behavioral skills, such as communication and group problem solving. The experience of the Northrop Corporation (1985) is representative. From a handful of quality circles on aircraft assembly lines, the company developed a Quality Circle Program Office that helped create interdepartmental task forces and management teams designed to solve specific problems across the organization. Over time, however, these programs often developed elaborate and costly parallel structures involving a large staff isolated from line operations.

In other cases, the experience with such parallel structures as quality circles and problem-solving teams has been a first step toward forming self-directed teams as the basic work unit. At General Motors' Packard Division, for example, the employee-involvement program evolved into autonomous work groups (Kochan, Katz, and Mower 1984). As we review below, firms such as McDonnell Douglas Electronics, Corning, Xerox, and many others that have moved to more team-based production strategies began with experiments in quality circles more than a decade ago.

In our analysis here and in appendix B, we make a clear distinction between parallel (or off-line) groups and production-based (or on-line) teams. We think this distinction is significant because in the first case the organization of work and the roles of worker and supervisor usually remain unchanged, whereas in the second case, a fundamental change occurs in the way work is done. In reality, the distinction may not be so clear, and this is an issue that requires further research. If, for example, workers in off-line problem-solving teams are involved in redesigning job tasks (enlarging or enriching jobs) or deciding which new equipment to purchase, then they may substantially affect the way work is organized. But even in these cases, the off-line teams are likely to involve only a small subset of workers who suggest changes to management, who in turn may implement the changes in a broader work unit. This off-line process is significantly different from one in which all workers on the production line are involved in day-to-day decisions through self-directed teams.

COMPENSATION STRATEGIES

In the last decade or so, firms have experimented extensively with a wide array of alternative pay strategies for managerial and nonmanagerial employees. What we refer to as "alternative strategies," other researchers and consultants refer to as "nontraditional," "innovative," "incentive or performance-based," or "contingent." "Traditional practices" generally refer to the use of a base wage (hourly for front-line workers, salaried for managerial and professional) set in reference to the local labor market and industry standards plus annual across-the-board wage increases. In the unionized sector, annual increases were collectively bargained, linked to seniority, and sometimes included cost-of-living adjustments (COLAs). Nonunion firms tried to keep pace with union standards of wages and benefits, but tended to rely on merit increases. More successful firms tried to attract high-quality workers by offering wages above the market rate, often by pegging entry-level pay to the sixtieth or seventy-fifth percentile of the industry average. Thus, consistent or patterned compensation practices existed within industries, allowing firms and unions, to a greater or lesser extent, to "take wages out of competition." By contrast, managerial and professional workers have traditionally received salaries plus merit raises and/or annual bonuses. Because performance appraisal systems are difficult to administer, however, and because managers often find it difficult to give low performance evaluations, merit increases in nonunion companies are often indistinguishable from across-the-board increases based on another year of service. We will use the term *traditional pay* to describe these various arrangements.

Writers and consultants tend to lump together everything that does not fit these patterns as "innovative," or "nontraditional," including such practices as profit sharing (which originated in U.S. companies in the 1800s), gainsharing (which emerged in the steel industry in the 1930s) (Lesieur 1958), and pay systems such as piecework or work on commission, which are incentive pay systems that historically have been common in certain industries.[5] Similarly, although group-based pay for performance is termed "innovative incentive pay," collectively bargained (e.g., group) wage increases linked to gains in productivity, negotiated by the United Auto Workers (UAW) and other unions in the post–World War II era, are considered "traditional across-the-board" increases. Another example comes from a recent survey by Towers Perrin, which found that although most American HR professionals expected to increase variable pay but decrease individual merit pay in the future, the Japanese said they planned to emphasize merit pay to improve competitiveness (reported in Gerhart, Milkovich, and Murray 1992:204). Thus, discussions in the literature of what is innovative (and by implication "better") are often confusing.

What is "new" about the new pay policies is the use of compensation as a strategic variable to improve firm competitiveness (Shuster and Zingheim 1992). In the past, firms certainly used pay to "attract, motivate, and retain" high-quality employees and to improve productivity through incentives such as piece rates, commissions, or merit pay. Currently, however, employers are experimenting with compensation to shape a wider range of employee behavior and to link workers' performance more closely to the goals of the firm. If firms increasingly treat pay as a strategic variable, then we would expect to find a much wider range of diversity in pay practices at the firm or even the establishment level. This, in fact, is what the survey evidence corroborates.[6]

If total compensation is defined as having three components—base pay, variable (or contingent) pay, and indirect pay (benefits)—most researchers and consultants have focused on the increased use of variable pay as the centerpiece of new pay strategies (see, for example, Shuster and Zingheim 1992). Variable pay includes gainsharing, winsharing, profit sharing, lump-sum bonuses, and individual and group-based incentive pay.

In gainsharing (such as the Scanlon, Rucker, and Improshare plans), workers and the firm share the gains from increases in productivity above a given baseline. Gains are usually shared at the work unit or suborganizational level and payouts are frequent so that workers see the relationship between their effort and the unit's gains in productivity. Gainsharing often has a participation component so that workers' suggestions help bring about increased productivity. Winsharing is a form of gainsharing. Profit-sharing plans pay out bonuses to workers for increases in firm-level profits above a baseline. Because profits are affected by the market and other factors, because payouts are based on organizationwide performance, and because they tend to be made on an infrequent basis (often annually), profit sharing provides a weaker incentive for employees to improve performance. Moreover, profit sharing probably has even less of an incentive effect if it is used as a deferred wage or pension plan, as it is in the majority of cases in the United States (Hammer 1988:334). Individual incentive strategies include "traditional" practices such as piece rates, commissions, and merit pay as well as the newer pay-for-knowledge or pay-for-skills programs, which link compensation to training, based on the implicit assumption from human capital theory that training improves productivity.

Employers like variable pay because they believe it creates flexibility and more marketlike conditions for employees—and they thereby increase their sense of ownership and assume some of the financial risks associated with the business. Variable pay also directly links labor costs to external market conditions so that wages (rather than employment) fluctuate with the business cycle (Weitzman and Kruse 1990).

For workers, variable pay enhances the potential to earn more than the average worker, but it also increases income instability; it may also decrease motivation and morale if too high a proportion of the wages are at risk. Workers appear divided on the question of variable pay. A 1988 nationwide survey, for example, found that most employees prefer a straight wage or salary over any form of incentive compensation. A sizable minority (22 percent) preferred individual incentives, however, and an additional 12 percent said they would be willing to use an overall corporate performance plan (Bureau of National Affairs [BNA] 1988:9).

In addition to using new forms of variable pay, employers are also experimenting by applying old pay strategies to new groups of workers and by changing base and indirect pay. Some, for example, are extending salaried pay and/or lump-sum bonuses to front-line workers. Others are putting managerial and nonmanagerial workers on the same group incentive plan.

Our understanding of the extend to which alternative pay practices are being used is weak but has grown, as indicated in the review in the previous section of the surveys. Practices such as profit sharing, gainsharing, and pay for skill have become more widespread in the last decade. A 1991 BNA survey also found that the use of these practices accelerated during the 1980s. Similarly, a 1987 survey of 1,598 companies by the American Productivity Center (APC) found that a sizable number of companies had significantly reduced or eliminated "traditional" pay practices: 36 percent of respondents had eliminated or significantly reduced the use of across-the-board pay hikes; 28 percent had reduced or eliminated COLAs, and 25 percent had reduced or eliminated merit increases (APC, *People, Performance, and Pay*, cited in BNA 1988:49). At the same time, all of these surveys also found that alternative pay strategies still affect only a small minority (less than 10 percent) of workers, even in the firms that have introduced the alternatives. Compared with other organizational practices, such as employee involvement, compensation systems appear particularly resistant to change.

The central questions raised by this diversity of practices is whether there is an emerging pattern to the mix of strategies firms are adopting. What is the relationship between changes in base, variable, and indirect pay? Do the mix of pay strategies used add up to a coherent whole or motivate an internally consistent set of behaviors? Are they consistent with other organizational changes undertaken? And do compensation policies lead or support other strategies?

These questions are central because each pay strategy motivates different behaviors. Thus, incentive pay, which re-creates market conditions inside the firm, increases individual competition and distrust, whereas the effect of salaried pay is just the opposite. Individual incentives tie individual behavior more closely to performance outcomes but undermine the cooperation necessary for teamwork. Piece-rate and commission systems tend to emphasize quantity over quality, although quality measures can constrain pay rates. Profit sharing focuses employee effort on relatively short-term (quarterly) profits or savings, gainsharing emphasizes short- or intermediate-term productivity, and pay for knowledge emphasizes skill development and continuous improvement over a longer time period.

The specific form of pay strategy that is used and the process by which it is implemented are also likely to be significant. Wide wage dispersion fosters competition; narrow dispersion favors cooperation and builds group cohesiveness. The portion of pay that is fixed versus variable shapes whether the effect on employees is to increase effort or to undermine income security and hence demoralize workers. To be effective, the relative pay rates among workers must be perceived as fair and the performance goals as realistic. The success of gainsharing and profit sharing, for example, depends on whether the target is set high enough to induce effort but realistically enough that workers enjoy rewards. Targets that are constantly moved upward are intended to induce "continuous improvement," but workers may perceive management as manipulative of the system. In addition to balancing these concerns, a major difficulty in creating an effective incentive pay scheme is the heavy data requirements needed to implement it.

Our understanding of the mix of pay practices used by firms is particularly incomplete. Most surveys, for example, ask firms about "new" (primarily variable) pay practices without asking about concomitant changes in base pay or benefit structures (Osterman 1993 is an exception). In fact, wage studies indicate that many firms have cut costs by freezing wage rates, introducing two-tiered systems, or replacing base pay with pay for skill (BNA 1988). By limiting the growth of base pay, firms have sought to limit or reduce the costs of benefits, which usually vary with base pay. Other studies show that firms have also reduced benefit costs by introducing flexible or "cafeteria" plans, by shifting from defined-benefit retirement plans to profit sharing, and by requiring more employee co-payments in such areas as health insurance and child care (Employee Benefits Research Institute 1990).

The cases we reviewed address some of these questions. The purpose of our analysis of case materials was to determine whether changes in compensation are an integral part of work reform efforts, whether particular compensation plans are associated with certain work reforms, and the extent to which compensation is a driver (versus a support) of change. We found that in most cases, changes in compensation systems are neither an integral part of employee-involvement efforts nor introduced as part of total quality management and that compensation tends to be based on individual as opposed to group incentives. Only in a few cases were compensation strategies leading or driving organizational change. More generally, in companies that have changed their pay practices, there seems to be little logic or coherence as to why one set of strategies was chosen over another (profit sharing versus gainsharing, versus lump-sum bonuses). The exceptions were several cases in which firms and employees established pay for skill in combination with gainsharing to support team-based production.

In firms in which compensation strategies constituted the central strategy for improving performance, we found a number of instances in which the central thrust was to increase variable pay substantially and reduce fixed labor costs. Firms used an ad hoc mix of "old" and "new" strategies to accomplish this end.[7] At Steelcase, for example, a company included in *The One Hundred Best Companies to Work for in America* (Levering, Moskowitz, and Katz 1984), the company combines a piece-rate bonus system and regular overtime with a profit-sharing system, so that workers receive more than 60 percent of their wages as contingent pay. Similarly, Lincoln Electric (1985) uses a piece-rate system, regular overtime each week, plus annual bonuses tied to individual performance evaluations based on cooperation, output, quality, and dependability. In another series of cases reported by Jay Shuster and Patricia Zingheim (1992), firms followed a coherent three-part strategy: (1) they allowed base pay to fall from the seventy-fifth percentile to the fiftieth percentile of industry market rates; (2) they froze indirect pay at current levels and introduced a flexible benefit plan as well as cost sharing of premiums by employees; and (3) they increased the proportion of variable pay in total compensation.

In cases in which pay strategies are intended to support organizational change, firms also use multiple compensation strategies (base pay, bonus, pay for skills, and profit sharing). The Nucor Corporation, for example, uses multiple incentive compensation policies that include profit sharing, a monthly stock investment plan, an employee stock ownership plan, service awards, and bonus payments based on extraordinary group performance. Employees receive bonuses if they produce a part in 90 percent of the time established to produce it. Employees who are late or absent a day lose their bonus for the day or week (Nucor, 1983).

In a minority of cases involving a shift to team-based production, management considers contingent compensation to be a central driver of work reform and the key to improvements in productivity and quality. At LTV Aerospace and Defense Company in Camden, Arkansas, for example, management introduced two complementary pay schemes—gainsharing based on group performance and a pay-for-skill program based on individual learning—in conjunction with the use of self-directed teams (LTV Aerospace, 1991). Gainsharing, introduced in 1988, rewards employees for savings above a predetermined baseline, set by LTV, which was the best performance employees achieved but were unable to sustain over time. Only workers in units that produced more efficiently than the baseline allocated hours received part of the payout. Average payout per employee was $2,000 in the first year. During the first three years of the program, $12.5 million in savings were realized, of which half went to employees and half to LTV. The pay-for-skill program, introduced in 1990, links all base pay increases to skill development along two dimensions: depth (through formal technical training courses at a community college) and breadth (skills across job functions or teams). The company credits the pay-for-skill program with making teamwork a success. In the first year of the program, defect rates on rockets produced dropped from 1.3 to 0.2 percent and rocket reliability rose from 96 to 99 percent.

Corning represents a similar case. In team-based plants, the company and union have established pay for skill to encourage training, gainsharing to induce group effort, and one profit-sharing plan in which managers and nonmanagers participate equally. All three pay strategies emphasize group participation and cooperation.

TRAINING STRATEGIES

Current interest in the shift to high-skill, high-performance work systems has led researchers, firms, unions, and policy makers to focus on education and training as a competitive strategy in its own right. The evidence is strong that the United States underinvests in training relative to its competitors (Kochan and Osterman 1991) and that when firms have made the investment, managers receive the training, often as part of their benefit package (Carnevale and Goldstein 1990:49). Several states have led the way in funding workplace-based training programs for production-level workers, with the goal of improving economic development and competitiveness, and interest is growing in a national employment training policy (Lynch 1993; Batt and Osterman 1993a).

Although most case studies identify training as an important human resource strategy, the type of training, its duration, and the recipients vary substantially. There are many cases in which firms have undertaken substantial technical training, often in conjunction with new technologies, but have left the organization of work or other human resource policies unchanged. This has been a central feature of state-funded "customized training" programs that train workers for firms willing to relocate plants to the state (see Creticos, Duscha, and Sheets 1990). This is also true of employment training programs such as California's Employment Training Panel (ETP) that do not involve smokestack chasing but fund the training and upgrading of workers in firms to improve economic competitiveness. These cases are documented elsewhere and are not included in our review (see Batt and Osterman 1993b; Creticos and Sheets 1991). Training by itself is a limited strategy for firms because employees who return to their old jobs are unlikely to use their new skills, and if they do not receive a commensurate pay increase, they are likely to look elsewhere for work.

Several other patterns emerge from the cases we reviewed. Unlike compensation programs, training is an integral part of most organizational change efforts, but the amount of training is minimal (one or two days) and tends to be focused on behavioral or soft skills (communication, group dynamics, team building) rather than on technical skills. The type and amount of training varies depending on the intervention. Programs involving parallel structures provide supervisors and employees with only minimal training and only in communication and team-building skills. Total quality programs tend to be associated with more training in quality, both in awareness and orientation, and in technical skills, such as statistical process control. Team-based production strategies involve the greatest commitment of resources to training across an array of areas, including soft skills (team building and group processes), broader skills (cross-training), and deeper skills (problem solving and the maintenance and repair of equipment).

Although conventional wisdom based on human capital theory links gains in productivity to basic education and job-related training, the case studies make clear that training in soft skills is a critical part of organizational change. Employers and managers indicate a much greater demand for training in process and behavioral skills than in technical skills, according to recent survey research (Capelli 1993), and perhaps too little attention in academic research has been paid to such training until now.

Most of the firms included in our study invest relatively small amounts in training. By contrast, the best-practice firms invest heavily—at least 5 percent of payroll and 15 percent or more in self-directed team-based systems, such as those at Corning. Best-practice firms often signal their commitment to training and continuous improvement by shifting to pay-for-skill systems, as Boeing (1991), Maxwell House (1989), and others did. Employee involvement in defining the skill sets as well as in deciding who should be trained in what sequence also seems to be an important attribute of these programs.

WORK REORGANIZATION AND TEAM PRODUCTION

The idea that teamwork improves performance derives from the sociotechnical literature from the 1950s on.[8] But the concept has a particular meaning in that literature. Continuous improvement originates from two sources: giving workers autonomy and treating work as a system rather than a set of individual jobs. The assumption is that workers rather than managers or engineers know best how to organize work in the most productive manner possible, using a given technology. To gain this level of efficiency, the work system rather than individual jobs must be the unit of analysis—hence, the importance of working in teams rather than individually. Technology is permissive rather than determinative of work organization, and workers are complementary to, rather than extensions of, machines. Productivity does not depend on technology, on the one hand, or human or social relations, on the other (e.g., human resource practices to improve morale or job satisfaction); rather, it depends on the fit between social and technical systems. Once teams of workers design the work process, they continue to look for ways of improving it if they are given the discretion to do so, so that workers themselves become the source of continuous improvement.

There are a few celebrated examples of U.S. firms that adopted sociotechnical systems in the 1960s, such as the General Mills food-processing plant in Topeka, Kansas (Walton 1982), but more widespread use of team-based production systems did not emerge in the United States until the 1980s. The approach has been most widely promoted by organizational development specialists and "action researchers" working in the Tavistock tradition (Goodman and Associates 1979; Goodman 1982; Guest 1982a; Macy 1982; Walton 1982; for a good review, see Trist 1981).

In the cases we reviewed, the concept of teams covers a much wider spectrum of behavior than that embodied in the sociotechnical approach. The meaning of teams varies considerably as defined by their involvement in different domains of decision making (work design, work processes, administrative/personnel issues) and their degree of autonomy or control over substantive decision making. The most telling indicator of whether firms follow a sociotechnical approach is whether workers are involved in the redesign of a plant, assembly line, or work process. This usually entails substantial lead time, investment, and commitment by management and workers to changing the process of production.

Earlier, we discussed management strategies that make use of groups of workers in such parallel structures as quality circles and problem-solving "teams." This application of the team concept is significantly different from the sociotechnical approach because it does not give workers autonomy and does not integrate group activity into the production process itself. As we noted earlier, however, introducing quality circles and problem-solving groups can serve as a first step in moving toward team-based production.

We identified three levels of autonomy in firms where production is organized around teamwork: (1) supervised teams, (2) semi-autonomous teams, and (3) autonomous teams. In supervised teams, a supervisor retains a central role in overseeing production, which is carried out by groups of workers. Hierarchical decision-making structures remain substantially in place, although frequently workers participate in decision making. The case study of the Naval Air Rework Facility (1986) is an example of such an organization, as is NUMMI (Adler 1990).

In semi-autonomous or self-directed teams, workers assume responsibility for most production decisions, but a supervisor or team leader with an enlarged span of control plays the role of "coach" or team leader. Many firms that have won manufacturing excellence awards or the Baldrige Award appear to have moved to this level of team-based production (Sheridan 1990; Stovicek 1991; Teresko et al. 1991; Manji 1992; U.S. GAO 1991a). Among those firms that report using teams, most appear to have semi-autonomous groups, although many do not explicitly state the level of autonomy of their workers or the specific areas of decision making over which they have control. This ambiguity makes it difficult to draw more than a tentative assessment. Examples include the Lord Corporation (1986), McDonnell Douglas (1987), Harley Davidson (1988), Maxwell House (1989), U.S. Shoe (1989), and Boeing Defense (1991).

It is also unclear from the case materials whether companies view the use of autonomous teams as an ultimate goal, since the cases represent firms at various stages of development, or whether they will continue to introduce new models of teamwork and autonomy. We expect that they do and they will. At a new facility of Lake Superior Paper Industries in Minnesota, for example, the company began with a purely management design team, then began hiring workers into supervised teams, and now plans to move over time to using semi-autonomous teams (Lake Superior Paper, 1989). In other cases, firms opening new facilities have used a sociotechnical systems approach from the start so as to involve workers in the design of the entire production process (Moore Marketing Response, 1991).

Few U.S. firms have moved to using purely autonomous teams without shift supervisors. Among unionized firms, Corning and the GM-UAW Saturn plant are among the few examples of firms where this has occurred. At the Specialty Cellular Ceramics plant, in Corning, New York, for example, a brownfield site, the 110 workers, who came from another nearby Corning plant, were actively involved in the design and layout of the plant and equipment. Teams work autonomously without shift supervisors, cross-train and rotate across semiskilled jobs, and communicate directly with engineers and other "support staff" (human resource, clerical, sales, and marketing) to solve production-line problems and to coordinate production deadlines and deliveries. They regularly receive business information so that they can understand the plant's competitive position. Teams have undertaken job analyses to develop their own pay-for-skills compensation system. They select who is to be trained when and participate in hiring decisions. Training covers four distinct skill areas with three levels of understanding, from the most mechanical to analytical and problem solving. Thus, workers in teams have enlarged responsibilities along the three dimensions: in breadth (job enlargement), in depth (job enrichment), and vertically (administrative tasks).[9]

The small, nonunion Rohm and Haas chemical plant in LaPorte, Texas, operates along similar sociotechnical principles (Rohm and Hass Bayport, 1985). Four teams of five to seven multiskilled technicians operate the plant, without shift supervisors, foremen, or plant guards, rotating jobs on a regular basis. Workers receive training in social and team-building skills as well as technical training in specialized jobs. Teams have assumed administrative responsibilities and were responsible for making changes over time in the compensation system, which began as a combined merit and pay for skill system and evolved into a pay-for-time-in-grade system because it was too difficult to differentiate the performance of individual workers.

In summary, when firms employ a sociotechnical systems approach, organizational change takes a very different form than when employees participate through parallel structures, isolated compensation or training strategies, or, as we discuss below, TQM programs. These strategies tend to be more top down, whereas the sociotechnical approach starts at the work site and is bottom up. It therefore requires management to give up much greater control over decision making along several dimensions. In the STS model, the focus is on giving groups of front-line employees the central role in all aspects of work, from the design and operation of the plant, the assembly line, and individual jobs to repair and maintenance and human resource decisions regarding hiring, discipline, training, and compensation.

SCIENTIFIC MANAGEMENT AND TOTAL QUALITY

In contrast to the decentralized sociotechnical systems approach, total quality programs are initiated by top management and apply scientific management principles of total quality developed by Deming (1984), Juran (Juran and Gyrna 1988), Crosby (1979), Ishikawa (1985), and others. The underlying assumption is that "85 percent" of problems originate with management; thus, the focus is on improving management methods or coordination. Theorists argue that continuous improvement results from the application of statistical methods to uncover bottlenecks in production, thereby leading to the reengineering of work processes. Though Deming and other quality experts have emphasized the importance of employee involvement in quality, this involvement does not necessarily imply the reorganization of work as in the STS model. In our cases, other human resource practices, such as changes in compensation or incentive structures, also play a role, albeit a less important one. The emphasis is on changing the engineered work process rather than on increasing an individual worker's effort or autonomy, although training designed to get workers to work smarter rather than harder may be part of the program.

Total quality programs have the potential to bring about significant improvements in the quality of work and the performance of employees, but much depends on how firms implement TQM and the extent to which worker participation, training, and other human resource practices are part of the process. Because TQM requires substantial top-down coordination, the danger is that companies will retain a hierarchical approach. Reported results on the effectiveness of TQM, therefore, are mixed. On the one hand, many companies report major improvements as a result of total quality, among them many of the Baldrige winners, which are the focus of part IV. On the other hand, as indicated earlier, recent surveys have uncovered evidence of considerable disappointment among firms regarding the effectiveness of TQM. Clearly, implementation matters.

Taken to the extreme, the emphasis on reengineering the work process has led to the latest in management fads, "reengineering." This approach focuses exclusively on cutting costs and improving cycle time by reengineering the work process to "eliminate redundancies," that is, to eliminate jobs (see Hammer 1990; Hammer and Champy 1992). Cigna Corporation, for example, a leading proponent of "reengineering," claims to have cut staff by 40 percent in its reinsurance unit and to have reduced policy-processing time by 90 percent as a result of reengineering (Hemp 1992).

A substantial number of the firms whose cases we reviewed and that are described below seemed to fall into the trap of overemphasizing performance measurement and outcomes at the expense of employee participation.

We found that many TQM programs tended to focus heavily on managerial control and measurement of the production process through the application of statistical methods and the reengineering of work processes to "eliminate redundancies." Objective measures of quality become part of employee evaluations. Statistical process control techniques identify deviations from mean standards of quality and provide management with information on where bottlenecks occur in the production process. A just-in-time inventory process may or may not be part of the system. Management information systems transfer data on employee performance to finance departments, where accounting systems incorporate measures of the cost of quality into financial analysis. All employees receive training in quality and customer consciousness, and often in statistical process control as well. The purpose of the training is to "align" the vision of all employees toward a common goal. In this sense, participation is mandatory or expected, rather than voluntary. Compensation tends to be based on individual rather than group criteria and may or may not be tied to performance. Incentives for participation tend to be nonmonetary.

The Ethyl Corporation's quality program provides an example (1986, 1990). The company developed a "management systems" approach so that it could move to a "quality-focused culture," introduced a quality and productivity measurement system throughout the organization, and set up management teams that received in-depth training in the quality principles of Juran, Deming, and Crosby to coordinate the effort. There is a heavy emphasis on annual budget planning, information sharing through publications and regular meetings (executive committee, staff meetings, analyst meetings, board meetings), and the use of a cost-of-quality system for feedback. Ethyl also has a companywide quality award to provide incentives for employee participation.

Similarly, the total quality program at a Capsugel manufacturing plant in Greenwood, South Carolina, centers on training in "total quality awareness," the application of statistical process control and just-in-time inventory to reduce defects and variability in the production of its capsules, quality improvement teams, and new measurement systems. The director of manufacturing emphasized that "there's hardly anything we've done in which we haven't had to go and change our measurement system . . . either our technique for taking measurements or the equipment we use to do the measurement" (1991).

Of the total quality programs we reviewed that included employee participation, it tended to occur more through such parallel structures as quality circles or problem-solving teams than through autonomous teamwork in the sense employed in the STS model. In addition, most of the programs did not include changes in compensation. Examples include Polysar Gulf Coast's implementation of a total quality program in a Texas production facility (1987), Allegheny Ludlum Steel Corporation's quality program (1986), ZEBCO, Inc.'s program (1984), Cutter Laboratories' quality program (1985), and the Los Nietos plant of National Supply Company, a division of Armco (National Supply Company, Armco, 1984).

INDUSTRIAL RELATIONS STRATEGIES: QWL AND JOINT COMMITTEES

Whereas nonunion firms began applying insights from organizational behavior to predominantly greenfield work sites in the 1950s, union firms began experimenting with quality of work life programs in the 1970s as a first step in overcoming the limits of Taylorism. The most serious effort in the 1970s involved experiments funded by the Ford Foundation and the U.S. Department of Commerce at twenty firms. Eight case studies were eventually pursued, and three became famous: the Rushton coal mine experiment in a militant United Mineworkers' local (Goodman and Associates 1979, Goodman 1982); the Bolivar, Tennessee, UAW/Harman Industries auto parts plant (Macy 1982); and the Tennessee Valley Authority (TVA) engineering department project (Tennessee Valley Authority 1976; see also Strauss and Hammer 1987).

A joint-labor-management steering committee oversaw each experiment, created lower-level joint committees and task forces where necessary, and liberally used consultants to provide guidance and academic researchers to evaluate the success of the programs. Borrowing heavily from sociotechnical approaches and what in Europe constituted a movement for industrial democracy, the experiments emphasized the redesign of jobs to humanize work and a shift to team-based production. Both management and the unions considered productivity improvement to be a secondary by-product.[10]

In the first few years, the experiments produced reductions in grievances and modest improvements in working conditions, health and safety, and worker satisfaction and participation in decision making. The experiments faded, however, as initiators or consultants left (in the case of Harman Industries, both the owner and Irving Bluestone, representing the UAW, left), workers lost interest, or economic crises arose. The greatest success with participation occurred among the professional workers at TVA (the only long-lived program), followed by Rushton, which had moderate success with its skilled workers. The least involvement occurred among the semi-skilled workers at Harman (Strauss and Hammer 1987:10).

Three characteristics of these experiments are notable: (1) though they were governed by representative committees, direction tended to be top down and committee structures were outside normal work structures; (2) the change efforts focused on workplace organization; and (3) the union and management considered the experiment separate from the collective bargaining agreement and signed "shelter agreements" that allowed either party to withdraw from the experiment at any time.

Widespread use of QWL did not begin until the 1980s, particularly after the recession of 1982,[11] and QWL programs took on a very different form from that suggested by advocates of sociotechnical ideas or industrial democracy.[12] First, they were negotiated in collective bargaining agreements and associated with concession bargaining—unions gained QWL or other joint programs in exchange for concessions in work rules or wages (Strauss and Hammer 1987:16). In this context and defined as "labor" programs, they were often perceived by management as a union benefit and by labor as a management attempt to co-opt the union—rather than as vehicles for changing the work process. Second, although they were collectively bargained, QWL and other joint programs were not subject to the grievance and arbitration procedure as other contract clauses are. Thus, joint structures existed outside collective bargaining and outside the organization of work. Third, they tended to focus on "local" concerns—on the work environment, including health, safety, and "cosmetics"—not on policies governing the way work was done. Similarly, although the celebrated Tarrytown QWL program introduced problem-solving teams, improved union-management communication, and lowered grievance levels, "the intrinsic nature of repetitive conveyor-paced jobs ha[d] not substantially changed" (Guest 1982a:104).

There are many examples of joint labor-management efforts whose primary effects have been an improvement in "the climate" of union-management relations and a reduction in hostility. Celebrated success stories often come from plants where labor relations were notoriously bad and a joint cooperative effort led to a complete turnaround in union-management relations. Examples include Eastern Airlines (which ultimately failed), the

NUMMI plant (Adler 1992), Tarrytown (Guest 1982a), and the Magma Copper Company, a mining company in Arizona (1991).

QWL programs and other forms of joint structures have given labor and management the experience of communicating and solving limited problems on a more informal and ongoing basis than is possible under legally sanctioned collective bargaining that takes place every two or three years. Problems previously dealt with through the grievance procedure could be dealt with more informally in committee meetings. But joint programs did not shift the balance of power or necessarily change the role of the union, which remained one of reacting to management's unilateral decisions, representing the rights of workers, and monitoring contract compliance. In this sense, these early programs were more behavioral than substantive in nature, and many were not long-lasting. For every case of success, there are many unwritten cases of failure ending in decreased trust and increased skepticism between labor and management.

QWL programs took three directions in the last decade. Many atrophied, continuing to exist only on paper. Others were linked with quality circles, giving them a more cost-saving orientation, or were part of total quality programs with a focus on quality improvement. In either case, they continued to exist outside line operations. A third group of firms and unions used the QWL joint steering committee structure to develop team-based work organization along sociotechnical lines. Joint labor-management programs became more common in part because of strong support from the Bureau of Labor-Management Relations and Cooperative Programs in the Department of Labor as well as from the Federal Mediation and Conciliation Service. Throughout the 1980s, these federal bodies served as clearinghouses for information and technical assistance to firms and unions involved in labor-management programs, sponsored conferences to generate interest, and conducted studies of program effectiveness.

A wide array of unions have been involved in QWL-QC joint programs (see table 6.1). These efforts include a combination of representative and consultative participation. They were undertaken at various times during the last two decades and continue to the present. Each makes use of a joint labor-management steering committee, which oversees joint participation in lower-level problem-solving teams or task forces that focus on a range of issues such as cost cutting, waste reduction, health and safety, quality, customer service, and administrative issues such as scheduling. The firms routinely report improvements in costs, productivity, product quality, job sat-

Table 6.1   *Selected Cases of Firms Involved in Union-Management*
Quality of Work Life and Quality Control Programs

Union	Company	Start date	Date of U.S. Dept. of Labor Report
Firemen and Oilers (IBFO)	Standard Oil Engineering Materials	1974	May 1, 1991
Machinists (IAM) and Bakery, Confectionery, & Tobacco Workers (BCTWU)	Philip Morris Manufacturing Center	1979	May 1, 1991
Allied Industrial Workers (AIW)	Wohlert Corp.	1981	May 7, 1991
Textile Workers Union (UTWU)	Johnson & Johnson Medical, Inc.	1983	Dec. 20, 1991
Chemical Workers (ICW)	Mobay Corp.	1984	March 25, 1991
Teamsters (IBT)	Thomas Lipton Co.	1988	Dec. 20, 1991
Rubber Workers (URW)	Bridgestone-Firestone, Inc.	1988	June 19, 1991
Steelworkers (USWA)	National Steel	1989	March 29, 1991
Electrical Workers (IUE)	Delco Chassis Division	1989	Dec. 13, 1991

isfaction, the rate of grievances, and communication. They also report that
plans or pilot programs are under way to implement self-directed or semi-
autonomous teams in parts of the production process.

In another group of firms, again involving a broad cross-section of
unions, a joint committee oversees self-directed or managed teams in production settings. Many of these firms began with quality circles or problem-
solving teams, and unions and firms continue to make use of ad hoc task
forces as needed. These cases therefore combine the three types of participation we have identified: consultative, substantive, and representational.
They vary in whether or not the participatory programs are covered by the
collective bargaining agreement; the extent to which teams are autonomous
or supervised; the extent to which training, gainsharing, and management
methods such as total quality are used; and the reported benefits of participation (see table 6.2).

Table 6.2   *Selected Cases of Firms Involved in Union-Management Team-Based Production*

Union	Company	Start date	Date of U.S. Dept. of Labor Report
UAW	Delco-Remy	1978	March 19, 1991
Aluminum, Brick and Glass Workers (ABGW)	Rohm & Haas, Knoxville	1980	April 26, 1991
Firemen, and Oilers (IBFO); Oil, Chemical, Atomic Workers (OCAW)	Rohm & Haas, Kentucky	1984	May 21, 1991
Smith Steelworkers (SSDALU)	A. O. Smith	1987	April 10, 1991
Susquehanna Valley Auto Association	TRW, Inc.	1987	April 29, 1991
Steelworkers (USWA)	Inland Steel Bar Co.	1988	Jan. 2, 1992
Autoworkers (UAW)	J. I. Case Co.	1989	Jan. 2, 1992
Machinists (IAM)	McDonnell Douglas	1989	April 26, 1991
Autoworkers (UAW)	L. E. Jones Manufacturing	1990	Jan. 2, 1992

Joint labor-management efforts have been and continue to be controversial among trade unionists and to divide unions into two camps: those who oppose cooperation and view themselves as "militant" or strong trade unionists and those who support cooperation and are often defined as weak or pro-management. Those who oppose "cooperation" argue that it equals co-optation, that it is cooperation on management's terms, that management disproportionately benefits from forums in which workers give away their knowledge (see, for example, Parker and Slaughter 1988). Given union experiences during the last two decades with management hostility toward union concerns—concession bargaining, widespread and continued plant closings, outsourcing, downsizing, and fierce opposition to organizing drives—this position continues to influence union thinking. Proponents argue that participatory programs do in fact make work more satisfying; ease worker-supervisor tensions; give workers recognition they deserve; and, given the current economic conditions and weakness of unions, serve as a survival mechanism to save jobs. Given the division of opinion, industrial relations scholars now identify two models of labor-management relations: "adversarial" and "cooperative" (Katz 1988; Kochan, Katz, and McKersie 1986).

More recently, a third position has emerged, which rejects the adversarial-cooperationist dichotomy as divisive and counterproductive and treats union participation in joint structures as a strategic decision, an extension of collective bargaining, and a vehicle for organizing. This perspective in part grows out of the positive experiences some unions have had in "managing participation" by carefully selecting committees with clearly defined objectives. Joint health and safety committees, for example, have evolved since the 1970s, following the passage of the Occupational Safety and Health Act. In the 1980s, several unions negotiated company funding ("nickel funds") for joint training programs to retrain displaced workers or upgrade current workers (Ferman et al. 1991; Batt and Osterman 1993b). The Communications Workers of America (CWA) negotiated a company-funded, jointly administered child-care program, and other unions have worked closely with management in developing employee assistance programs (for alcohol or substance abuse), which in some cases have evolved into work and family programs (Sonnenstuhl and Trice 1990). The CWA, UAW, IAM, Service Employees' International Union (SEIU), and other unions, have gained important benefits for members through these efforts. These narrowly defined joint problem-solving programs are more easily implemented than "participatory" programs because the limited programs are more clearly defined and of clear mutual benefit to those involved. The union can use the committee structure to increase membership participation in union-sponsored activities and build internal organizational strength. Union members often see immediate gains in areas traditionally ignored by collective bargaining.

It is not a far stretch, then, to apply what has been learned in these limited spheres to joint partnerships focused on the redesign of jobs and the reorganization of work. The difficulty is that participation at this level goes to the heart of American labor law: challenging management rights, shifting decision-making power over issues central to firm profits and workers' income and employment security, and requiring the union to play an economic rather than a strictly political role in the production process. Nonetheless, a few firms and unions are making this change with some success. In these cases, joint structures become an extension of collective bargaining.

The American Flint and Glass Workers Union (AFGWU) at Corning, for-example, views its "business partnership" with management in strategic terms, incorporates conditions for participation into a working document, and negotiates pay-for-skill rates into its contract (on-site visit and inter-views, Oct. 7–8, 1992).

There are several ways in which a union's participation on representa-tional committees can complement consultative or substantive arrange-ments. The union's leadership in and monitoring of the process is likely to increase trust between workers and managers and to provide workers with an independent source of technical assistance and information about what works best based on the union's experience at other work sites. Joint struc-tures at various levels help ensure management commitment at higher levels of the organization, where support is often reported to be problematic. An analysis of the 1987 GAO survey data, for example, found that participa-tory programs in unionized firms tend to be more substantive and effective and to involve more team-based production than in nonunionized firms (Eaton and Voos 1992). Unions also have a key role to play in making sure workers are equally treated, have equal access to training, and share in the gains associated with moving to higher-performance work systems.

7.

ORGANIZATIONAL CHANGE IN SERVICES

Most of the experiments in management methods, work reorganization, human resource practices, and industrial relations both in the United States and abroad began in manufacturing settings. In this chapter we examine the extent to which such reforms can be and have been applied to nonmanufacturing activities. We will focus on organizational change in the service sector, which the government defines in the Standard Industrial Classification (SIC) as nongoods-producing industries and which is divided into five two-digit subcategories based on similarities in the degree of capital intensity and final products.[1] We will also examine the production of services in manufacturing firms and the extent to which clerical, technical, professional, and managerial workers in these firms are involved in organizational change.

In considering restructuring in services, three questions are relevant: First, what reforms are theoretically applicable to services? Second, what is the impetus or need for change in this sector? And, third, to what extent have service industries and organizations actually adopted reforms to improve performance?

THEORETICAL CONSIDERATIONS

Although most models of organizational change originate in manufacturing settings, most theorists argue that their models are universal and apply equally to all work settings. Thus, production-line techniques based on Taylorism were applied to the mass production of low-quality, low-cost services. Industrial psychologists used Hawthorne and other experiments to develop a general theory of human relations. Sociotechnical systems theorists assumed that the benefits of autonomous teamwork were generalizable. More recently, Deming (1984), Juran and Gyrna (1988), and others have asserted the applicability of total quality management to services. The central question is whether differences in the nature of the production processes and markets for goods and services lead to differences in the application or relevance of these theories.

Our hunch is that some differences in the application of work reform theories do occur as a result of differences in the nature of work in manufacturing and services. We consider this issue below in conjunction with our analysis of case materials. But it also appears that conditions in product and service markets are converging. And to the extent that market strategies shape production strategies, goods and service production systems can be expected to converge even more quickly.

For example, international competition has forced manufacturing firms to compete on the basis of product quality and diversity. Customers measure product quality in terms of defects, how well individual specifications were met, quick response to customer requirements, and just-in-time delivery—the same criteria and performance measures that are used to judge the quality of services. Zero defects, for example, are particularly important in services because many are consumed as they are produced (meals, haircuts, medical services, education). There is no opportunity to order replacements for defective services. Quick response (in processing orders, mailing out policies) as well as timeliness and reliability in delivery are equally critical.

Thus, U.S. manufacturing firms have had to rethink their business strategies and to treat products more like services—a reversal of the Taylorist approach to services. This is evident, for example, in the total quality movement and in the heavy emphasis in the Baldrige Award application on market-driven criteria and close customer ties. In this sense, the quality movement has been central in making manufacturers think more like service providers, starting first with an analysis of the market and customer demand, and in organizing production strategies to meet that demand.

Similarly, the internationalization of service markets is forcing service providers to act more like manufacturers of traded goods—to be more cost conscious and to look for ways to improve productivity in the service sector, which has traditionally lagged behind productivity in manufacturing.[2]

Just as national oligopolistic product markets have eroded, service providers can no longer be assured of captive domestic markets. Service firms have increasingly looked to manufacturing strategies to cut costs and improve productivity.

WHY CHANGE IN SERVICES?

Services are increasingly important to the national balance of trade both indirectly as inputs to manufacturing and directly through international trade. The latter role has become more important because of the revolution in information technologies and telecommunications, which allows many service firms to be located anywhere. Financial, information services, and communications networks serving multinationals, for example, may be owned and operated out of any country or location. For a number of reasons, therefore, many service industries no longer enjoy captive markets or isolation from international trade.[3]

Until now, those service firms that were concerned about improving their performance largely tried to increase their productivity through Taylorist methods of automating, routinizing, and eliminating jobs. Managers applied Taylorist modes of work organization to workers in those areas of service industries that could be rationalized and deskilled—clerical workers, back-office processors, telephone operators, and customer service representatives.[4] Thus, firms "produced" some services following a high-volume, production-line mentality. Managers believed that the application of computer and communications technologies to services would allow even more service activities to be handled on such a production-line basis.

There is convincing evidence, however, that relying on the Taylorist implementation of microprocessor-based technology has not been effective. U.S. service industries currently spend more than $100 billion each year on new technologies and own 85 percent of the country's installed information technology. Capital investment in information technology per white-collar worker has doubled since 1982, when it stood at $6,000 per worker. Yet white-collar productivity is about the same as it was in the 1960s (it peaked in 1973, declined till the early 1980s, and then began to return to prior levels). Manufacturing appears to use technology more efficiently than services do (Roach 1991:85). This has suggested to some service firms that office automation alone does not improve productivity and that it will be necessary to restructure and change human resource strategies.

Another segment of the service sector—the public sector—is also under new pressure to change. The fiscal crisis of governments at all levels, the tax revolt, and the threat of privatization have led public agencies and public sector unions to begin reexamining their work processes to serve the public better. The need to improve public sector performance is important not only to public sector workers, who want employment security, but to the taypayer as well. Given the low-performance record of many private sector firms, a simple transfer of ownership from public to private hands is no guarantee of improved accountability or use of tax dollars. Private entrepreneurs lobby as hard as public agencies for tax dollars. Indeed, the history of cost-plus military contracts suggests that private contractors can be more costly and less accountable to the public.[5]

EVIDENCE OF CHANGE

Organizational change is occurring among three different groups of service workers: (1) front-line or "production-level" workers in service firms; (2) professional, technical, and managerial workers in services and manufacturing industries; and (3) public sector workers. Employees *within* each of these groups are similarly situated in the labor market and similarly affected by particular external forces for change.

Low-level office workers, the first group, are often in nonunionized, Taylorized jobs, and the reform needed is similar to that occurring in manufacturing firms—to improve customer service by enhancing the skills and decision-making capacity of these front-line workers and redesigning their jobs accordingly. Increased competition as a result of deregulation and foreign penetration into services provides incentives for such change.

Professional and managerial workers, the second group, already have the skills, education, flexibility, and at least some of the decision-making authority that many change efforts are attempting to give lower-level workers. Workplace changes for professional and managerial workers, then, often include practices that increase their interaction with front-line workers, the use of cross-functional teams, and the introduction of performance measurement systems—all of which are designed to get professionals to work smarter and more efficiently. The growth of bureaucracy and the need to reduce costs, coupled with the failure of earlier changes in work systems that focused only on production-level workers, has led manufacturing and service firms alike to reduce their layers of management and demand higher productivity from their white-collar workers.

Public sector workers, the third group, have the particular task of "serving the public," that is, producing an amorphous public good. They are similar to private sector workers who work in hierarchical bureaucracies with little decision-making responsibility, but are different in that they are more highly unionized and protected from the external labor market by civil service rules that grant them substantial job security. And because the market mechanism is not at play, they receive little information or feedback from the public consumer on how they are performing. Reforms that reduce hierarchies, decentralize decision making, and increase accountability to the public are particularly relevant for these workers.

Based on our review of case materials, several generalizations emerge. Generalizations about the service sector are difficult to make, however, because of the immense diversity in the occupations, work, and size of the organization involved, among other factors. Our cases cover most service industries, including financial services, insurance, utilities and telecommunications, and business services, but the cases include primarily large organizations and exclude many professional occupations. We note some of the limitations of our findings in the discussion below.

First, despite the recognized need for restructuring, service organizations have lagged behind manufacturing in restructuring work systems, and where efforts have occurred, they have been largely piecemeal and marginal. Second, many more examples exist of programs that involve employees in parallel structures or total quality management than in teams or a sociotechnical approach.[6] TQM appears to be particularly popular or useful to service sector organizations because it helps firms develop performance measures in areas of work traditionally thought of as "unmeasurable" or "uncontrollable"—service quality among front-line workers and knowledge work among white-collar professionals and managers. In a number of cases, the application of TQM to services has only this narrow focus on performance measurement.

Third, total quality concepts appear to be more difficult, or at least less obvious, to apply to services because of the nature of service work. This argument depends importantly, however, on which service occupation we consider.[7] Quality appears more difficult to control in instances in which services delivered as they are produced (e.g., customer service, retail) or in transaction-based activities (e.g., financial, communications, insurance, retail services), where multiple transactions create multiple opportunities for errors. Variability in employee attitudes and behavior also directly affects customer service and is more likely to affect quality directly than in manufacturing.

At first glance, the way managers and employees use team concepts also appears to be different in service-producing than in goods-producing industries. This observation again depends on the service activity in question. Workers in a manufacturing plant must coordinate their activities around producing each product. Many workers are directly involved in the production and assembly of an automobile or a piece of apparel. Even in plants where jobs have been redesigned to include a wider range of tasks, no one worker is responsible for producing an entire product. Moreover, even in plants where workers have customer contact, it is not part of their daily assignment.

Service contact work, by contrast, requires individual employees to work with individual customers. The way to enhance this work is to increase the breadth and depth of workers' skills so that they can handle most or all of the customers' needs. In customer service occupations, there is the concept of a "universal" representative—what a universal service representative was, for example, to telephone customers thirty years ago. The analogy in goods production is a craft worker. Over time, the service representative comes to know his or her clients and may develop the kind of relationship with them usually associated with professionals such as tax accountants or lawyers.

Our cases suggest that in customer-contact occupations, the customer-employee link becomes as important as the employee-employee relationship. A closer look at this professional model in organizations, however, suggests that there are limits to the extent to which jobs can be broadened without loss of in-depth technical expertise. This is a relatively unexplored area in the literature, and we can only flag it here as an important arena for future research. There are trade-offs between breadth and depth of knowledge; teaming provides one solution by enabling co-workers to emphasize knowledge in particular areas while keeping abreast of developments in related areas. This is in fact what many professionals do. A tax office, for example, may handle both the personal and business taxes of a client, providing "one-stop shopping" as it were. But within the office, different accountants handle business and personal tax returns. Similarly, in the cases we discuss below, front-line service employees work in teams as knowledge workers to meet the diverse needs of a customer. We discuss these ideas in greater detail in the following section.

PARALLEL STRUCTURES, PERFORMANCE MEASURES, AND TQM

Quality circles and problem-solving teams in services have the look and feel of such activities in manufacturing—they open up communication between lower-level workers and supervisors, whether they occur in a computer company (Control Data Corporation, 1980), a bank (Norwest Bank St. Paul, St. Paul, Minnesota, 1983), or a news organization (Beaumont Newspaper, 1989). Some manufacturing companies learned early on that improving performance only among front-line workers (a quarter of the work force in many large corporations) has limited returns, so they have extended quality circles into white-collar areas (Northrop Corporation [1982], Shell Oil Company [1980]). Because total quality programs start at the top and try to "align the vision" of all employees of the firm, TQM particularly has the effect of involving managers and other professionals in organizational change. TQM efforts usually involve white-collar workers through training sessions and problem-solving task forces or quality circles.

TQM became popular among service firms in the 1980s in part because of its heavy emphasis on starting with the customer to reorient management and on developing measurement systems that account for quality and customer service—"intangible" dimensions traditionally considered too difficult to measure or control. Both Deming and Juran argue that total quality concepts are applicable to service work but for several reasons they are more difficult to apply than in manufacturing.[8] They argue that because the service is not tangible, workers may not have the kind of direct feedback that manufacturing workers do when they produce a product. Quality is more difficult to measure in services, and measures of defect rates rely on a proxy, the by-products of services, or the paper trail left in arranging for services (applications, orders, policies, transmission slips, and so on) (Deming 1984:183–247; Zimmerman and Enell 1988). They also argue that services involve many individual transactions and multiple transactions with an individual customer, so there are more opportunities for mistakes and multiple opportunities to alienate the customer. Although this attribute also provides multiple opportunities to build long-term relationships, arguably any one negative interaction does more harm than a positive one does good. And once a customer is lost, it is difficult to regain her or his confidence.

Managers who leave manufacturing for services routinely complain that it is more difficult to control quality in services because they are delivered as produced (no preinspection), because quality depends so heavily on day-to-day variability in employee attitudes and behavior, and because managers supervise "a large army" of front-line servers, often in hundreds of locations close to customers (Heskett, Sasser, and Hart 1990:112).

Given traditional problems of measurement and quality control in services, it is not surprising that firms in a number of the cases we reviewed made performance measurement systems the centerpiece of their TQM efforts. First Seattle National Bank, for example, claimed a 10 percent improvement in productivity as a result of introducing a measurement and reporting system (Murray and Mertes 1989). At Continental Insurance (1983) and Zurich-American Insurance (1991), the quality programs focused heavily on developing measurement systems to improve productivity, as did Baxter's corporate finance office (1987). Sewall Village Cadillac, a car dealership in Dallas, built its quality program around a measurement and reporting program in which it publicly displayed the sales and service performance of each employee on a board in the dealership, presumably to increase individual competitiveness (1987).

The application of total quality principles has also had a measurement focus in many professional occupations. At Southern Company Services, for example, an engineering and technical firm that services utility companies, the total quality programs involved two dimensions: a heavy expenditure of effort to develop a productivity measurement system that would take account of effectiveness, efficiency, quality, quantity, and timeliness; and a quality circle program to improve communication (Southern Company Services, 1984).

Measuring performance is the dominant theme even in firms with a more classic TQM approach. American Express, for example, piloted a quality effort at its Phoenix, Arizona, card operation. The company emphasized the importance of defining quality from the customer's point of view and of carefully measuring service delivery. It reexamined work flows to eliminate unnecessary steps and to restructure lines of reporting. Employee involvement consisted of soliciting ideas for improvement from groups of employees, establishing new performance standards, providing quality training, and educating employees on how the new standards had become a part of each employee's performance appraisal. Recognition programs provided incentives for increased effort. After three years, the company claimed that quality had improved by 78 percent, expenses per transaction had dropped 21 percent, and the time to process new accounts had been cut in half. The company went on to develop a "Service Tracking Report" to track one hundred service measures worldwide as the basis for a statistical process control program and an exacting quality target (American Express, 1988; Welch 1992).

Similarly, First National Bank of Chicago began a quality improvement program with a strong emphasis on measurement and customer feedback and some on the redesign of jobs and work. Beginning in 1981, the bank identified new corporate services that could become profit centers, restructured the organization into strategic business units based on individual products, and developed an extensive measurement system to track weekly product performance according to minimum acceptable performance (MAP) standards. MAP standards were continually adjusted upward to induce improvement, and managers' compensation was linked to reaching these goals. To encourage employee involvement, the bank introduced a suggestion system, "quality improvement teams" (similar to quality circles), and monthly recognition awards. The bank boasts significant drops in error rates and claims the program saves $7 to $10 million annually. In 1988, the bank became the first financial institution to receive the International Customer Service Association's Award of Excellence (First National Bank of Chicago, 1987, 1990).

Given the deregulation in banking services in the last decade, numerous financial institutions have attempted reforms to improve customer service, perhaps more so than in many other service industries. A survey of quality programs in financial institutions, for example, found that 70 percent of respondents had a quality control program (Hopkins 1989).[9] The programs often did not alter how the organization functioned, however; only about half the respondents used error information to correct procedures or to prevent future errors. And only a quarter of the respondents used statistical methods to analyze or control errors.

JOB ENLARGEMENT, DECENTRALIZATION, AND SELF-DIRECTED TEAMS

Only a few of the service sector cases we reviewed involved the use of self-directed teams, a sociotechnical approach to work redesign, or significant changes in the structures of power. Where "teams" exist, they are often designed to improve motivation or effort, rather than to reorganize work roles and authority relations. When firms speak of "empowerment," they often mean decentralizing profit centers or decision making to middle managers or enlarging the scope or responsibilities of front-line workers without necessarily changing decision-making hierarchies (see, for example, the case studies of clerical work in Roose 1992).

An early experimenter in job enlargement was Citibank, which began a reorganization effort in the mid-1970s. The company had been a highly centralized, functional organization that processed all transactions—business and residential—in the same manner. Managers and workers had responsibility for particular functions, and no one oversaw the process for any one customer from start to finish. Management introduced structural changes at two levels of the organization: it organized work units around particular markets, and it redesigned clerical jobs so that there was less emphasis on a particular, narrow function and more focus on the customer. In the decentralized, customer-oriented structure, each manager had control over a total transaction for a particular set of customers, defined by type of customer (business, government, residential) and geographic location.

The individual jobs of front-line workers expanded to allow them to handle all the steps necessary for a customer request. The purpose of this job enlargement was to reduce monotony and improve motivation, personal responsibility, and productivity, but no use was made of teamwork. A change in technology from a mainframe to mini-computers faciliated decentralization. A detailed process review or "content analysis" identified areas for automation, and labor-intensive areas were heavily automated. Results were significant. In the letter of credit unit, for example, productivity increased, revenues tripled in three years, and expenses, which had been increasing at an annual rate of 15 percent, were held constant (Matteis 1979; Walters 1982). What Citibank did in the 1970s is very similar to what TQM programs attempted in the 1980s.

Another example comes from a telemarketing office of a large telecommunications firm. After going through the quality training process, workers who took orders for telephone installation identified an area in which they had little control—another office was responsible for checking installation dates and doing customer follow-up calls. These additional tasks were brought under the jurisdiction of the order clerks, who received training on the appropriate computerized database and enlarged their scope of responsibility. Although the work continued to be done on an individual basis, the group refers to itself as a "team." The sense of teamwork or cooperation in the office arose from the quality training, which improved communications among workers and between workers and managers. The entire process has significantly improved employee morale (personal interview, Nov. 1992).

In another case, a sales and marketing unit of a communications firm, management organized telephone sales representatives into "teams" by geographic area and type of business customer. Team members worked with an account executive, received training in marketing, and enlarged the scope of their jobs to include visits to business clients rather than just phone work. The team or cooperative environment provided the support for individual workers to move into a more client-oriented role, though teamwork in the sense of job rotation or working together on a single project was not a regular part of the job itself (personal interview, Oct. 1992).

Yet another example is AT&T's Universal Card operation in Jacksonville, Florida, a winner of the 1992 Baldrige Award. Its competitive advantage in entering the market was to offer credit cards with no annual fee for the first subscribers and a lower and variable interest rate overall. AT&T retains customers by emphasizing customer service: customer service representatives can handle a wide array of questions and can resolve problems without contacting supervisors. Electronic monitoring, including spot checks of phone conversations by supervisors and 110 measurements reported daily, ensures the quality of service. "Teams" behave like quality circles, meeting once a week to discuss problems on the jobs (Waggoner 1992).

These cases draw on the experiences of customer-contact service occupations. The nature of this work differs from that of making a product, and, arguably, this difference shapes the different role that teamwork plays. In manufacturing, for example, front-line workers produce a tangible product in relatively close physical proximity to one another. Their work is interdependent. Improving performance depends on improving the coordination between workers and understanding how what is done at one point in the process affects another point. There are a number of discrete tasks, and workers improve their understanding of the work process by rotating across jobs as well as by deepening their analytical abilities.

By contrast, successful performance in customer-contact jobs requires individual workers to develop a close relationship with individual customers. Examples include office workers such as receptionists; customer service representatives in insurance, real estate, finance, telecommunications, sales and marketing, business or repair services, educational services, hotels and restaurants; tellers in banks; and clerks in payroll, billing, and accounting departments of most businesses. In these settings, the way to improve service is to move away from an impersonal, assembly-line mentality toward a more "professional" or personal model of client contact. Front-line workers need to expand their ability to handle a number of issues for any one customer in order to reduce the time it takes to solve a problem and the confusion for the customer of talking to more than one person. Reliability therefore improves because the customer can develop a longer-term relationship with a particular customer service representative. Moreover, workers are likely to need a deeper understanding of the services the firm offers as well as a command of information or computer systems to answer a range of customer questions with accuracy. The advantage of teamwork in these cases appears primarily to be the mutual gains achieved by employees in learning from one another, problem solving, and offering support.

This thesis is consistent with the ideas of some theorists concerning how service industries can move away from a Taylorist model to a high-performance work system. Leonard Schlesinger and James Heskett (1991a, 1991b), for example, contrast a (Taylorist) cycle of failure with a (high-performance) cycle of success. In the first instance, high-volume markets with low profit margins lead firms to take a low-cost strategy: hiring low-skill workers at low wages, designing narrow jobs to accommodate these workers, using technology to control quality and rules to control workers. For workers, this approach creates dissatisfaction and poor service, high turnover, and therefore a lack of continuity between employees and customers. Failing to develop customer loyalty, the firms experience high customer turnover as well and need to devote extensive resources to marketing and attracting new customers.

The success cycle works in reverse: with a focus on higher profit markets, firms hire more skilled workers, invest in training, increase wages, and reduce turnover. Satisfied employees make satisfied customers, and cost savings arise from lower customer turnover and lower marketing costs (Schlesinger and Heskett 1991a). Job enlargement and skill enhancement rather than sociotechnical work design and self-directed teams are seen as central to continuous improvement.[10]

There are other cases in which service organizations have shifted to self-directed teams in addition to enhancing individual jobs—particularly when there were a variety of technical tasks to accomplish to provide the service or the work was more blue-collar in character (as in installation and repair). We have identified examples of this approach among three types of service employees: front-line office workers, field workers, and professional-managerial workers.

Among front-line office workers in one large telecommunications company, teamwork, job rotation, and cross-training were found to be useful and offered flexibility in work units that had responsibility for several specialized tasks. This was true, for example, in a payroll and accounting office where there were specialized tasks and computer programs for a number of functions (e.g., current payroll, pensions, health-care benefits). Cross-training in the different systems enabled workers to understand how errors that entered the system at one point had repercussions at other points; it also allowed for more flexible coverage and deployment of workers in the various jobs in the unit. The requirements of each job were sufficiently technical that it would have been inefficient for each employee to handle all systems simultaneously. This group was in the process of moving to more self-directed teams, in which the supervisor would serve as a "coach" (personal interview, Oct. 1992).

Another example comes from the Shenandoah Life Insurance Company, which, beginning in 1983, used a sociotechnical approach to redesign work flows and introduced self-directed teams at some of its Virginia offices. Employees assumed responsibility for personnel as well as work-related issues and undertook cross-training in a pay-for-learning compensation system. Supervisor/employee ratios dropped from 1:7 to 1:37 (Shenandoah Life Insurance Company, 1991).

Field-based teams are a way firms can involve workers in decentralized field operations, such as trucking and delivery jobs or installation and repair in telecommunications. The switch to self-directed teams coupled with the use of hand-held devices or mini-computers installed in trucks and vans has proved effective in improving performance in these hard-to-monitor jobs.

At Federal Express, for example, couriers have always been responsible for scheduling their own routes and for making changes so they can handle unscheduled pickups (tasks typically handled by supervisors in other firms). They have broader jobs than typical couriers because they act as assistant sales representatives as well, using their knowledge of customers and routes to inform existing customers about new services. "Teamwork" developed as computers installed in the trucks allowed the couriers to communicate directly with each other, help each other, and "balance routes" between those who had unexpectedly large shipments and those who had lighter loads. Today, these teams exist in addition to ad hoc problem-solving teams (Commission on the Skills of the American Workforce 1991).

Installation and repair teams in Bell telephone companies work in a similar fashion. In the conventional system of work, still used in most places, installation and repair technicians report to a garage, receive orders from a dispatch office through a supervisor, follow the orders, and solve narrowly defined problems. If a customer wants additional services, she has to place another order. If the repairperson finds additional difficulties in the network or lines, he or she has to call the supervisor, who then has to come to the location to approve the additional work, causing considerable time delays. Workers are not allowed to "double-up" on jobs; supervisors monitor work by driving around and spot-checking workers on the street.

By contrast, a self-directed team at a Bell company has a geographic turf and tries to develop more personal relationships with customers. Because the team "owns the turf," workers have more incentive to do preventive work, thereby keeping customer complaints to a minimum. The team receives a group of orders at the beginning of each day and divides the work among members. Whenever possible, repeat work is given to the member who did the initial work, because he or she is more knowledgeable about the job in question. Teamwork also fosters training and cross-training in different skills. On difficult jobs, workers team up to save time. If one member is having difficulty on an order, he can beep another member for technical advice. If a customer has additional requests, installers can do the work on the spot. Performance is measured not by the number of jobs done by individual workers (which pushes workers to do many narrowly defined jobs), but by quality measures such as repeat repair rates and network failures measured at the work unit or group level (personal interview, Oct. 1992).

Among professional and managerial workers, the advantage of teamwork appears to be in the use of a collaborative process to solve problems, come up with more innovative products or processes, or improve the quality of work.

McDonnell Douglas Astronautics, in St. Louis, for example, took a sociotechnical approach to white-collar productivity improvement in a pilot project in the mid-1980s. In a financial work unit, management grouped professional workers into teams at the work unit level to analyze and redesign their work flow, identify training needs, develop *group* performance measures appropriate to the work they do, and figure out more efficient uses of technology. The group was involved in financial analyses for management; late analyses and labor hours per analysis dropped by more than half as a result (McDonnell Douglas, 1987).

Examples from research and development in engineering often point to the added value and reduction in product development time arising from the use of cross-functional teams. By overlapping product and process engineering, for example, Japanese automakers have far outpaced Americans and Europeans in model renewal. By the 1980s, however, many U.S. firms and suppliers in the auto industry had shifted to concurrent engineering and "multi-functional task forces" (Clark and Fujimoto 1991).

INDUSTRIAL RELATIONS STRATEGIES

AT&T, BellSouth, and U.S. West provide examples of firms in the service sector that have developed joint efforts with the unions that represent their employees to improve employee participation and reorganize work to improve quality and customer service. The task of coordinating consistently high-quality, customer-oriented service in telecommunications network operations in hundreds of geographically dispersed units is immense. In these companies, union and management leadership in the development of participatory work systems coupled with joint structures at various levels of the organization are central to the diffusion and sustainability of high-performance work systems.

Under the old Bell system, experiments in employee participation in decision making began in 1980 when AT&T, the Communications Workers of America, and the International Brotherhood of Electrical Workers (IBEW) negotiated the Quality of Work Life Program. Between 1980 and 1984, more than 100,000 Bell system employees participated in the program, the largest such effort by any company or union in the country (U.S. Department of Labor Bureau of Labor-Management Relations 1985). As with many QWL programs, this effort was later criticized by the participants for being overly focused on "cosmetic" or superficial issues rather than on improving work processes, jobs, and quality (U.S. Department of Labor Bureau of Labor-Management Relations 1985). Nonetheless, it provided managers and employees with practical experience in participating in joint problem solving at the local level. The local leaders and managers who most fully embraced the program were those who had been open to other recent joint efforts to reorganize work and improve customer service in more substantive ways.

AT&T

Following divestiture in 1984, deregulation and changes in technology brought new entrants into telecommunications markets and led to the erosion in market share of AT&T in the long-distance market. More recently, deregulation in local markets has increased the competition for the Regional Bell Operating Companies (RBOCs), such as BellSouth. As a result, the companies formed from the old Bell system face daunting strategic and organizational dilemmas. On the one hand, they must cut costs to compete with the new entrants—carriers with low overhead using nonunionized labor and installing new technology with lower maintenance costs. On the other hand, they have had to maintain and improve a switching and transmission infrastructure built on what is now obsolete technology. At the same time that they seek to reduce costs, AT&T must make sure that it does not alienate its massive loyal customer base or the commitment of the work force, both of which are central to providing high-quality customer service.

AT&T went through a period of radical downsizing and reorganization into strategic business units following divestiture, resulting in the reduction of about 40 percent of the managerial and nonmanagerial work force. Despite notable efforts to create cooperative relations, such as the jointly operated training program known as The Alliance (Batt and Osterman 1993b), employee morale and labor-management relations suffered overall.[11]

During the past few years, efforts to improve quality and customer service through the use of quality improvement and self-directed teams have emerged at local work sites and business units. The challenge for AT&T has been to develop a coherent structure to translate these isolated experiments and "islands of excellence" into organizationwide gains in performance. For the unions, the challenge has been to develop a strategy to safeguard the employment security and income growth of their members in an industry in which technological change and market fragmentation will necessitate ongoing changes in work processes, the design of jobs, and the demand for skill.

In 1992, the CWA, IBEW, and AT&T, in an agreement known as the "Workplace of the Future," agreed to create a joint structure to address these issues. The agreement anticipates joint union-management participation in four representative bodies at three levels of the corporation: the workplace, the business unit, and corporate levels. Through this tiered structure, the parties anticipate "interactive planning, both top down and bottom up" (Bahr and Ketchum 1993).

At the work-site level, the unions select employee representatives to be involved in planning how work will be done. The contract language construes workplace change broadly to enable local managers and employees to devise "workplace models" to meet local needs. Suggested models include employee participation initiatives, self-directed teams, quality improvement teams, and new systems of work organization. Workplace models must be jointly designed and approved before implementation.

Business Unit Planning Councils, which are composed of top-level department managers and union representatives, provide critical arenas for union involvement in business planning around such issues as technological change, work organization, and job content. AT&T has established more than twenty strategic business units, and three business unit planning councils have already been created, as envisioned in the Workplace of the Future. Although the contract does not call for equal numbers of management and union representatives or union veto power on these planning councils, it clearly provides for substantive information sharing and substantial union influence in strategic business decisions, particularly as they affect employment levels and skill requirements. According to the contract, "The Company recognizes that gaining employee involvement and commitment to the *Workplace of the Future* model, which targets customer satisfaction and market flexibility, requires the Company to be sensitive to employees' needs regarding employment security" (Bahr and Ketchum 1993).

A third body, the Constructive Relationship Council (CRC) consists of four top-level union and management representatives (two from each side) who handle issues that arise in the Business Unit Planning Councils that affect the negotiated contract. The CRC is a mechanism for integrating ongoing changes into the contract so that labor-management participatory structures are extensions of, rather than alternatives to, collective bargaining.

Finally, a top-level Human Resources Board consists of representatives of top management, the unions, and outside experts in human resource issues who consider long-term strategic issues on a global scale.

BellSouth

Unlike many companies in which quality and employee-involvement programs are at odds or implemented as separate, seemingly unrelated efforts, BellSouth's strategy has been to build total quality principles into the existing structure of the quality of work life programs jointly administered by the union and management since 1980. According to managers and union leaders alike, this integration is central to the successful mobilization of employees around improving customer service. The QWL program has been popular among employees in the Bell system because it represents the first time that managers agreed to participate with employees in problem solving around workplace issues. Although committees initially ended up dealing with issues that concerned the quality of employees' work life more than the quality of their work performance, the committees have contributed to improved labor-management relations and employee goodwill at the local level. And although the activism of QWL committees ebbed and flowed in the 1980s, as of 1990, 600 QWL committees were still active throughout the corporation. Through this structure, the company has invited local union presidents in cities across the South to attend district and state-level business meetings with department managers to discuss QWL activities.

By the late 1980s, BellSouth had embraced a total quality program as a strategy to improve quality and customer service. It discussed this initiative with the CWA district leadership during the 1989 contract negotiations, and the parties reached an agreement to sponsor a joint "Excellence through Quality" program similar to that launched by Xerox and ACTWU. The company and union set up joint quality training teams at local, state, and corporate levels in which equal numbers of trainers are selected by the union (from rank-and-file members) and by management (from mid-level managerial ranks). These teams of trainers have developed curriculum and provided training in quality for employees throughout the BellSouth system.

The program goes beyond simple training in quality principles or techniques, however. By working with what were the QWL committees and what are now called quality action teams, the trainers provide technical assistance in undertaking a variety of workplace innovations, job redesign efforts, initiatives to improve work processes, and self-directed teams. The former management director of the QWL program now works as the corporate leader for the development of self-directed teams throughout the company. Approximately 150 such teams currently exist, and the number is expanding rapidly.

Also under the "Excellence through Quality" program, union leaders' participation in company business meetings has increased. Now, union leaders often attend monthly business meetings at the district, state, and corporate levels. Whereas in the past they would stay only for that part of the agenda that concerned the QWL program, they now stay for the entire meeting. This structure provides an ongoing forum for the company to share information about the business and for union leaders to have input into business decisions.

Central to the union's active involvement in supporting quality efforts has been the company's long-term recognition of the union and its institutional security. At the time of divestiture, for example, when BellSouth set up a separate subsidiary known as Advanced Systems, Inc. (ASI), it negotiated a separate contract with the CWA rather than operate ASI as a non-union subsidiary. In the first round of bargaining after divestiture, BellSouth was the only RBOC to agree to the union's request for regionwide bargaining (as opposed to the more decentralized approach of bargaining with each telephone company in the region). Since 1986, BellSouth and the CWA have jointly operated a program to provide workers with training in career planning and thereby improve the potential for employment security. During the 1989 negotiations, the company agreed to several clauses that improved job security and union membership levels. One agreement set up a joint union-management task force to study the content of managerial jobs and to return to the bargaining unit those jobs that were not managerial. As a result, 550 jobs were returned to the bargaining unit between 1989 and 1992. In 1992, the union and company agreed to set up a series of additional joint task forces to develop pilot innovative work arrangements, including self-directed teams and telecommuting.[12]

U.S. West

The 1980 QWL program negotiated by AT&T and the CWA and IBEW also became the basis of an expanded employee involvement program negotiated by the union and management at U.S. West in 1986 negotiations. The program was oriented toward building labor-management problem-solving teams at local work sites. By 1989, the CWA and the company agreed to further institutionalize the employee participation program by setting up a corporate-level employee involvement quality center, with a staff of forty organizational consultants. The company committed $9.5 million to fund forty contractual change agents, twenty chosen by the union and twenty chosen by management. Their job was to assist local union and management leaders and workers in developing joint approaches to problem solving and to provide training in such areas as team building. By the 1992 contract negotiations, the CWA and management focused the employee involvement program more centrally on quality and customer service and integrated the organizational consultants into decentralized service and marketing units.

In the meantime, a more dramatic joint labor-management effort evolved in the company's home and personal services business unit. Beginning in 1992, the CWA, IBEW, and management jointly redesigned the jobs of over four thousand customer representatives serving residential customers. As part of the process, the company agreed to a union demand that there would be no layoffs or pay downgrades resulting from the redesign effort and that the unions would be fully involved as equal partners in the decision-making process. The design team used a sociotechnical systems approach to integrate the technological (computer systems) and social (particularly customer contact) aspects of the work and developed the job of service consultant, increasing the diversity of workers' tasks and decision-making discretion. The redesigned jobs, which the company and unions began piloting in 1993, had the goal of reducing the monotony and tight supervision experienced by workers on the one hand, and improving the quality of customer service on the other (see U.S. Congress 1993).

PUBLIC SECTOR CASES

Although organizational change is occurring much more slowly in the public than the private sector, government agencies at all levels have been exploring the application of employee involvement, teams, total quality, and joint labor-management committees to public service. The process of implementing these programs as well as the obstacles do not appear to differ markedly from those in the private sector, with the exception that the change efforts are more constrained by civil service rules, which fall outside the jurisdiction of both the union and management. Many of the cases we reviewed began in response to fiscal crises and the call to privatize services, which threatened managerial and nonmanagerial jobs alike. Unions that represent public sector workers, such as the American Federation of State, County and Municipal Employees (AFSCME), the SEIU, the American Federation of Teachers (AFT), and the National Education Association (NEA) have undertaken a number of joint projects to improve quality and save jobs.

An early example comes from the U.S. Customs Service at Houston Intercontinental Airport, where recommendations for changes from a quality circle resulted in dramatic improvements in efficiency. To respond to employee concerns of overwork and low morale as well as customer complaints of long waiting times, the quality circle came up with an honor system whereby passengers tell customs workers whether they have anything to declare, rather than requiring everyone to be checked. Spot checks and roving inspectors control contraband. The facility went from processing four hundred people per hour to processing one thousand (U.S. Customs Service, 1985).

Another early case involved the Copyright Office in Washington, D.C., where an AFSCME local participated in a QWL program to improve productivity and employee morale. The program focused on employee participation in decision making and put particular emphasis on training in problem solving, team building, and management-employee relations. Using a sociotechnical approach, employee-management task groups redesigned jobs so as to convert an assembly-line system for processing copyright applications into a "product-line" approach in which semi-autonomous teams handled all of the paperwork for the product line in question. Turnaround time dropped from as much as four months to two weeks. After four years, the labor-management committee reported a 15 percent gain in productivity, which saved taxpayers $5 million (U.S. Copyright Office, 1984).

Employees at state and local agencies have worked through similar joint labor-management committees and employee-participation programs to improve productivity, service quality, and retain jobs, as well as to reduce costs. In New York, for example, professional employees represented by SEIU and state administrators set up a statewide labor-management committee to convert Job Service and Unemployment Insurance offices into "one-stop" community service offices. The restructuring enabled the state to offer more comprehensive services to the unemployed, to introduce greater flexibility into its deployment of staff, and to provide workers with better job security and career opportunities (SEIU, 1992).

In another case involving the SEIU, this one at San Francisco General Hospital, an employee suggestion to apply the hospice model of treatment for AIDS patients resulted in a 40 percent reduction in the average cost of AIDS treatment. Similarly, through an employee-participation program in state mental hospitals in Connecticut, employees redesigned staffing schedules to reduce costs as well as injury rates, resulting in $300,000 in savings in the first year. Finally, in New York City, mechanics in the Bureau of Motor Equipment in the Department of Sanitation used a union-management program to reorganize work, resulting in decreased costs, improved productivity, and the receipt of the 1992 Award for State and Local Government Service by the John F. Kennedy School of Government (SEIU, 1992).

Local public schools have also experimented with a variety of participation and team concepts to improve education. At the Duluth, Minnesota, local of the AFT, public school faculty and administrators used a QWL structure to face a fiscal crisis and decide how to achieve $5 million in savings (Duluth Public Schools, 1991). In "building-based management programs" in Seattle, Washington, teachers make decisions about the curriculum, monitoring of the classroom, and discipline policies, among other matters, while principals serve as facilitators. In other districts, such as the one in Orange County, Florida, teachers are using a "teamwork approach" to formalize teacher-support networks within the district (NEA, 1988, 1992).

Efforts to introduce total quality programs into government service have also expanded in recent years, spurred by the President's Award for Quality and Productivity, similar to the Baldrige Award in the private sector. A 1991 winner was the Air Force Logistics Command at Wright-Patterson Air Force Base in Ohio, where the use of cross-functional "process action teams" led to reported improvements in on-time delivery rates, repair rates, and rework rates. The Patent and Trademark Office of the Department of Commerce reduced processing time for patents from thirty-seven days to eighteen. And the Veterans Affairs Medical Center in Kansas City, Missouri, used TQM methods to reduce the average length of a patient's stay by 15 percent and the mortality rate by 20 percent (Jasper 1992). The GAO also introduced a quality program in 1991 but has not yet reported the results (U.S. GAO 1990, 1991b).

Clearly, public sector agencies can benefit from the use of new management methods, work reorganization, and human resource and industrial relations practices developed in the private sector. For these strategies to be successful, however, they must be used not simply to cut government costs under the threat of privatization but to improve work force skills and decision-making capabilities so as to provide high-quality services.

Innovative practices have the potential to improve quality and reduce costs in services as well as in manufacturing, and in public sector organizations as well as in private companies. Small or partial changes, however, have small effects. In the last few years, some firms have been able to build on the experiments of the last decade or more to develop or adopt coherent high-performance production systems. Two distinct models have emerged. We discuss them in the next chapter.

PART IV.

THE SOLUTIONS

8.

AMERICAN MODELS OF HIGH

PERFORMANCE

I n our review in part III of nearly two hundred case studies of workplace change in American firms, we observed that managers and employees frequently combine practices drawn from very different production models to create a new model they hope will lead to improved efficiency or quality. It is now commonplace, for example, for American firms to benchmark their practices against those of "best-practice" companies in the United States and abroad. In some instances, union leaders have accompanied corporate managers in visits to their European and Japanese counterparts to gather new ideas for improving production and human resource practices.

The Japanese system of lean production has received the most attention in the popular press, but it is not the only source of work innovation. Some strategies, such as total quality management via statistical control processes, originated in the United States in the 1920s at Bell Labs and were central features of war production in American companies during World War II before being adopted by the Japanese (Walton 1986:8; Eidt 1992). The American human resource model, developed from the 1950s on by firms such as IBM, Procter & Gamble, Cummins Engine, Texas Instrument, and Hewlett Packard, continues to have an influential effect on work reorganization efforts. Following this model, managers draw on the principles of organizational psychology to build incentive programs designed to improve worker motivation and management-employee communication. The concept of pay for performance, for example, grows out of this tradition and gainsharing, a group-based system for sharing gains in productivity, was developed by the United Steel Workers in the 1940s (Lesieur 1958).

In their search for better production methods, U.S. firms have also isolated and experimented with the distinctive features of work systems developed in other national contexts. The current widespread interest in self-managed teams (SMTs) draws on the sociotechnical systems approach, which emerged in Britain and Norway in the 1950s and first gained attention in the United States in the 1960s and 1970s (Trist 1981; Zager and Rosow 1982). The Swedish version—exemplified by Volvo's Uddevalla plant, among others—emphasizes low-volume, customized production using autonomous teams of highly skilled craft workers. From Japanese lean production, American firms have copied quality circles, total quality engineering, and just-in-time inventory systems. Italian and German industrial districts have offered examples of how networks of firms can collaborate in ways that enhance product innovation and provide flexibility—a model of "flexible specialization"—for responding to rapidly changing product demand. State governments have supported the development of such small-firm networks as a vehicle for regional economic development (Bosworth 1992; Batt and Osterman 1993b; Harrison 1993); and there is growing interest in expanding this model to larger companies on a more national scale (Nagel and Dove 1991).

More recently, researchers and policy makers have focused on the German system of diversified quality production—on the critical role of the publicly funded training system jointly administered by the government, unions, and firms (Oosterman 1988; Berg 1993), on the centrality of works councils in representing employees in day-to-day production-level decisions; and on the practice whereby unions are involved in strategic decision making in enterprises (Freeman 1991; Rogers and Wootton 1992; Wever, Berg, and Kochan 1993).

Many U.S. firms put together a "menu" of human resource policies and organizational tools.[1] The advantage of this "eclectic" approach is that it has the potential to create new human resource practices, allows for more variety within the organization, and enables firms to adapt production methods to the particular requirements of a product line or to the specific interests of workers and managers. The danger, however, is that firms may adopt fragments of production systems that, taken out of context, do not produce the ongoing improvements they do in their original settings—as occurred with quality circles in the early 1980s (Drago 1988; Lawler and

Mohrman 1987; Kochan, Katz, and Mower 1984) and may be happening with some applications of total quality management (Gilbert 1992; Boyett, Kearney, and Conn 1992; Mathews 1992; McLagan 1991). These failures fuel worker cynicism with workplace change and encourage management fadism. The central questions are whether this menu approach adds up to a coherent whole, and whether, within the new production model, there are opportunities for organizational learning and continuous improvements in performance.

Our review of the evidence points to the emergence from a sea of variation of two distinctly American high-performance work systems. Both draw on quality engineering and management concepts, and both use incentives developed in the American human resource model. In other words, they draw on similar management tools and techniques to improve performance. As a result, the demarcation between the two systems tends to be fuzzy, and there can be considerable overlap in the practices employed in each.

The approaches differ, however, in the extent to which they locate the source of continuous improvement as their front-line work force and, consequently, in their use of human resource practices such as worker participation in decision making, whether they provide extensive training for non-managerial employees, and whether employment security provides employees with the opportunity, capability, and motivation to contribute to upgrading quality and efficiency. They differ as well in the extent to which employee participation extends beyond the immediate work process and involves workers or their representatives in a broad range of operational and business decisions.

The first system is an American version of lean production, perhaps best characterized by the criteria for the influential Baldrige Award, which emphasize the use of top-management–driven quality systems.[2] The second is a more decentralized system that we refer to as "American team production." It combines the principles of Swedish sociotechnical systems and self-directed work with those of quality engineering.[3] Performance improvements in both cases appear impressive. These findings contradict the view held by many, and expressed most emphatically in *The Machine That Changed the World* (Womack, Jones, and Roos 1990), that the Japanese model of lean production is superior to all other production models and should be applied in every industry.[4]

The distinction between these two systems, in other words, centers largely on differences in human resource and industrial relations policies rather than on differences in product markets, technology, or organizational strategies. The American team production approach relies heavily on decentralized decision making through collaborative teamwork and on joint labor-management structures that allow workers to be represented in decision making at every level of the company—operational, tactical, and strategic. The American version of lean production is more centralized in its approach—tending to implement or mandate a set of human resource policies such as training in quality or employee involvement across the entire organization. This approach emphasizes some elements of total quality management more than others. It focuses, for example, on process management or the reengineering of work flows, data collection and performance measurement, and a centralized approach and "alignment of vision" between the goals of the company and those of the employees. Although quality theorists such as Deming discuss the importance of employee involvement, American firms using this approach do not rely on innovations from front-line workers in the way envisioned in the more decentralized team production approach. Employee involvement, for example, usually takes the form of a selected subset of workers participating in problem-solving committees directed by first-line supervisors or other managers.

Several researchers have noted that a dilemma exists in balancing decentralized decision making and self-directed work teams, on the one hand, and total quality management, on the other: the bottom-up logic of the self-directed team approach and the top-down logic of TQM appear to be contradictory, insofar as total quality principles do not challenge management to decentralize decision making to the extent implied by the self-directed team production model (see, for example, the survey of management practices in Lawler, Mohrman, and Ledford 1992:101–3; see also Klein 1991). Total quality is too easily adapted to an existing hierarchy without making fundamental changes in human resource and industrial relations practices. Companies are likely to resolve this contradiction by adopting one approach or the other, but not both. The risk of the decentralized approach is substantial variation in performance and insufficient coordination across the organization; that of the centralized approach is inadequate employee involvement and autonomy so that continuous improvements in performance do not materialize (on the latter point, see Beaumont, Hunter, and Phayre 1993).

Where unions have the organizational capacity and leadership to become involved in production decisions, they appear to provide an organizational

Japanese transplant, employment security provides the basis for employees to participate in continuous improvement, or *kaizen,* efforts. In both settings, employees have a commitment from the firm to a no-layoff policy; they also have protection against unjust dismissal through collective bargaining agreements. As a result, workers are able to contribute ideas for improvement without jeopardizing anyone's employment security, and without putting themselves at risk of recrimination if the ideas prove unpopular with management.

Baldrige Criteria and TQM

It is important to understand the Baldrige Award because it has already affected the behavior of thousands of managers across the country. In the first five rounds since its inception in 1988, approximately five hundred applicants have entered the competition.[5] It often takes two, three, or more years to prepare to enter the competition and put into place the management practices suggested by the criteria for the award, so that many more companies have been influenced by the competition than the number of applicants indicates. In 1992, for example, 240,000 companies requested copies of the award criteria and application (Miller 1992:1). Moreover, the award has spurred networking and benchmarking among firms by requiring winners to respond to requests for information. Baldrige winners have thus given hundreds of lectures and conferences to managers from firms interested in replicating successful techniques (Main 1991).

Many firms use the Baldrige criteria as a "road map" for success (Garvin 1991; Main 1991). Many companies have begun doing "mock" applications as part of their annual performance evaluations, and some are submitting applications as a way to get feedback from the Baldrige examiners.[6] Many other companies have begun their own internal quality awards. In 1990, for example, Westinghouse required all ninety of its corporate divisions to compete for its internal George Westinghouse Total Quality awards, modeled after the Baldrige (Main 1990). IBM, whose Rochester, Minnesota, facility won the Baldrige Award in 1990, recently announced that it is awarding cash and equipment grants to nine U.S. colleges and universities that will work with IBM in an effort to accelerate the teaching, research, and use of TQM principles (*Corporate Giving Watch*, Dec. 1992, 3).

Baldrige examiners judge companies by criteria that fall into seven categories and twenty-eight subcategories, each of which receives a point value that in total adds up to 1,000 points.[7] The point value for each category clearly signals to managers which areas are most valued or considered most critical in developing a high-quality, high-performance system.

The Baldrige criteria reflect a version of total quality management that emphasizes the strategic role of top management and quality management systems in improving competitiveness.[8] Consistent with the TQM adage that 85 percent of problems reside with management and 15 percent with employees, 85 percent of the points in the Baldrige Award application are for improvements in management methods and processes. These include 30 percent for customer service (including marketing, product development, cycle time); 23 percent for top-management leadership, strategy, and management of information systems; and 32 percent for process management and operational results. By comparison, only 15 percent of the points are rewarded for improvements in human resource practices.

In the customer service category, the emphasis is on improved methods for incorporating customer feedback into marketing and product development, particularly through such methods as customer surveys and focus groups. Closer attention to customer demand is required as a result of advances in technologies and the proliferation of differentiated products, which make it more difficult for companies to anticipate the demand for their products. Customer surveys provide constant feedback, whereas focus groups help create customer loyalty. A key objective measure of quality and customer service is cycle time (both quality and speed are often by-products of the same source—for example, the integration of engineering and manufacturing). To achieve this level of quality service, the Baldrige model draws on other elements of the TQM approach for improving internal management and production processes: top management provides leadership; develops a strategic plan; ensures quality engineering processes; gets feedback through data collection, performance measurement, and management information systems; and measures operational results.

The remaining 15 percent of the formula is for improvements in human resource development and management: overall human resource management counts for 2 percent; employee involvement, 4 percent; education and training, 4 percent; employee performance and recognition, 2.5 percent; and, finally, employee well-being and morale, 2.5 percent. The Baldrige Award provides no special incentive for the involvement and empowerment of front-line workers per se but suggests that companies involve different categories of employees according to company goals or occupational responsibilities.[9]

Recommended measures of well-being and morale include "satisfaction, safety, absenteeism, turnover, attrition rate for customer-contact personnel, grievances, strikes, and worker compensation" (U.S. Department of Commerce 1992:19). With the exception of employee satisfaction, these indicators have cost and productivity implications as much as they measure employee well-being.

Several omissions are notable. There is no mention of those measures that employees would consider central to their well-being: employment security, wage growth, promotions, due process guarantees, conflict resolution procedures, or employee voice. The award criteria mention the role of unions only once in the entire thirty-five–page instruction booklet in a footnote concerning human resource planning (U.S. Department of Commerce 1992:17; this comment is repeated in the introduction, on page 4).

The Baldrige Award criteria, therefore, provide a model of lean production that emphasizes improvements in performance by combining total quality marketing and production processes with a more traditional hierarchical organization and with employment policies such as the careful selection of new employees, training, and performance evaluation drawn from the American human resource model.

Although industrial relations issues and human resource practices are slighted in the Baldrige Award criteria, most Baldrige *winners* pay careful attention to some human resource policies. They tend to be more selective in hiring practices and to invest more substantially in training in quality, group process, and job skills than conventionally managed companies and are more likely to tie compensation to performance in a variety of ways. Despite the low weight assigned to worker participation in the award *criteria*, the award *winners* tend to make use of quality circles, problem-solving teams, or cross-functional teams.[10] These team structures mobilize the information and knowledge that hourly workers have in order to make process improvements and are an important form of employee involvement, but they are different from production or work teams and they do not involve employee participation in management. They are parallel structures that co-exist with the "normal bureaucratic organization and hierarchical authority, but leave these arrangements untouched" (Hill 1991:549).

Baldrige Award Winners

There is a diversity in management practices among the Baldrige winners that is greater than that observed among the Deming winners (Gomez del Campo 1993), but the Baldrige winners share certain characteristics.[11] Most discovered the total quality teachings of Deming, Crosby, and others earlier than other American firms and experimented for several years with refining quality principles to fit the peculiar characteristics of their own industries and organizational cultures. Many were spurred by a profit crisis or decline in product market share that led top executives to make a single-minded commitment to quality and customer service and to make radical changes in production processes to achieve those ends. We draw on case studies of Baldrige winners, focusing on the experience of two companies, Marlow Industries and the IBM plant in Rochester, Minnesota.[12] Headquartered in Dallas, Texas, Marlow is a small privately held corporation that employs 160 people and supplies half the world market in thermoelectric coolers. The IBM Rochester plant employs a work force of eight thousand in the design, development, and manufacturing of the AS/400 computer and hard-disk storage devices.

Marlow Industries. Raymond Marlow, the founder and current president of Marlow Industries, launched the firm's total quality management system in 1986 soon after learning about statistical process control techniques required by Hughes Aircraft of its "Blue Ribbon Suppliers." After exposure to the total quality principles of Crosby through meetings with representatives from Texas Instruments, Marlow organized the Texas Quality Consortium, a group of small companies formed to spread the costs of TQM training. Once some of his senior management and department heads had gone through the training, Marlow brought them together in a Total Quality Management Council to spearhead quality as a philosophy within the company. That council was later expanded to include all senior management as permanent members plus rotating members from the customer and supplier base.

Marlow took the quality philosophy to all employees to gain their commitment to the company's pledge of quality. The TQM Council sets up "quality improvement teams" and other ad hoc committees to make improvements in such areas as the cost of quality, safety, communications, and employee recognition. The TQM Council also oversees and approves the goals and resources for "action teams"—problem-solving teams at the corporate, departmental, and production levels of the firm. Employees receive recognition for their quality contributions through monthly awards of $100 plus a color TV. The Total Quality Management Council also conducts an "employee quality survey" to get feedback on the extent to which employees adopt the quality values of senior management.

Training plays a central role in efforts to empower Marlow employees. Through a "professional qualification system," supervisors develop job-skills training and annual recertification procedures. The company also provides training in team building, problem solving, and quality tools (pareto, flow, yield, and attribute charts; scatter plots and histograms; cause and effect diagrams). Training increased from an average of thirty-two hours per employee per year in 1990 to fifty-five hours (2.7 percent of employee hours) in 1991.

Marlow's top managers participate in developing annual five-year strategic business plans that include goals for capital investment, quality, operations, human resources, training, and implementation. The quality assurance program is built around international (ISO 9001) standards for design control, reliability, documentation control, statistical techniques, audits, and supplier control. An extensive information management system collects more than five hundred data/information points to measure progress toward the "strategic quality initiative" as well as daily operations.

Taken together, Marlow's total quality program has produced dramatic results. Between 1988 and 1991, productivity per employee improved by 56 percent and manufacturing yields increased by 61 percent. The company reduced its number of critical suppliers from 204 in 1988 to 100 in 1991. During the same period, the company registered a 66 percent decline in cycle time and a 49 percent drop in cost of quality.

IBM Rochester. The IBM story builds on a corporate history of commitment to quality which made it a leader in the development of such modern quality assurance concepts as stress testing, indirect poor-quality cost, and process qualification. Increased competition from new entrants in the 1980s led the company to refocus on quality and to incorporate the ideas of Deming, Crosby, Juran, and Ishikawa into its management processes.

The IBM Rochester plant went through four phases of quality programs. Beginning in 1981, top management drew on the work of Crosby to develop a "zero defects" program that focused heavily on cost reductions in manufacturing and that was designed to fit with IBM's corporate strategy of becoming a low-cost producer. A second program, initiated in 1984, emphasized efficiency and process effectiveness by paying more attention to the complete product cycle.

A crisis in a new development project ushered in a third period of innovation in 1986, this time focused on improving responsiveness to customers and reducing development cycle time. The goal was to reduce the development cycle time of a new computer system by about half—to two or three years. The system under development, known as "Silverlake," was the AS/400. Led by the director of the development lab, Tom Furey, the group concentrated on changing the plant from a "technology-driven" to a "market-driven" organization.

To help lead and communicate the change process, Furey created the "Rochester Management Board" composed of eighteen top managers from across the plant who met biweekly to discuss major decisions. Furey communicated his vision with employees through roundtable discussions.

A central obstacle to quality was that management lacked information about its product markets and its customers. Furey helped elevate planning, market research, and forecasting to the status of engineering and programming. To incorporate customer feedback into the planning process, he developed a cross-functional customer satisfaction team to respond to customer problems. The marketing department also adopted new methods for identifying market segments by industry and establishment size, targeting growth markets, and analyzing how to prioritize new customer demands for product development. Additionally, the plant developed a more open-door policy with its suppliers and customers, which fostered better communication and feedback on products and services.

At the same time, Furey shifted from a sequential to a "parallel" development process to reduce product development cycle time. The parallel process involved designing the product and concurrently testing for defects using computer simulation. Manufacturing built a number of prototypes, rather than having engineering construct just one. This allowed manufacturing to move down the learning curve, engineering to focus on refining the design, and software development to begin ahead of its normal schedule.

IBM chose the Rochester plant to represent the company in the 1989 Baldrige competition, and this initiated the fourth phase of the plant's quality effort. The goal was to integrate quality efforts into a comprehensive plan through the Baldrige application process.

IBM Rochester's human resource or empowerment strategy has focused on getting its managerial staff to delegate more responsibility to technical employees, who together with managerial staff comprise about 60 percent of the work force. This goal has been achieved by redesigning the performance planning, counseling, and appraisal system to clarify employee responsibilities and establish more objective standards for employee evaluations, which occur annually and may range from unsatisfactory to excellent. Technical staff are involved in setting their own performance goals and schedules. They participate in technical training programs, prepare a career development plan, and are encouraged to publish professional papers and reports.

The results of the AS/400 project are impressive. The project cycle time was halved to twenty-eight months, rework and scrap declined by 55 percent, and engineering changes decreased by 45 percent.

AMERICAN TEAM PRODUCTION

The American model of team-based high performance begins with sociotechnical job design and the use of self-directed teams, but incorporates an eclectic set of ideas from other sources: just-in-time inventories from the Japanese, total quality and statistical process control from Deming via Japan, incentive and compensation structures developed in the American HR model, and a uniquely American form of labor-management partnership that emerged out of the American experience with collective bargaining and joint quality of work life activities. The American team-based model leads to a real redistribution of power and authority in the workplace. Among the cases we examined, this model is most fully articulated at the Xerox facilities in Webster, New York; at GM's Saturn plant in Spring Hill, Tennessee; and at some of Corning's plants—the new or "greenfield" catalytic converter plant in Blacksburg, West Virginia, and the converted or "brownfield" specialty cellular ceramics (SCC) plant in Corning, New York.[13]

Many other companies have adopted important elements of this model with notable results. Ford, for example, has active joint steering committees at almost all its locations, makes extensive use of voluntary problem-solving teams led by facilitators who may be managers or hourly workers, applies just-in-time and quality principles, and has begun to promote natural work teams as the basic production unit (Banas 1988; Smith 1986; Sheridan 1990; Templin 1992). Joint partnership processes have been implemented at Magma Copper in Tucson, Arizona, and at a number of steel plants, including National Steel's Great Lakes and Midwest plants, LTV's LSE plant, and Inland Steel's I/N Tek finishing plant. Involvement of front-line employees generally consists of department committees with off-line quality or problem-solving groups. At LTV's LSE plant and at Inland's I/N Tek plant, the work process has been restructured around self-directed teams and innovative compensation plans (Camlin, Scharf, and Walton 1993). More recently, service sector firms such as BellSouth, U.S. West, and AT&T have begun experimenting with this approach.

In the following sections, we outline the main features of this model, which include a sociotechnical organization of work; employee participation in human resource issues such as the selection of work unit participants, training, and compensation systems; industrial relations built around joint labor-management decision-making structures; and total quality principles involving the use of such techniques as quality process improvement, just-in-time inventory systems, and statistical process control.

Sociotechnical Work Systems and Self-Directed Teams

The sociotechnical systems movement, which began in the 1950s, argued that autonomous teamwork improves performance. Continuous improvement is expected to occur as a result of two conditions: the decision-making autonomy of employees and the treatment of work as a system rather than as a set of individual jobs. The STS approach assumes that because of their intimate knowledge of the work process, workers, rather than managers or engineers, know how to organize work to make most productive use of a given technology. Employees are more likely to come up with process innovations if they can look across a work system rather than at a narrow job—hence the importance of working in teams rather than individually (Simmons and Mares 1983). Continuous improvement, therefore, does not depend solely on technology, on the one hand, or human or social relations, on the other (e.g., human resource practices to improve morale or job satisfaction); rather, it depends on the fit between human and technical systems. Once teams of workers design a work process, they can become the source of continuous improvement if they are given the discretion and incentives to do so.

The high-performance plants of Xerox, Corning, and Saturn all take a sociotechnical systems approach to technology and work organization that involves production workers in the selection of machinery and the design of work systems to ensure that human and technical requirements are integrated into the work process. Employees have used their understanding of the work process to optimize the technical system, organizational structure, and quality of work life. In each case, employees, in conjunction with managers and union officials, have borrowed and experimented with ideas from a broad array of sources.

As early as 1978, managers at Xerox began looking at human resource issues from the point of view of sociotechnical job redesign, did benchmarking with firms in Norway, and drew on the knowledge of outside consultants who had been trained at Tavistock, the British institute best known for its elaboration of STS principles. At about the same time, Xerox officials used their corporate relationship with Fuji-Xerox of Japan, which won the Deming Award in 1980, to establish internal benchmarks for manufacturing costs, quality, and design time. Then, in 1982, the co-managers of Xerox's "Joint Process Architecture"—a union-management initiative to improve production methods—visited Japanese companies to observe their manufacturing methods and human resource practices.

A similar process occurred at Saturn and Corning from the mid-1980s on. Workers and the union participated in every phase of the design and construction of the Saturn plant. A committee composed of plant managers, supervisors, union leaders, production workers, skilled workers, GM managers, and UAW leaders known as the Group of 99 participated in a series of fact-finding missions. Teams from the Group of 99 visited forty-nine GM plants and sixty benchmark companies all over the world (including Xerox's Webster complex) to develop a new production system that could compete effectively (LeFauve and Hax 1992). The integration of technical and social work organization is an organizing principle at Saturn that extends to the electronic data systems, which track information on everything from human resources and the flow of materials to financial data, manufacturing, product engineering, marketing, and service. At Corning, where plant managers have responsibility for the plant as a cost center and the freedom to make operational decisions, the managers, workers, and union at several plants jointly agreed to convert to a high-performance work system and worked out the details for the particular plant "architecture."

In these three cases, the basic production unit is a team or collaborative work group, but the composition and degree of autonomy vary both within and across the three sites. The key is that front-line employees participate fully in shaping their areas of responsibility based on the type of product, technology, and preferences of those involved. Work teams at the Corning and Saturn plants have substantial autonomy not only over work-related decisions but also over human resource issues, as we discuss below. Work groups at Xerox show more variation in composition and discretion than groups at the other two companies.

At the Corning SCC plant, teams work autonomously without shift supervisors, cross-train, rotate across semiskilled jobs, and communicate directly with engineers and other "support staff" (human resource, clerical, sales, and marketing) to solve production-line problems and to coordinate production deadlines and deliveries. They regularly receive business information in order to understand the plant's competitive position.

At Saturn, the basic work unit is a six- to fifteen-member team that is self-managed and has the responsibility and authority to address work flow, quality, and human resource issues. Teams elect their own leaders, who remain working members of the unit. Interrelated teams form modules, which are then integrated into three business units. Each business unit has a joint labor-management "decision ring" or committee to address plant-level operational issues. There are also decision rings at the module level. Other joint structures are the Manufacturing Action Council, which covers the manufacturing and assembly complex, and the Strategic Action Council, which does long-range planning at the corporate level.[14]

The basic work unit at the Xerox Webster plant is the Business Area Work Group (BAWG), a group of thirty-five to sixty people that includes all employees—production workers, maintenance personnel, managers, engineers, union representatives—responsible for producing a specific output (Lazes et al. 1991). These small business teams make their own decisions about how to get the work done, as long as production quotas, schedules, and quality standards are met. The BAWGs use a variety of participatory practices and tools—including problem-solving and quality improvement teams; just-in-time application projects to improve the velocity of paper through offices and materials through plants; production design teams; task forces for new product development; and study teams to tackle longer-term problems (Lazes et al. 1991; Lazes and Costanza 1984). The BAWGs also have the authority to establish self-managed work teams. These are voluntary and are established if 80 percent of the members of a work group want such a team and the managers agree. As a result, although employee participation in the BAWG decision-making structure is high, the degree of self-management varies. Autonomous work groups, semi-autonomous work groups, and work groups with supervisors co-exist in the same facility.[15]

The organizational structure at both Corning and Saturn is flat. Xerox retained its traditional structure throughout the 1980s but created a leaner organization by increasing the training and responsibilities of front-line employees and decreasing the reliance on engineering and support staff. More recently, Xerox has undertaken a restructuring effort that levels its hierarchy and reduces the number of production-level job classifications. In machining, for example, the number has been reduced from twenty-five to five broad bands.

Human Resource Policies: Hiring, Compensation, Training

The STS approach provides workers with the discretion to improve the work process, but their participation in setting human resource policies provides the incentive to do so. At the Corning SCC plant, for example, the self-managed teams came up with a set of disciplinary rules governing appropriate behavior on the job and help in the selection of new entrants to the team by participating in job interviews and explaining to new applicants what is entailed in autonomous team production. By gaining full exposure to how the system works, job applicants who are not interested in self-managed work tend to self-select out of the hiring process. The fit between incumbent and new team members has worked better as a result.

Corning teams also undertook job analyses to develop a new set of job classifications and a three-tiered skill hierarchy (from mechanical understanding to a more analytical and problem-solving focus) that is the basis for a pay-for-skills compensation system. All team members must achieve basic competence in four jobs through which they rotate regularly. Within two years, they must reach competence in all jobs at the second-tier level; beyond that, members specialize and together decide who is next in line to receive training and in which skill areas. The union and management negotiated the pay formula associated with the pay-for skill system so that it is comparable to wage rates in other local Corning plants. Additionally, the SCC employees (both managers and workers) receive 5 to 7 percent of their wages through a gainsharing plan (linked to achieving plant-level performance goals) and a profit-sharing plan (linked to corporate performance).

Teams at Saturn do their own hiring and are responsible for developing and administering policies regarding absenteeism and the replacement of absent workers. Wages at Saturn are set at 80 percent of the industry wage, paid as an annual salary rather than an hourly wage, and workers receive an additional 20 percent if performance goals, including goals for customer satisfaction, are met, and they may receive up to another 20 percent if goals are exceeded.

At Xerox, workers are not generally involved in the hiring process. An exception is trades people, who interview new workers who may be joining them on the mod squads to be sure they are qualified. The union and management have jointly developed a training program and have negotiated a gainsharing plan that allows workers to share the rewards of gains in performance. Gainsharing is based on workers meeting quality, cost, scheduling, safety, and attendance goals.

Training budgets at all three work sites are extensive. In the set-up phase at Corning, training costs ran as high as 23 percent of payroll. Now that the new organization is functioning smoothly, the plant manager budgets 15 percent of worker time for training. Initial training of workers at Saturn is extensive, although the work force consists entirely of experienced auto workers. Following their initial training, workers at Saturn devise individual training goals and are expected to spend 5 percent of their time (ninety-two hours annually) in training activities.

Training has always been extensive at Xerox, which has a highly developed mechanism for internal training. The company puts all production workers through a qualification course and has a four-year apprenticeship program for workers in the skilled trades. Since 1980, training for front-line workers in problem-solving techniques, quality practices, and how to present material or facilitate a meeting has been an integral part of Xerox's strategic shift to a joint partnership focusing on employee involvement and quality of work life programs and the establishment of problem-solving teams. A few years later, despite the economic crisis it faced, the company put everyone through forty hours or more of this training. Xerox spent $9 million for trainers in 1985, and employee time spent in training in a three-year period had a value of $70 million (Marshall and Tucker 1992:97).

Industrial Relations

At Xerox, Saturn, and Corning, a distinctly American form of "partnership" between plant management and the union has emerged, which emphasizes the development of a "shared business vision" and joint union-management committees at every level of the organization. Shop-floor participation, though important, is viewed as insufficient to gain the full involvement of the work force in the organization. Production and problem-solving teams are viewed as most effective at refining a given production process and at improving conformance quality—that is, conformance to specifications and approaches that reduce defects. To go beyond these incremental changes requires joint processes and "architectures" that involve workers or their representatives in broader operational and strategic issues. Officials at these three companies credit worker and union representation on joint policy committees with improving the planning process and the quality of the decisions that are made. In addition to providing a vehicle for tapping knowledge, sharing information, and obtaining a buy-in on decisions from both sides, the joint committees are an important expression of mutual respect.

At Saturn, the partnership between UAW and GM leadership encompasses strategic planning at the corporate level through the Strategic Action Council, which meets weekly to address relations with dealers, suppliers, and stockholders and long-range business issues. In addition, union and management partnerships are responsible for tactical planning and for operational planning and performance in most areas of plant operation through decision rings, problem resolution circles, and partnering by the union and management in middle-management positions (LeFauve and Hax 1992). Business unit leaders (plant managers) are partnered with elected union executive board members. This partnering of a union member with a manager in hundreds of staff and line positions may be the most innovative aspect of Saturn's governance system (Rubinstein, Bennett, and Kochan 1993).

Among the major elements of the ACTWU/Xerox joint process structure at the Webster complex are the executive and policy committee, which meets semi-annually to set overall strategic goals; the joint planning committee, which meets quarterly as a steering committee to determine how the overall strategy should be deployed; and the plant advisory committees, which meet monthly to decide how to implement the strategy. In addition to the plant manager, union leader, and other management and union representatives, the advisory committee also includes shop-floor workers.

The joint committees at these three companies—made up of approximately equal numbers of representatives from management and the union—as well as the negotiating process are extensions of, rather than alternatives to, collective bargaining. They grow out of the American experience with bargaining at plant and local levels. The collective bargaining process is expanded as joint decision making creates implicit contracts, which are often made explicit in memos and company documents. Negotiating itself has become an ongoing process.

Central to the flexibility inherent in these companies' labor contracts is a strong commitment to employment security. This commitment makes economic sense for firms that have invested heavily in training their workers and where multiskilling allows for more flexible internal deployment. Workers at Xerox's Webster plants have had employment security since the 1983 contract, although they may be transferred to different BAWGs and even to different plants in the Webster complex as necessary. The Saturn contract guarantees workers there will be no layoffs except in the case of a catastrophic event. This commitment to employment security was recently tested when the fourteen-member team responsible for assembling doors suggested that some machinery be rearranged to improve quality and productivity. By implementing the suggestion, however, the number of workers required to perform the work would be reduced to twelve. Rather than lay off the two workers who were no longer required, management transferred them to another part of the plant (*Business Week* 1992).

Quality

Quality is a central focus of the organizational transformation at all three companies. Xerox won the Baldrige Award in 1989, and Corning was a finalist. And quality tools and techniques are used for far more than the control of variance. Corning began introducing total quality concepts in 1982, making statistical process control available to plant managers to use as they deemed appropriate. The Corning SCC plant incorporates SPC responsibilities into the jobs of front-line production teams, as does Saturn; and SPC has been an important quality tool at Xerox since 1983. As noted above, problem-solving and self-directed teams are at the heart of the very substantial performance gains reported by all three companies.

Xerox adopted just-in-time production as a key element of the third strategic shift in its production system in 1988 and "time-based competitiveness" as part of its fourth shift in 1993 (Argona 1992). Just-in-time production techniques were also an integral part of the high-performance systems put in place in the late 1980s at Saturn and Corning. In addition to the tight management of buffers and "pull" production and scheduling, steps have been taken at all three companies to minimize set-up time, to streamline supplier relationships, to distribute the workload more evenly within teams or work groups and across the plant, to reduce equipment downtime, and to improve the throughput of materials.

All three companies have also built customer feedback into the quality control system; and customer satisfaction ("internal" as well as "external" customers) drives design changes in products and delivery systems. Saturn's on-line tracking system, for example, tracks all repairs at dealerships, thereby identifying very quickly any problems in cars that have moved out of the factory.

A critical feature of the quality programs at all three companies has been the role of the union in creating the level of "mass participation" needed to make quality efforts successful. At Corning, for example, although management initiated a total quality program in 1982 and put all employees through training, the program did not really take hold until the late 1980s after the company and the union negotiated an agreement that embodied a shared vision and a partnership structure for the union in business decisions and planning.

At Xerox, the process occurred in reverse: Team Xerox, the joint process first ratified in the 1980s collective bargaining agreement, laid the groundwork for the Leadership through Quality program introduced by top management in the mid-1980s. As with total quality mangement generally, the training was "cascaded down" from top management to lower levels of management to employees. When total quality training finally reached the shop floor and skilled trades, workers found that, although the terminology was unfamiliar, they had already mastered the skills required. The total quality processes introduced at Xerox had a firm basis for success because shop-floor workers had experience with similar training and activities. At the prodding of the union, what started as a top-down mandate for change was blended with the commitment to employee involvement and joint processes already in place. The slogan at Xerox became "Total Quality through Employee Involvement."

DO HIGH-PERFORMANCE SYSTEMS ACHIEVE RESULTS?

One explanation for the reluctance of U.S. firms to overcome the obstacles to change and embrace broad-based efforts at organizational transformation must surely be the fragmentary and self-interested nature of the evidence that supports claims of high-performance. With few exceptions, careful studies of what has been accomplished by instituting far-reaching changes in management methods and work organization, or of the role played by clusters of innovations or particular practices have not yet been undertaken. Exceptions include studies of the auto industry that document performance gains in lean production systems (MacDuffie 1991; Womack, Jones, and Roos 1990); studies of the steel industry that show improvements from a cluster of HR innovations (Ichniowski, Shaw, and Prennushi 1993); and of Xerox that find gains from team production (Cutcher-Gershenfeld 1991; Klingel and Martin 1988).

A comprehensive review of the effects of participation on productivity (Levine and Tyson 1990) concluded that "the size and strength of the effect [of participation on performance] are contingent on the form and content of participation." Based on this review, it appears that four features of a firm's human resource practices and industrial relations system affect how participatory arrangements influence performance: whether the gains from improvements in productivity are shared with the workers (gainsharing), whether the workers have employment security, whether the firm has adopted measures to build group cohesiveness, and whether there are guaranteed individual rights for the employees.

The lack of systematic evidence on the outcomes of high-performance work systems is in part a product of the newness of the models described in this chapter. Just five years have elapsed since the first Baldrige Award and even less time since the transformations at Corning or the production of the first Saturn car. Most of the evidence of improved performance currently available is self-reported by firm managers, although the Baldrige Award has stringent requirements with respect to measurement and record keeping on an array of performance criteria. Because of confidentiality requirements, however, the federal agency that oversees the award is unwilling to release aggregate data for independent analysis (Garvin 1991).

With these caveats in mind, performance gains reported by companies that have transformed their production processes appear to be impressive. Managers report improvements in quality—reductions in cycle time, defects, and waste; improvements in customer satisfaction; improvements in productivity; and gains in market share or return on investment. In a 1990 study of twenty companies that were high scorers on the Baldrige Award in either 1988 or 1989, the General Accounting Office found that adopting the quality management practices embodied in the award led to improvements in corporate performance, including financial areas (U.S. GAO 1990). Response rates on many questions were quite low, however, averaging only nine companies per answer.

Among the Baldrige winners, Milliken & Company reported a significant increase in on-time delivery and a 50 percent reduction over ten years in defects in goods. Motorola developed methods for measuring quality in white-collar settings and improved quality tenfold between 1981 and 1986. Solectron Corporation reported a 50 percent improvement in the average product rejection rate between 1987 and 1991. The Wallace Company increased sales by 69 percent between 1987 and 1990 and raised market share from 10 to 18 percent. Granite Rock cut truck-loading time by 70 percent and meets a quality standard for its ready-mix concrete of just 3.4 defective loads per million.

Among firms with team production systems, Xerox reports that defects in its component parts dropped from 10,000 parts per million in 1980 to 360 in 1989, and Corning reports that scrap is down by 46 percent and productivity up by 30 percent in its transformed plants. Return on investment, which had slipped at Corning in the 1980s, increased to 15 percent in 1991, putting the company back in the top quintile of Fortune 500 companies. Although it is too early to report on improvements in productivity or quality performance at Saturn, there is already evidence of accomplishment in the dealers' performance and in customer satisfaction. J. D. Power and Associates ranks Saturn second in dealer satisfaction, just behind Lexus and ahead of Infiniti, and third in 1991 for total new vehicle gross profit per dealership, behind Lexus and Infiniti. Saturn ranks well ahead of the industry in overall satisfaction among owners, in sixth place behind cars that compete in the luxury segment, and in first place among the top-five basic small performers.

Thus, the evidence suggests that high-performance firms perform well in the areas of efficiency and quality. We hope, however, that future research will provide an independent comparison of the performance of transformed and untransformed plants on a consistent set of outcome measures. More importantly, the outcome measures used to evaluate the success of work systems must be expanded to include the impact of *all* stakeholders—including shareholders, suppliers, customers, unions, managers, and front-line employees.

9.

OBSTACLES TO CHANGE

U.S. firms seek to maximize profit, and economists have assumed that, in a competitive system, this is sufficient to drive inefficient producers out of the market and to guarantee that only those that have efficiently allocated labor and other resources survive. As a result, most economists have treated the firm as a "black box" whose inner workings could be ignored and have confined their interest at the microeconomic level to the production function relationship between inputs and output while advocating that the role of government intervention should be largely limited to ensuring the existence of competitive market conditions. It was on this basis that the Reagan and Bush administrations looked to deregulation to promote productivity growth and the competitiveness of U.S. firms.

The assumption that profit-maximizing firms are inevitably efficient may not hold. The competitive advantage achieved by foreign firms whose management methods and work organization differ markedly from those in U.S. companies, and the enormous performance gains in both efficiency and quality reported by domestic producers that have fundamentally reorganized the production process, suggest that a more efficient organization of the factors of production may, in fact, be possible. In contrast to the neoclassical assumption that the most efficient use of technology is both available to firms and easily achieved, a more dynamic theory suggests that efficiency is affected by management structures, organizational systems, and company strategies (Chandler 1990, 1992; Teece 1993). These structures and strategies, in turn, are shaped by the institutional framework within which the firm operates. Most important are the financial system, which affects the firm's ability to invest in new technology and in such intangibles as work reorganization and training, and labor market institutions, which govern skill acquisition and the terms on which labor can be hired (Porter 1992; Wever and Allen 1992). The realization of new and more efficient production systems may therefore be slower and more difficult than envisioned in the neoclassical theory of the firm; the discipline of the market may not be sufficient to guarantee their timely adoption.

In the United States, the pace of organizational change has been relatively slow. Several factors account for this. First, given the current skills of front-line workers and the current levels of expenditure on civilian research and development, *static* allocative efficiency considerations may dictate that U.S. firms economize on the use of such scarce resources as highly skilled front-line workers and sophisticated process technologies. Although this approach may yield least-cost outcomes for individual firms in the short run, in the long run U.S. firms will lose out to foreign competitors that are investing more heavily in worker skills and in the development of manufacturing process technology.

Second, the institutional framework of the United States was developed to support the old, mass-production system, which led to the creation of standardized products that competed on the basis of price. Now that the basis of competitive advantage in the advanced industrial economies has changed, U.S. economic development is constrained by the very institutions that previously assured its competitive success.

Third, the incentive structure in U.S. firms rewards what Stephen Smith (1991) has termed "managerial opportunism": managers are rewarded, for example, for appropriating the ideas of their subordinates or for improving the bottom line in the short run and then moving on to other positions before the long-term implications of the strategies they have adopted make themselves felt. The result is that managers may be reluctant to implement change.[1]

Fourth, the erosion of the concept of "ownership" of publicly held corporations and the rise of the market for corporate control have made the maximization of the current stock price the chief goal of publicly held firms in the United States. This has impaired the ability of these firms to make financial commitments to other stakeholders or to make investments that pay off over the long run (Porter 1992).

Fifth, and finally, most workplace innovations consist of practices borrowed piecemeal from one or another alternative to mass production. Managers themselves are often uncertain as to what is required in a transformed production system to achieve continuous improvements in quality and efficiency.

This analysis leads to two conclusions: First, if profit-maximization alone does not ensure efficiency, then transforming the organization of production could lead to gains in both productivity and quality. Second, adopting a dynamic view of industrial development suggests that there is a role for government policy in building a new institutional framework that defines and supports high-performance work organization.

The analysis of case materials presented in this book suggests that a more efficient organization of the factors of production is, in fact, possible. The competitive advantage achieved by foreign competitors whose management methods and work organization differ markedly from those in U.S. firms, and the enormous performance gains reported by domestic producers that have fundamentally reorganized their production processes, are evidence that organizational transformations that mobilize workers' intelligence and capabilities in production and that provide workers with the necessary skills and work structures to apply those capabilities can improve efficiency.

Despite the reported gains in performance and the apparent acceleration of experiments with innovative practices, the overwhelming majority of U.S. workplaces are traditionally managed. In this chapter we examine the obstacles impeding organizational transformation.

AMBIGUOUS ROLE OF TECHNOLOGY

While during the last two decades some firms turned increasingly to contingent employment contracts and flexible mass production in response to intensified competition, others experimented with workplace innovations. Both approaches have led firms to replace dedicated equipment with more flexible technologies. But the technology, quite clearly, has not dictated the outcome.

The role of technology in organizational transformation is thus ambiguous. Not all transformed production systems involve the implementation of new technology, and, indeed, alternatives to mass production predated the widespread use of microprocessor-based technologies (Trist 1981; Piore and Sabel 1984). One might argue that the virtue of transformed organizations is that the new forms of work organization make the most intelligent use of whatever technology is in place. Nevertheless, the shift in process technology, from electromechanical to computer and information technologies, has facilitated increases in product variety and improvements in quality; has increased the product areas in which customization is a cost-effective option; and has provided communication and information management capabilities that support the decentralization of large companies and the creation of interfirm networks. The shift in technology has also made possible reductions in time to market by accelerating various stages of the production process, from product design and process engineering to throughput of the final product. Microprocessor technologies have replaced equipment dedicated to producing a particular component, part, or product with equipment that can easily be programmed to produce highly diversified outputs. Microprocessor technologies have also made it possible for small firms to be cost effective while producing small batches and for large firms to maintain high-volume output while introducing a variety of customized, quality-competitive products. In services, microprocessor-based computer and communications technologies have made possible a wide range of new services and have altered the production process in industries largely untouched by electromechanical automation.

There is no technological imperative driving organizational transformation, however. As Shoshana Zuboff (1988) observed, the new technologies can be used either to automate or to informate. That is, they can be used to increase flexibility in some aspects of the production process (scheduling deliveries, controlling inventories) while perpetuating and even intensifying the standardization, specialization, and fragmentation of the work process; or they can be used to transform organizations and to restructure work in fundamental ways (Kelley 1990).

DILEMMAS FACING FIRMS AND MANAGERS

Barriers for Firms

Individual firms face numerous difficulties as they attempt to transform their production systems. These include the high initial costs for training (in excess of 15 percent of payroll) that may be associated with the adoption of innovative work organization practices, the high cost to small firms of training workers at all, and the absence of a clearinghouse for sharing information on innovative practices and of accounting standards for measuring quality or valuing investments in research or human capital.

In addition, there are "boundary" problems—problems of interfirm coordination, as well as what economists refer to as externalities or market imperfections. Examples include the recruiting by one firm of workers trained by another firm and the problems of integrating into a participative work system employees and equipment that belong, say, to the telephone company but that are located on a customer's premises and are essential to the customer's performance.

Finally, problems have been created by the recent rise of the market for corporate control, which requires a firm's top officers to satisfy the demands of portfolio investors (who favor firms with high-dividend payout rates) rather than invest the earnings of the company in such difficult-to-measure activities as training or research and development. The proportion of after-tax corporate profits distributed as dividends by U.S. firms, which was 45 percent in the 1950s and 1960s, rose to 60 percent in the 1980s and to 72 percent in 1990 as profits fell and dividends climbed (Lazonick 1992: 459). Current corporate governance structures in U.S. companies make it difficult for top management to make intrafirm commitments to the development of new production processes or to long term employment relations or to make interfirm commitments to stable, collaborative network relationships with suppliers. Yet many researchers have argued that such commitments are essential characteristics of high-performance production systems (Brown, Reich, and Stern 1991; Brown et al. 1993; Levine 1992; Levine and Tyson 1990; Helper 1991; Helper and Levine 1992).

We are not suggesting that individual firms can never transform their production systems successfully in the absence of a supportive institutional environment. Clearly, as the evidence in this book demonstrates, this is not the case. But we would argue that it has proven inordinately expensive and unnecessarily difficult for U.S. companies to make the transformation. As a result, work systems have tended to be transformed when three conditions are occurring: a crisis threatens the product line or market share, the company has the resources to gamble on a high-risk strategy, and top management is willing to take that risk. Such crisis conditions, however, often have the opposite effect—they can cause a company to downsize or outsource production and to renege on the commitments it has made to its hourly workers and middle managers on gainsharing or employment security.

Managerial Resistance to Change

Several factors account for the inertia and resistance to organizational change among U.S. managers. First, as described above, the incentive structure in U.S. firms rewards "managerial opportunism" (Smith 1991). Unless corporations restructure the reward system, managers will be reluctant to implement change.

Second, sharing power, authority, responsibility, and decision making is uncharted territory for most U.S. managers, and many are reluctant to cede power to workers on and off the shop floor. This is particularly true in view of the widespread downsizing and reductions in managerial ranks undertaken by many firms. Companies that wish to reorganize work systems must define new roles for managers—more than just as "coaches"—which give them new responsibilities for coordinating across functions, improving quality, or responding more directly to customers or suppliers.

Third, as discussed above, earlier rounds of work reform and employee involvement were "ideological," in that they were intended to improve worker attitudes and avoid unionization and only indirectly to affect firm performance. For that reason, training, job enlargement, and other workplace innovations were seen as discretionary actions by management that could be cut back in times of crisis to reduce costs. It is only since 1980 that some managers have come to see organizational transformation as a part of their firms' competitive strategy and not as a tactical tool for dealing with workers. Disagreement on this point among managers continues to be prevalent and in some cases may account for the failure of successful transformations to diffuse from one site to another even within a company.

Finally, as the examples in previous chapters have shown, most workplace innovations consist of practices borrowed piecemeal from one or another alternative to mass production. Managers themselves are often uncertain as to what is required in a transformed production system to achieve continuous improvements in quality and efficiency. The result, in the U.S. context, is that management inertia has been difficult to overcome (Milkman 1991) and attempts at change have often been partial or halfhearted.

UNIONS' AND WORKERS' AMBIVALENCE TOWARD PARTICIPATION

Many unions now recognize the value of participation in management decision making. As the central conflict between labor and management has shifted from wage bargaining to saving jobs, unions have recognized the need to represent members' interests by taking a proactive rather than a reactive stance on corporate decisions that affect the ability of the company to remain profitable in an increasingly competitive environment. Long-term management decisions with respect to capital investments, product development, technology, and work organization determine the viability of a facility. If unions are not involved early on in the decision-making process, they will have little opportunity later to shape the course of events. In addition, employee participation at the workplace in problem-solving teams often results in cost savings and quality improvements that save jobs. There are a growing number of examples of employee committees that have identified sufficient improvements to prevent work from being outsourced or that resulted in new work being brought in-house.

Joint labor-management programs have been established at approximately half of all unionized establishments (Cooke 1991) and, as we have shown, many of the best-known examples of high-performance production systems are occurring in unionized plants—such as Corning, Saturn, Xerox, Levi Strauss, NUMMI, and AT&T. Many more unions have had positive experiences working on joint committees focused on such specific issues as training or health and safety (e.g., Ferman et al. 1991). Union participation in these committees is less problematic, however, than participation in quality-oriented committees, because the subject of discussion in the former case is generally clearly delineated and unlikely to impinge on collective bargaining issues.

According to case studies (for example, Adler 1992) and surveys of workers, such as a recent survey of AT&T employees jointly admininstered by AT&T and the CWA, many employees also genuinely like participating in problem solving, self-directed teams, and other workplace programs that draw on their ideas and input.

The locus of debate within unions, therefore, has largely shifted from whether to participate to *under what conditions* and *how*. These questions continue to pose daunting dilemmas for unions. A union local at a large manufacturing plant that recently won a quality award refused to participate in the company's quality efforts when invited to do so because management unilaterally set the terms and conditions of participation and retained the right to select the employees who would be involved. Under these conditions, participation was not attractive to the union. The question of *how* to participate also poses problems. Participation puts major new demands on the administrative, leadership, and technical capabilities of unions in a period of dramatically reduced organizational and financial resources. Few unions currently have the necessary capabilities to assume "partnership" responsibilities.

Union members may be called on to make decisions about two different levels of participation: whether to support *worker participation* in management-led committees such as problem-solving teams and whether the *union* should participate in joint union-management structures. Two interrelated principles guide union decisions on these questions: the welfare of members and the institutional integrity of the union. The two principles are closely linked because the institutional strength of the union determines how well it can represent the interests of members in the long run. The welfare of the members is dependent on the firm making improvements in working conditions and providing employment security and income growth. Thus, the decision by union members to participate in work reorganization depends largely on their ability to negotiate two guarantees: that workers will share in the gains from the work reorganization and that the union's security will be preserved and its ability to organize new members unimpeded.

Sometimes, however, work restructuring and the pruning of middle management result in increased burdens and speedups for hourly unionized employees, who may be poorly prepared by the company to undertake their new responsibilities. In other cases, participation may be used to provide managers with access to workers' tacit knowledge, which may then be used to reorganize work at foreign subsidiaries or elsewhere, at the cost of the jobs of the original workers (Richardson 1992).

Although self-directed teams provide greater autonomy for workers, management by one's peers introduces the potential for new conflicts, including the illegitimate use of peer pressure to intensify work or to carry out management by stress. Further, conflict resolution among workers and between workers and managers is likely to be more complex in a transformed workplace than in a more traditional setting. Some of these new conflicts can be resolved through contract language that builds in mechanisms for gainsharing, employment security, and the retraining and placement of workers displaced by technology or by process and quality improvements.

Worker involvement in management-led committees raises two concerns for unions that relate to their institutional integrity. First, in nonunion settings, companies have used employee-involvement programs to discourage union organizing. In the *Electromation* and *Dupont* cases, the National Labor Relations Board (NLRB) determined that such committees, with management-appointed members, constitute illegal company unions. Second, in unionized settings, unions are concerned about their ability to uphold collective bargaining principles. Even some unionized companies have attempted to use QWL or other committees to marginalize the union. Quality or process improvement teams in which management selects volunteers to participate pose even greater concerns. These teams focus on ways to change the working conditions and skill content of jobs (for which the union has negotiated specific wage rates). These are issues of mandatory bargaining under current labor law. Even under the best of circumstances—where management does not intend to undermine the bargaining relationship and the union selects participants—legitimate concerns arise regarding the use of informal labor-management committees in decentralized work sites. These committees essentially engage in ongoing negotiations and may reach agreements that contravene broader contract agreements. Workers representing their own interests at one site may not be aware of the adverse effects of their decisions on workers at other sites. The union, however, has the legal responsibility to represent all workers. Unions also are concerned about the potential for joint work-site committees to allow management to engage in "whipsawing"—in which locals are made to compete against one another or are compelled to match changes made at other sites.

These dilemmas have led some unions to negotiate joint structures and oversight committees at several levels of the organization. The 1992 contract between AT&T and its unions, the CWA and IBEW, which established the "Workplace of the Future," takes this approach, as do the collective bargaining agreements between Xerox and ACTWU and Saturn and the UAW. These structures require unions to reorganize internally, however, and to strengthen their leadership and administrative capabilities at several levels. They require large investments by the unions to train staff to monitor the decentralized agreements and to develop the technical expertise to analyze and contribute to the new technological and organizational strategies. Moreover, establishing such structures necessitates shifting decision-making power to lower-level union leaders. Work-team leaders, QWL facilitators, and worker representatives on operations and strategic management committees can threaten the authority of the elected union leadership if they are not fully integrated into a revamped union organizational structure.

Even where unions have developed joint structures and capabilities, mutual trust from the union perspective depends, at the very least on management agreeing to remain neutral with respect to union organizing at any nonunionized company work sites. Finally, the involvement of union leaders in operational and strategic management decisions and the performance of traditional management responsibilities on the shop floor by workers in self-managed teams raise legal questions. In 1980, the U.S. Supreme Court ruled that employees performing managerial work were not covered under the National Labor Relations Act.[2] How this ruling applies to participatory workplaces will have to be clarified.

In nonunion settings, the question of how workers are to be represented in power-sharing activities is an equally difficult one. The legality of the paternalistic solutions favored by some companies, especially those that have adopted the American HR approach, has been challenged by the December 1992 ruling of the NLRB in the *Electromation* case.[3] The issue is whether workers' interests are represented in labor-management committees when management selects the workers who will participate.

INSTITUTIONAL BARRIERS

In the U.S. context, no "institutional imperative" shapes the transformation of production systems. In a sense, the institutional framework in the United States can be characterized as permissive—institutions neither require nor support change—which may account for both the diversity and the difficulty firms face in making such changes. Moreover, U.S. labor law—in which only wages and working conditions are mandatory subjects of collective bargaining and business decisions are management prerogatives—hinders the transition to high-performance work systems.

Unlike their German counterparts, U.S. firms are under no legal mandate to share company information with employees or to allow employees to participate in corporate decisions about the choice of new technology (Turner 1991). Unlike their Japanese or Swedish counterparts, U.S. firms do not have access to an infrastructure of organizations capable of diffusing new ideas and work practices, such as the Japan Federation of Employers' Associations, the Japanese Union of Scientists and Engineers (JUSE), or the technical department of the Swedish Employers' Confederation (SAF) (Cole 1982). Unlike their counterparts in the Italian industrial districts, employees and owners of small firms in the United States cannot rely on local governments to provide collective goods—day-care centers and low-cost housing for workers, training institutions and marketing consortia for firms—that reduce costs and encourage labor-management compromise (Trigilia 1990). The weakness of U.S. trade unions means that U.S. firms are not constrained, as are those in Germany or Sweden, to seek out high-productivity solutions to problems of competitiveness; in the United States, low-wage, low-productivity alternatives remain available. Moreover, firms that choose to pursue a high-skill alternative face great difficulties in obtaining skilled workers given the lack of national training standards or programs for training and retraining the 70 percent of workers without college degrees. These difficulties have become all the more acute as the nature of organizational innovation has changed over time, from partial measures designed to improve employee satisfaction and increase productivity to more basic and wide-reaching measures intended to lead to continuous improvement.

The absence of an institutional framework external to firms that could shape opportunities, constrain outcomes, and support the diffusion of successful innovations within companies leads to certain patterns of change in the United States. The failure to develop an infrastructure that supports change means that major organizational transformations are more likely to occur in response to crisis conditions than as a result of the implementation of a vision. In the absence of a crisis, such changes are likely to be both difficult and slow in occurring.

One result is that major changes are more likely to occur in manufacturing than in services, since manufacturing is more subject to the adverse effects of increased global competition and the loss of market share. Moreover, the concern with organizational change as a means of improving international competitiveness has focused attention on industries that produce traded goods. Indeed, the models of transformed systems that social scientists and organizational development consultants draw on all come from the experiences of manufacturing industries, particularly automobiles.

Yet service industries will have to change as well. Services account for more than 75 percent of U.S. employment and 50 percent of real gross domestic product. Failure to improve performance in these industries will restrict U.S economic gains overall. Equally important, both private and public sector services—as diverse as financial services, communications, health care, hotels, air travel, and public infrastructure—affect the costs (and hence the competitiveness) of manufacturing enterprises.

That change in the United States is likely to be undertaken in response to economic crisis explains in part why workplace changes tend to be adopted piecemeal. Organizational and industrial relations theorists are well aware that major changes in work systems are most successful when they include employment security, gainsharing or other pay-backs for workers, and participatory structures that encourage cooperation backed by an independent role for worker voice and interest representation. Firms that adopt organizational changes under crisis conditions are often unable to make such commitments. Indeed, as they attempt to transform production they may be simultaneously engaged in more direct cost-cutting measures, such as subcontracting out work and laying off workers, which demoralize employees and undermine trust.

Furthermore, the lack of an institutional infrastructure to shape developments means that major organizational change is overly dependent on the personalities and commitments of key individuals—the CEO, plant manager, and, where relevant, local and national union officials. Lacking union research centers, employers' associations, or organizations like JUSE to guide the transformation of production and the reorganization of work, managers in the United States turn to consultants and come under the influence of one guru or another. Thus, U.S. companies often import pieces of production models—sociotechnical systems, lean production, diversified quality production, or flexible specialization—that were developed in other institutional contexts. Such models may be implemented successfully in one or another company without the support of external institutions, but it takes a leadership dedicated to change and a very large commitment of financial and other corporate resources to make widespread organizational change possible.

In the absence of an institutional setting that socializes some of the costs of high-performance production systems, it may be unprofitable in the short run for individual firms to introduce more efficient forms of organization. The design stage (hiring consultants, developing a vision, persuading managers and workers to buy into change) and the training of employees that is required to implement the changes impose high costs on individual firms in money, management time, and time spent in training by workers. Firms incur all these costs in advance of the gains from higher quality and/or lower costs. These up-front costs hinder the ability of all but the most convinced or most desperate firms to change to a transformed system.

Finally, the move to high-performance systems involves several other obstacles to success. One major obstacle is that, in the short run, low-wage competitors can undermine U.S. firms while they are attempting to make fundamental changes, before the improvements made possible by the changes have materialized. Given the very high start-up costs of organizational change in the U.S. context, firms are especially vulnerable in the initial stages of the change process. Predatory pricing by low-wage competitors can threaten the survival of the transformed firms, or at least of the innovations they have adopted.

There is some fragmentary but alarming evidence to suggest that low-wage competitors are, indeed, undermining the efforts of U.S. firms to change. As part of its project to evaluate the impact of the National Institute of Standards and Technology/Midwest Manufacturing Technology Center, the Industrial Technology Institute studied 250 small and medium-sized manufacturing firms (Luria 1992). The 1992 study includes a sample of firms that sought advice from the Manufacturing Technology Center and a second sample of randomly chosen firms. The study identified three types of firms. Type A high-performance work organizations exhibit high-average blue-collar wages and a high proportion of skilled employees, "spend more than average to train shop employees, and exhibit high labor productivity, widespread multi-skilling, low worker turnover, and significant worker authority" (Luria 1992:1). Many are unionized, and the firms in this category have much higher than average rates of technology use and labor productivity. The surprising finding, however, is that, as a group, these firms are shrinking because they are losing market share to firms in the other two categories. These other two categories are (1) low-performance work organizations that "train less, use fewer quality management and lean production techniques than average, often do no statistical quality control, and seldom have groups or teams of any kind"; and (2) type B high-performance work organizations, which employ some quality mangement and lean production techniques and have reduced the amount of indirect labor, but are no more likely than average to use problem-solving groups, work teams, setup teams, or maintenance teams (Luria 1992:2). The latter two types of firms use lower-skilled workers and pay wages substantially below those of type A high-performance firms. Despite their lower productivity, however, these lower-wage firms have grown by attracting domestic customers away from the higher-wage, higher-productivity firms, thereby undermining their position in the market. Significantly, they have *not* grown by increasing exports (interview, Dan Luria, Nov. 19, 1992).

The dangers of allowing this "market solution" to prevail are evident in

Michael Best's 1987 study of furniture firms in North London (cited in Pyke 1992). Faced with increasing competition, the firms sought to maintain market share by cutting prices and costs. They perceived their problem to be excessive wages and competition from neighboring firms, and they reacted by hiring less-skilled workers, automating or increasing the intensity of work, and cutting prices in an effort to drive other firms out of business and pick up their customers. These responses, however, left the North London firms with worsening relations with their workers, slimmer margins, and, eventually, insufficient financial capacity to survive. They were thus less able to respond to the real problem, which was neither their workers nor their local competitors but the emergence of foreign competitors organized around new principles. As a result, twenty-five North London furniture firms that in 1960 employed 16,000 workers were reduced by 1987 to a single firm employing about 550 workers.

Yet another problem is that the lack of legal, bargained, or cultural restrictions on the ability of most U.S. firms to lay off workers, and the ideological opposition in the United States to such restraints, make it difficult for transformed firms, which rely on mutual trust, to honor commitments they have made to employment security during periods of recession. Competitors who have not adopted a high-commitment model of production will reduce costs during a recession by laying off workers, putting firms that have promised employment security under pressure to renege. Finally, unions engaged in a rear-guard action to protect jobs and wages at companies pursuing an intensification of mass production and a low-wage path exhibit an understandable uncertainty about the intentions of firms pursuing alternative systems of work. Unions fear that if they give up traditional means of exercising power—such as job control and grievance procedures—they will be unable to compel companies to uphold their commitments to worker participation in mangement and other new forms of power sharing. Thus, to the extent that firms adopt flexible mass production or other low-wage paths to competitiveness, the obstacles facing firms that attempt high-skill, high-commitment alternatives will increase.

This analysis of the impediments to the diffusion of high-performance work systems suggests an important role for public policy in developing an institutional framework that would support, rather than undermine, the transformation to high-performance work systems. A more hospitable institutional setting might enable nascent or newly emerging high-perform-

ance systems to survive the challenges posed by low-wage, low-skill competitors and by poor macroeconomic performance. The role of public
policy in developing such a framework is discussed in the next, and final,
chapter.

10.

POLICIES TO PROMOTE HIGH-
PERFORMANCE SYSTEMS

The evidence from this and a growing body of research is that the American business landscape is populated by many firms that continue to pursue the low-wage path, many others that are struggling to adopt piecemeal reforms without the institutional supports they need, and a small number of best-practice firms that have transformed their production systems. To move beyond the current landscape and diffuse high-performance work systems more broadly requires an interrelated set of public policies that address the issues that firms and workers on their own cannot tackle. Economists generally agree that dealing with externalities and market imperfections is an appropriate role for the government. A labor force that possesses a high level of skills reduces training costs and improves the efficiency of all firms. Similarly, publicly supported interfirm consortia that achieve economies of scale in research and development or in technical assistance and training diffuse the costs associated with high-performance work systems. Although some of these initiatives require government spending or changes in existing regulations, many require little of the government in the way of spending or intervention other than in an initial role as "honest broker" to help the private sector establish these institutions.

We have grouped policy options into five areas. These include policies to improve training institutions, enhance employee participation, increase the commitment of firms to their stakeholders, support interfirm collaboration, and rule out the low-wage path. Rather than providing detailed prescriptions, we have outlined a number of principles and policy alternatives for achieving these goals.

JOB TRAINING

There is considerable evidence that front-line employees currently receive less training than is required to support high-performance work systems (Kochan and Osterman 1991). Broad support from communities, firms, workers, and unions now exists for federally supported policies to enhance training for a broad cross-section of the U.S. population. Unlike past efforts that centered on disadvantaged workers and were viewed as social welfare programs, the current support for training initiatives grows out of concerns about the United States' competitiveness and the need for high-wage, high-performance jobs. The outlines of a national policy for workplace training are developed in reports by the Economic Policy Institute (Batt and Osterman 1993a; Lynch 1993); we briefly review the recommendations here.

In addition to apprenticeship programs focused on youth and the school-to-work transition, training for high-performance work systems must reach the 70 percent of the American work force that does not have a college degree. Building a technically trained work force requires programs that are workplace-centered so that training can occur on state-of-the-art technology and be integrated into work reorganization efforts. Throwing dollars at training is unlikely to produce performance gains unless firms simultaneously undertake organizational changes that allow employees to use their newly acquired skills and problem-solving capabilities.

To support a work force that produces continuous improvements in production processes requires training opportunities that go beyond individual programs—it requires *training systems* that have a strong local institutional base and that can evolve and respond flexibly to new demands on labor from changing technologies or products. Employees must be able to return again and again to formal training as needed throughout their lifetimes and to integrate this process into the normal course of their working lives.

Such a systemic effort at publicly supported training runs the risk of creating large subsidies to firms for training they would undertake anyway in the normal course of doing business. To avoid such subsidies, training programs should be administered as grants or contracts with targeting and performance criteria.[1] States administering such contracts could establish the appropriate criteria. One alternative is to target firms and workers most in need and unlikely to have the resources to undertake training on their own—small and medium-sized firms; front-line rather than managerial workers, who now receive most of the training (Carnevale and Goldstein 1990); and minority workers and women, who are the least likely to receive training (Lynch 1989). States should provide targets or incentives to reach these underserved constituencies.

Another alternative is to require larger firms to provide matching funds, to demonstrate how publicly funded training supplements existing efforts, or to show how higher-performance standards will be met through public subsidies. States could also target particular training related to high performance and to total quality and collaborative teamwork. States such as Illinois and California have already developed some of these alternatives (Batt and Osterman 1993b).

To enhance system building and create a strong institutional constituency, state-administered training programs may want to provide incentives to create training networks among small firms in conjunction with community organizations, trade unions, community colleges, and local employment offices. Within the workplace, labor-management training committees provide another vehicle for building institutional support for training, for ensuring that training programs meet the needs of the work force, and for monitoring programs to ensure quality and accountability.

Another risk in the creation of workplace-centered training is that the training tends to be specific to the particular workplace or firm in which it is given and therefore does not provide employees with more general or portable skills that more broadly enhance their employment security. To guard against this, training programs should build in occupational certification requirements that can be administered on a state-by-state basis. The development of occupational skill criteria and the accreditation of training programs offered by community colleges, technical schools, vendors, and in-house training staff reduce the costs to firms of identifying appropriate training curricula and increase the portability of worker credentials.

PROMOTING EMPLOYEE AND UNION PARTICIPATION

There is ample evidence that perverse incentives exist that discourage managers from adopting participative work systems (Smith 1991; Wever and Allen 1992). Several policy alternatives exist to counter these incentives. The most direct route, put forward by a number of researchers and policy makers (Rogers and Wootton 1992; Freeman and Rogers 1993), is to mandate elected employee councils, modeled after European works councils, at establishments with more than fifty employees. These councils could replace existing employee-involvement programs that, as in the *Electromation* case, violate American labor law because they are essentially company unions. Legislation could clarify the rights, responsibilities, and sanctions available to such councils, including their involvement in issues of work reorganization, training, health and safety, and conflict resolution.

Alternatively, Congress could build on existing legislation that provides special tax treatment to firms with employee stock ownership plans (ESOPs) under the Employee Retirement Income Security Act (Levine 1992). Support for ESOPs grew in the 1980s in part because some thought that giving employees stock in a company would increase their sense of ownership and hence their participation in performance improvements. The empirical evidence suggests, however, that meaningful employee participation occurs only when real structures are in place to provide a vehicle for participation (Levine and Tyson 1990; Eaton and Voos 1992). Tying ESOP tax subsidies to the creation of employee councils and of worker representation on the boards of companies would help establish this critical link.

Employee councils should not be viewed as an alternative to union representation but as an immediate way to increase participation in unionized as well as nonunionized workplaces. Trade union leaders play an active role in employee councils in Germany, and such councils have a legal responsibility to enforce union contracts at work sites. A strong trade union movement is viewed as a necessary condition for the success of the employee councils (Knuth 1991; Wever, Berg, and Kochan 1993). Indeed, as employee councils develop at nonunionized work sites, they may seek the leadership and technical assistance of unions to represent the interests of workers more effectively.

Any new policies would not take the place of reforms needed in existing labor legislation to overcome the obstacles to participation facing unions. The case studies in this book clearly demonstrate that where firms respect the institutional integrity of unions and where unions have the resources and capability, unions enhance employee participation and help diffuse and sustain higher-performance work systems. The lack of enforcement of current labor laws has created obstacles to union organizing, long delays in union elections, and managerial disregard for duty-to-bargain contracts, all of which drain union resources and deter unions from assuming the kind of leadership role required in partnership activities. Additionally, given the increasingly widespread use of self-managed teams, current interpretations of labor law (e.g., *Yeshiva*) that exclude from coverage workers with some supervisory responsibilities must be reconsidered. Indeed, there is no reason to exclude from protective labor legislation lower-level supervisors and managers who are not confidential employees and whose working conditions, degree of employment security, and work responsibilities increasingly resemble those of front-line employees.

A major obstacle to greater participation, as we have noted, is the lack of employment security both at the individual level because of "employment at will" and, more generally, restructuring and downsizing. The United States is the only advanced industrialized country in which employers may hire and fire "at will." In the last decade, however, the employment-at-will doctrine has been increasingly challenged in courts through tort law, and unjustly fired employees have won large awards. As a result, with broad support from the business community, one state (Minnesota) has already passed legislation prohibiting unjust dismissal, and as of 1991, seventeen other states were also considering such legislation (Tomkins 1988; Hahn and Smith 1990; Krueger 1991; Edwards 1993). As in other areas, these state initiatives set an example for the federal government.

The broader issue of employment stabilization must be addressed by macroeconomic policies as well as by labor market policies that support the adoption of high-performance work systems and enhance the viability of small and medium-sized, locally tied firms through regional economic development strategies. In addition to the policies discussed in more detail below, the development of officially sanctioned clearinghouses to determine and promote best practice in process technologies and associated work organization would reduce uncertainties not only for firms planning to implement them (Cole 1989) but for financial institutions that would otherwise be reluctant to lend to companies for this purpose. Such clearinghouses would help overcome the inherent bias in capital markets against hard-to-monitor investments in human capital. Imperfect information about the impact of investments in intangibles leads to underinvestment in training and participation. Additionally, Congress could reexamine the criteria for the Malcolm Baldrige National Quality Award and give greater weight to human resource and industrial relations innovations that promote employee participation.

INCREASING FIRM COMMITMENT TO STAKEHOLDERS

Both U.S. law and the operation of American capital markets favor the interests of a firm's shareholders over those of other stakeholders—its employees, managers, directors, suppliers, customers, and the community in which it is located. Moreover, shareholder value tends to be narrowly defined as current stock price (Porter 1992). Managers who sacrifice short-term stock price for other goals face the threat of a hostile takeover, a shareholder revolt that replaces top management, or a lawsuit for not managing the company in the interests of the shareholders who are the company's owners. This may happen, for example, if a firm increases retained earnings in order to invest in intangibles such as R&D, organizational redesign, or worker training and thereby reduces dividends, causing a sell-off of the stock and a short-term decline in its price. Retained earnings are the major source of investment in new technology and organizational change. Yet American managers today are penalized for retaining company earnings, even though doing so may maximize long-term shareholder value.

This problem is especially acute in the United States. In contrast to the German or Japanese systems, in which the dominant investors in a firm are corporations or institutions that hold large stakes and are permanent owners, more than 85 percent of the stock of publicly traded companies in the United States is owned by individuals and institutional investors that act as agents for individuals (Porter 1992). The goal of institutional agents (e.g., pension funds, mutual funds), who are evaluated on a quarterly or annual basis by the appreciation of the stocks in their funds, is rapid appreciation of their shares in relation to some stock index. Thus, both individuals and institutional investors in the United States are transient owners, always ready to move to another company in search of higher short-term gains.

This strategy leads American investors into short-term speculative behavior that erodes the concept of ownership in the corporate sector and has a profound effect on corporate governance, especially with respect to corporate control (Crotty and Goldstein 1993). Corporate managers today are prevented from making financial commitments to the long-term development of their companies and from recognizing their obligations to all their stakeholders, not just investors who own stocks or bonds, by the rise since the 1950s of what is called the market for corporate control. This term refers to the ability of current or potential stockholders to exercise control over the investment decisions of corporate managers, most notably, though not exclusively, through the threat of a hostile takeover of the company (Lazonick 1992).

Both the focus on short-term performance and the rise of the market for corporate control inhibit the shift to high-performance work systems. First, they undermine the ability of large shareholders to act as "patient" capitalists. Second, they reduce the ability of managers to invest in research and development, new process technology, new work organization, and training. Third, and finally, they undermine the ability of a firm to undertake long-term employment contracts with its hourly and managerial employees (Lazonick 1992). As a result, the firm is unable to make and honor commitments to other stakeholders, especially its employees.

A number of policy measures to reduce the focus on short-term stock price performance and to increase the financial commitment of firms to all their stakeholders, not just the owners of stocks and bonds, have been proposed (Crotty and Goldstein 1993). These include taxing short-term capital gains at significantly higher rates than long-term gains; subjecting securities transactions to a modest trading tax to weaken the incentives for speculation and churning; and adopting or strengthening state laws regulating hostile takeovers to protect the rights of employees, restrict "greenmail," and give longer-term shareholders more of a voice. Workers should have a larger role in deciding the policies of their pension funds, and managers of pension funds should be encouraged to engage in long-term shareholding and to take a more active role in the companies in which they hold stakes. Finally, all the stakeholders of a company—its employers, suppliers, customers, and community—should be represented among the outside directors, and the board of directors should be encouraged to play a larger role in the affairs of the company (Porter 1992).

BUILDING INTERFIRM COLLABORATION AND QUALITY STANDARDS

Transformed production systems require new forms of interfirm cooperation and coordination. Total quality production depends on reducing the arm's-length relationships between firms and building strategic alliances between competing firms or vertical links among tiers of suppliers and customers (Grabher 1991; Campbell 1992). Some state governments have already taken an active role in facilitating network relations among firms to enhance research and development, the adoption of new technologies, and the provision of related technical training; others have encouraged public-private partnerships to promote exports. These efforts should be evaluated and further diffused, perhaps as part of an industrial extension program. A system of state or regional-level industrial extension programs could provide a vehicle for disseminating information and providing guidance to firms on the adoption of new work organization and human resource practices. Industrial extension programs could also provide assistance to firms in meeting quality standards.

The ability of firms to meet quality standards could also be enhanced through the establishment of a third-party registration system whereby the federal government would certify auditing companies as qualified to rate the ability of suppliers to comply with their customers' quality standards. This would facilitate the customers' ability to take quality as well as price into account in choosing suppliers. Many European countries have such government-certified auditing companies, which audit companies that wish to demonstrate that they meet the quality standards of the International Standards Organization in Geneva. The certified auditing companies then issue "registrations" to those suppliers that qualify (Holusha 1992). The American National Standards Institute, a private industry group, and the American Society for Quality Control, an association of corporate quality-control executives, have begun issuing registrations in the United States, but no government agency has been authorized to bring the standards in line with total quality principles or to certify these or other auditing organizations.

RULING OUT THE LOW-WAGE PATH

Many proposals put forward in other contexts have the effect of limiting the excesses of predatory pricing behavior by firms following a low-wage strategy. These policies include a national health-care plan; a national family-leave act; the pro-rating of pension, vacation, and other benefits for part-time workers; the provision of mandated portable benefits for temporary workers; the indexing of the minimum wage to one-half the average wage; the elimination of tax code provisions and Agency for International Development (AID) program abuses that encourage firms to move production jobs out of the United States; and the development of international labor standards to accompany trade agreements (Rothstein 1993).

These policies are "preventive" (Sengenberger 1990) in that they make it more difficult for firms to follow a competitive strategy based on low wages. It is important to rule out this option if firms are to be encouraged to pursue a high-performance strategy. In the early stages of organizational change, the costs associated with reorganizing work, improving quality, and training workers are high, and firms pursuing a high-performance strategy are especially vulnerable to competition from low-wage firms. Thus, it may be unprofitable for an individual firm to transform its production system—despite the potential efficiencies of team-based production, total quality management, and more participatory structures—if it can be undermined in the short run by firms following a low-wage strategy. Ruling out the worst excesses of such behavior removes an important obstacle to organizational transformation in firms that wish to pursue this path.

CONCLUSION

U.S. firms face numerous obstacles to the implementation of transformed production systems. These include the dilemmas facing unions, the perverse incentives for managers, and the barriers to diffusion that arise from an outmoded institutional framework. An industrial strategy adopted by the federal government should include measures to support the transformation of production processes in U.S. firms and to promote a more efficient combination of the factors of production. Competition among national economies in the coming decades will be waged not only in the domain of critical new product technologies but in the domain of process technology and work organization as well. Government policy has a key role to play in facilitating the transformation of work processes in the United States.

INCIDENCE OF ORGANIZATIONAL CHANGE AMONG U.S. FIRMS: EVIDENCE FROM SURVEYS

A.1 New York Stock Exchange Survey

Year	1982
Sample	Stratified sample of 6,131 firms with 100 or more employees; responses weighted
Number of firms responding	1,158 (26.5%)
Median size	Responses weighted to be representative
Types of firms	50% mfg. 50% nonmfg.
Unionization	Not reported
Types of programs or practices	Human resource programs to stimulate productivity; might include QCs, formal training, job rotation, incentive plan

Incidence of programs or practices

Percent of firms with program or practice

No programs or practices	84.7
At least one program or practice	13.9
Program or practice in planning stage	1.4

Among firms with program or practice, percent with this type

Job design or redesign	46
Job enlargement	22
Job rotation	18
Formal training	76
Organizational structure	40
Scheduling work flow	43
Suggestion systems	38
Labor-management committees	25
Labor advisory groups	6
QCs	44
Production teams	16
Task forces	35
Employee surveys	45
Salaried blue-collar workers	6
Group productivity	7
Profit sharing	25
Stock purchase plans	21

A.2 Bureau of National Affairs Personnel Policies Forum Survey

Year	1983–84
Sample	Unclear
Number of firms responding	195 (approximately 66.7%)
Median size	53% are less than 1,000 47% are greater than 1,000
Types of firms	45% mfg. 27% nonmfg. 28% nonbusiness
Unionization	Not reported
Types of programs or practices	Productivity improvement programs

Incidence of programs or practices

Percent of firms, by firm size, with program or practice

	All firms	Large firms	Small firms
Formal productivity improvement program (including training)	41	48	35
Group incentive plan	32	38	27
Profit sharing	19	20	19
Stock ownership	18	25	12
Gainsharing	2	3	—

Percent of firms, by firm size, that have established a new program during the last five years (1979–83)

	All firms	Large firms	Small firms
Training and development	50	61	41
Worker participation	44	52	37
Work simplification	29	32	27
Job enlargement	28	28	28
Job enrichment	27	33	22
Rotate assignment	19	22	17
Job specialization	16	18	15

Percent of firms, by business type, with program or practice

	Mfg.	Nonmfg.	Nonbusiness
Formal productivity improvement program (including training)	48	43	27
Group incentive plan	45	42	4
Profit sharing	22	34	2
Stock ownership	29	17	2
Gainsharing	1	4	—

Percent of firms, by business type, that have established a new program during the last five years (1979–83)

	Mfg.	Nonmfg.	Nonbusiness
Training and development	46	66	42
Worker participation	53	30	44
Work simplification	31	43	13
Job enlargement	30	26	27
Job enrichment	23	36	25
Rotate assignment	23	19	13
Job specialization	15	23	13

A.3   U.S. Department of Labor, Survey of Human Resource Policies in American Firms (Delaney, Lewin, Ichniowski)

Year	Fall 1986
Sample	Executives from 7,765 business units from COMPUSTAT data tapes
Number of firms responding	495 business units (6.5%)
Median size	7,884 employees
Types of firms	45% mfg. 55% nonmfg.
Unionization	10% of professional employees 16% of clerical employees 32% of manufacturing employees
Type of programs or practices	All human resource management practices; >1,000 variables
Incidence of programs or practices	

(mean rating: 1 = not at all; 5 = a great deal)

Selected practices	Current	Planned
Allow employees to supervise selves	1.9	2.1
Training and retraining programs	3.0	3.5
Gainsharing	1.9	2.4
Profit sharing	2.7	3.2
EI/participation	3.1	3.7
QCs	1.9	2.3
Employee team building	2.6	3.3
Semi autonomous work groups	1.9	2.3

Percent covered by formal training	varies from 32% clerical to 50% professional and technical
Cost per employee	varies from $346 for some blue collar employees; to $1,408 for some professional and technical employees; to $1,343 for managers

A.4 Government Accounting Office Survey of Employee Involvement: Lawler, Ledford, Mohrman Analysis

Year	1987
Sample	Fortune 1000 firms
Number of firms responding	476 (51.0%)
Median size	9,000 employees
Types of firms	50% mfg.
	50% nonmfg.
Unionization	8% of nonmanagers unionized
	58% of unionized operations had EI programs
Type of programs or practices	Employee-involvement programs or practices
Incidence of programs or practices	

Percent of all firms reporting significant change in way workers managed   25

Percent of firms with employees trained for EI

	% of firms with more than 60% of employees trained in last 3 years	% of firms with more than 20% of employees trained in last 3 years
Group decision- & problem solving	5	57
Leadership	4	63
Business	4	50
Quality & statistical analysis	6	42
Team building	5	52

Percent of firms with pay or other reward systems

	Have	Don't have	Those without but plan to have
Profit sharing	35	65	na
Gainsharing	74	26	na
Stock ownership	39	61	na
All-salaried	29	71	na
Knowledge- or skill-based	60	40	na
Flex benefits	66	34	na

177

Percent of firms with participation programs

	Have	Don't have	Those without but plan to have
Quality circles	39	61	42
Other participation	30	70	62
Union-management QWL committee	70	30	20
Employee survey	32	68	65

Percent of firms with work reorganization programs

Job enrichment or redesign	40	60	48
Self-managing work teams	72	28	23
Mini-enterprise units	75	25	19

Extent of worker involvement

Percent of firms with this proportion of workers in pay or reward system

	0–20%	21–60%	≥61%
Profit sharing	55	15	30
Gainsharing	93	5	2
Stock ownership	47	8	44
All-salaried	44	23	33
Knowledge- or skill-based	85	9	6
Flex benefits	73	7	21

Percent of firms with this proportion of workers in participation programs

	0–20%	21–60%	≥61%
Quality circles	71	25	3
Other participation	63	30	6
Union-management QWL committee	90	9	2
Employee survey	54	23	23

Percent of firms with this proportion of workers in work reorganization programs

	0–20%	21–60%	≥61%
Job enrichment or redesign	78	18	5
Self-managing work teams	92	7	0
Mini-enterprise units	93	5	1

A.5 Government Accounting Office Survey of Employee Involvement: Eaton and Voos Analysis of Union/Nonunion Differences

Year	1987
Sample	Fortune 1000 firms (934 firms because of mergers)
Number of firms responding	476 (51.0%)
Median size	9,000 employees
Types of firms	50% mfg. 50% nonmfg.
Unionization	8% of nonmanagers unionized 58% of unionized operations had EI programs
Types of programs or practices	EI programs or practices

Incidence of programs or practices

Percent with this type of program or practice

	Union present (179 firms)	Nonunion (134 firms)
Profit sharing	63	66
Gainsharing	33	15
Stock ownership	65	58
Knowledge- or skill-based pay	47	29
QCs	71	48
Other participation	79	61
Union-management QWL committee	46	1
Employee survey	74	62
Job enrichment or redesign	66	60
Self-managing work teams	35	19

	More employees covered by program in firm where
Profit sharing	no union
Gainsharing	no significant difference
Stock ownership	no significant difference
Knowledge- or skill-based pay	no significant difference
QCs	union present
Other participation	no significant difference
Union-management QWL committee	union present
Employee survey	no significant difference
Job enrichment or redesign	no significant difference
Self-managing work teams	no significant difference

A.6 Lawler, Mohrman, Ledford Survey of Employee Involvement and Total Quality Management

Year	1990
Sample	Fortune 1000 firms (987 firms because of mergers)
Number of firms responding	313 (32.0%)
Median size	9,000–10,000 employees
Types of firms	53% mfg. 47% nonmfg.
Unionization	Not reported
Types of programs or practices	Employee-involvement and total management programs

Percent of firms reporting EI activity

Low level	36
Average level	34
High level	7
Reward	7
Other	16

Percent of firms with employees trained for EI

	% of firms with more than 60% of employees trained in last 3 years	% of firms with more than 20% of employees trained in last 3 years
Group decision- & problem solving	6	55
Leadership	3	54
Business	2	39
Quality & statistical analysis	9	43
Team building	8	56
Job skills	35	84

Percent of firms with pay or reward system

	Don't have	Have
Profit sharing	37	63
Gainsharing	61	39
Stock ownership	36	64
All-salaried	36	64
Knowledge- or skill-based	49	51
Flex benefits	46	54
Team incentives	41	59

Percent of firms with participation programs

	Don't have	Have
QCs	34	66
Other participation groups	14	86
Union-management QWL committee	60	40
Employee survey	23	77

Percent of firms with work reorganization programs

	Don't have	Have
Job enrichment or redesign	25	75
Self-managing work teams	53	47
Mini-enterprise units	72	28

Percent of firms with total quality practices

	Don't have	Have
Self-inspection	10	84
Work simplification	13	85
Monitor cost of quality	18	82
Collaborate with suppliers on quality	13	83
Just-in-time delivery	24	74
Work or mfg. cells (doesn't add to 100 in original)	41	59

Percent of firms covering this proportion of workers in pay or reward systems

	0–20%	21–60%	≥61%
Profit sharing	56	11	33
Gainsharing	89	9	2
Stock ownership	45	9	46
All salaried	54	24	23
Knowledge- or skill-based	83	13	3
Flex benefits	79	16	6

Percent of firms with this proportion of workers in a participation program

	0–20%	21–60%	≥61%
QCs	70	26	6
Other participation	49	41	11
Union-management QWL committee	86	13	1
Employee survey	49	25	27

Percent of firms with this proportion of workers in a work reorganization program

	0–20%	21–60%	≥61%
Job enrichment or redesign	68	29	3
Self-managing work teams	90	10	0
Mini-enterprise units	95	4	1

A.6 Lawler, Mohrman, Ledford Survey of Employee Involvement and Total Quality Management (continued)

Percent of firms with this proportion of workers participating in total quality practices

	0–20%	21–60%	≥61%
Self-inspection	35	45	14
Work simplification	39	45	14
Monitor cost of quality	53	35	11
Collaborate with suppliers on quality	50	38	8
Just-in-time delivery	55	33	10
Work or mfg. cells	68	28	4

Year	1990
Sample	NEA's K–12 local associations
Number of firms **responding**	5,747 (45.0%)
Median size	Not reported
Types of firms	K–12 schools
Unionization	100%
Types of programs **or practices**	Site-based decision making

Incidence of programs or practices

Percent with site-based decision making	*Don't* *have*	*Have*
	61	30

Percent of projects where these groups participate in decision making

Teachers	98
Support personnel	45
Administrators	96
Parents	51
Students	26
Other	13

Percent of projects where this subject is covered in decision making

Curriculum	84
Budget	49
Staff development	79
Student grouping	49
Student assessment	53
Program evaluation	71
Instructional materials	65
Other	26

Number of schools, of 1,735, with local association involvement

Joint management	362
Representation on district-level governing board	433
Association sign-off required	244
Other	412
No role	421

Year	1990
Sample	Team survey; 1,108 individuals known to be involved with teams
	Executive survey: stratified random sample of executives drawn from 300,500 subscribers to *Industry Week*—mfg. only, 1,000+ employees, $100 million+ sales
Response rate	
Number of firms responding	team: 272 (25.0%) executives: 862 (23.0%)
Size of firm	one-quarter 75,000+ one-quarter 20–75,000 one-fifth 5–20,000 one-third 500–1,000
Average size	1,000–5,000
Types of firms	team: 71% mfg. 29% nonmfg.
	executives: 100% mfg.
Unionization	39% have union affiliation
Types of programs or practices	Self-directed teams: have day-to-day responsibility for managing selves and their work; handle job assignments, plan or schedule work, make production-related decisions, take action on problems; not QCs or cross-functional teams
Incidence of programs or practices	

Executive Survey
Percent of firms with at least one self-
directed team   27

Percent of firms with this proportion of workers in self-directed team

	Now	In five years
0–10%	59	10
11–50%	31	43
≥51%	10	47

Percent of firms with a compensation system for team members

Gainsharing	21
Production bonuses	19
Pay for skills or knowledge	41

Team Survey

Production tasks	Percent of firms in which practice not done by team	Percent of firms in which team shares responsibility	Percent of firms in which team has sole responsibility
Prepare budgets	55	39	6
Set production goals	22	49	29
Work with external customers & suppliers	22	44	34
Select work methods	8	54	38
Process improvements	7	51	42
Routine maintenance	11	44	45
Stop production line	12	42	46
Work with internal customers & suppliers	8	39	53
Assign daily tasks	12	30	58
Safety/housekeeping	3	28	69

Personnel functions	Percent of firms in which practice not done by team	Percent of firms in which team shares responsibility	Percent of firms in which team has sole responsibility
Compensation	70	23	7
Performance appraisals	46	37	17
Individual performance problems	41	45	14
Select members	24	42	34
Training decisions	14	53	33
Schedule vacations	29	27	44

Year	March 1990
	Oct. 1991

Sample — HR executives from the 645 companies that participated in original Workforce 2000 study

Number of firms responding — 287 (44.5%)

Median size — Not reported

Types of firms — Idiosyncratic identification scheme

33% mfg. (approx.)
67% nonmfg.

Unionization — Not reported

Types of programs or practices — Cultural diversity, women in work force, changing worker values, labor shortage, skills mismatch, aging

Incidence of programs or practices

Percent of firms, as of March 1990, with plans for work reform and organizational change

	Have	Plan
Quality improvement	—	—
Employee surveys	47	13
Self-managed work teams	12	4
Gainsharing	12	6
Skill-based pay	—	—
Flexible benefits	—	—
Retraining	25	8
Remedial training	16	13

Percent of firms, as of Oct. 1991, with plans for work reform and organizational change

	Have	Plan
Quality improvement	69	16
Employee surveys	58	19
Self-managed work teams	36	18
Gainsharing	21	18
Skill-based pay	29	16
Flexible benefits	53	29
Retraining	47	17
Remedial training	35	15

A.10 Grant Thornton Survey of American Manufacturers/Managing Quality

Year	Dec. 1990
Sample	Random sample of executives selected from Dun & Bradstreet; mid-sized mfg. firms, sales of $10–$500 million, SIC 20–39
Number of firms responding	250
Median size	48% of firms have sales of $10–$19 million
Types of firms	100% mfg.
Unionization	Not reported
Types of programs or practices	What manufacturers are doing about quality

Percent of firms citing the importance of quality

Say quality is a high priority	83
Say they have TQC or TQM in firm	70
Calculate total cost of quality	31
Might enter Baldrige competition in next 3 years	18

Percent of firms citing the single most important step taken to improve quality

Training program	20
Production workers responsible for quality	16
Increase inspections	13
Eliminate steps	7
Upgrade equipment	6

Percent of firms citing other steps taken to improve quality

Quality assurance/inspection	96
Statistical control and preventive maintenance	79
Total quality control	70
Stop-line inspection program	67
Zero-defect program	34

Percent of firms that inspect for quality

100% inspection	48
Sampling	49
Doesn't inspect	3

Percent of firms in which this department is involved in quality efforts

Production	99
Purchasing	87
Accounting	55

Percent of firms in which CEO meets best customers

< once a month	36
> once a month	55

Percent of firms in which quality standards

Exceed customer expectations	48
Just meet customer expectations	46
Other	6

Percent of firms citing this as most important competitive factor

Quality	35
Speed	6
Service	24
Price	29
Other	6

Percent of firms that imposed a quality program on supplier

End product mfg.	69
Supplier	75

Year	Fall 1991
Sample	Executives drawn from sample of 1,000 largest manufacturing companies, 100 largest service companies, 50 largest utilities and other
Number of firms responding	500
Median size	All large
Types of firms	90% mfg. 10% nonmfg.
Unionization	Not reported
Types of programs or practices	Are firms adopting TQM
Incidence of programs or practices	

Percent of firms with a quality program

Company has quality program	93
Program consists of task forces working on improvements	35
Program consists of changing companywide processes and culture	58

Percent of firms finding it difficult to juggle employee, customer, owner needs

Agree	18
Disagree	30

Percent of firms with no real fundamental change in way we conduct business

Agree	14
Disagree	58

Percent of firms with no strategic framework to focus quality efforts

Agree	12
Disagree	54

Percent of firms where TQM efforts have had significant impact on competitive position	36
Percent of firms where TQM efforts will have significant impact on competitive position in next 3 years	62

A.12 Osterman Survey of Work Organization and Human Resource Practices

Year	1992
Sample	National random sample of establishments with 50 or more employees
Number of firms responding	875 (694 used in analysis)
Median size	Representative of establishments
Types of firms	Not reported in preliminary results
Unionization	23.7%
Types of programs or practices	Work organization, TQM, human resource practice
Incidence of programs or practices	

Percent of firms with this type of quality practice

	All	Mfg.
Self-directed teams	54.5	47.7
Job rotation	43.4	57.6
TQM	33.5	15.6
Quality circles	40.8	46.8
Nothing	21.8	14.2

Extent of worker involvement

Percent of firms at 50% level of penetration

	All	Mfg.
Self-directed teams	40.5	32.1
Job rotation	26.6	38.8
TQM	24.5	32.1
Quality circles	27.4	31.5
Nothing	36.0	31.0

APPENDIX B.

SUMMARY OF CASE STUDIES, 1970–92

EXPLANATION OF CATEGORIES AND DEFINITIONS

The following explains the categories used in the summary of case studies:

- Source: The majority of studies are drawn from a series of cases conducted by the American Productivity and Quality Center (APQC) in Houston and the U.S. Department of Labor's Bureau of Labor-Management Relations (USDOL). Cases from journal articles or academic researchers are referenced by author with the full citation listed in the references.

- Publication date (Pub date): cases are listed chronologically.

- # Years: The number of years refers to the number of years the program was in operation at the time the case study was published. Whether the program continued after that time is not known.

- # Workers: This refers to the total number of employees at the worksite or division affected by the innovation, not the actual number of employees participating in the program (which usually is smaller but which was often not reported).

- Sector: mfg = manufacturing; srv = service
  Occupation: bl = blue collar; wc = white collar

The categories discussed below evolved out of the case materials and include areas of innovation only. They are therefore not inclusive. Under management methods, for example, we include methods identified by researchers, managers, and consultants that are part of a new approach. The list of categories corresponds to the column headings across the charts that follow.

Management methods: new methods of coordination adopted by management, including:

- Approaches (broadly defined): STS (sociotechnical systems) and TQ (total quality).

- Techniques: JIT (just-in-time inventory); SPC (statistical process control); performance measurement (any system designed to measure organizational performance); cost of quality (measures designed to quantify the cost of quality).

- Structure: downsizing (whether downsizing is part of management strategy); delayer management (whether reductions in management are part of management strategy); integrate suppliers (whether management develops methods to develop more long-term relations with suppliers or require that suppliers apply quality processes or other production techniques.

Work organization: includes the use of new technology, job redesign, and job rotation.

- New technology: adoption of more flexible or microprocessor-based technology.

- Broad jobs: redesign of jobs through job enlargement (increased breadth) or job enrichment (increased depth).

- Job rotation: rotation of workers through different job tasks.

Worker participation: distinguishes between parallel structures (off-line) and teams (on-line).

- Parallel structures: structures that are outside or parallel to the production process. These include: suggestion systems (SS), quality of work life programs (QWL), and quality circles and problem-solving teams (QC/PS). This last category covers an assortment of groups that usually meet on a regular basis (once a week) to discuss work-related problems and arrive at solutions.

- Teams: work units that are organized by groups of jobs rather than by individual jobs. Teams vary in their degree of decision-making autonomy. Supervised (super.) teams retain a supervisory structure; self-directed teams (SDT) are semi-autonomous; a supervisor serves as a "coach" or "facilitator." Autonomous (auto.) teams have no supervisor.

Type of participation: whether participation is voluntary (vol.) or mandatory (man.).

Level of participation: whether workers participate in decisions at the level of the work unit (within dept.), across work units or across functions (across dept.), or on an organizationwide basis.

Domain of participation: area of decision making in which workers participate.

- Technology/job design: the choice of technology and the design of jobs.

- Work process: the way technology is used or products are produced.

- Administrative/scheduling (admin./sched.): traditional supervisory responsibilities with regard to administration, scheduling, personnel.

- Strategic: strategic business planning.

Human resource policies

Education and training

- Information sharing (info. share): the sharing of business information with employees.

- Behavioral. interpersonal skills, including team building, group dynamics, problem solving.

- Total quality: awareness of total quality principles and techniques; alignment of employee vision with that of management.

- Skills: technical training in job-related skills.

- Cross: cross-training in skills for jobs related to the one currently performed.

- Statistical process control (SPC).

Nonmonetary Incentives

- recognition: verbal recognition for job well done.

- job security: no-layoff pledge by company.

Monetary Incentives

- Gainsharing: firm and employees share unit or suborganizational productivity gains above baseline.

- Profit sharing: firm and employees share organizationwide profits above given baseline.

- Employee stock ownership plan (ESOP): employees receive stock option.

- Pay for skill (PFS): base pay determined by skill level, with opportunity for increases based on employer-provided training.

- Award: small cash award for service.

- Bonus: lump-sum (usually annual) bonus.

Unit of pay: whether new pay is based on indivdiual or group performance.

Industrial relations

Institutionalization: how new programs or policies are institutionalized in the organization

- Union present: whether union is present or not.

- LM committee: whether joint labor-management committees are established.

- Union contract: whether workplace innovations or participation programs are negotiated in the union contract.

- Company policy: whether the workplace innovations are instituted by the company only.

Type of system: whether system is consultative, substantive, or representative (may exist separately or in combination).

- Consultative: management consults employees but reserves right to make decisions.

- Substantive: employees have right to make substantive decisions (e.g., regarding work process, scheduling, and so on without management approval).

- Representative: union represents workers in joint decision-making bodies.

Improved performance outcomes: reported results of new programs and policies. Categories include profits, savings, productivity (prod.), quality, cost of quality, cycle time, customer service, reduced inventories, reduced ratio of employees to supervisors (red. empl./sup.), reduced grievances, improved cooperation (imp. coop.), improved morale, improved QWL (includes better working conditions, health and safety), reduced turnover, reduced absenteeism, and improved wages (base pay or contingent).

B.1 Summary of Case Studies

Name of firm	Source	(Pub. date)	Program started	# Years	Location	# Workers	Sector	Occupation
Solar Turbines Int'l	APQC	(1980)	1978	2	3 worksites	120	Mfg	BC
Columbus Auto Parts	APQC	(1980)	1979	1	1 worksite	715	Mfg	BC/WC
Shell Oil Co.	APQC	(1980)	1975	5	8 worksites	1,800	Mfg	WC
Texas Am. Bancshares	APQC	(1980)	1978	2	1 worksite	175	Srv	WC
Control Data Corp.	APQC	(1980)	1978	2	11 worksites	360	Mfg/Srv	BC
Beech Aircraft Corp.	APQC	(1980)	1976	4	companywide	8,982	Mfg	BC
Allen-Bradley Co.	APQC	(1980)	1975	6	1 worksite	5,300	Mfg	BC/WC
Waters Associates	APQC	(1980)	1979	1	1 worksite	70	Mfg	BC
Morse Borg-Warner	APQC	(1980)	1978	2	1 worksite	325	Mfg	BC/WC
Babcock & Wilcox	APQC	(1980)	1978	1	1 worksite	1,500	Mfg	BC/WC
Arcata Redwood	APQC	(1980)	1978	1	1 worksite	390	Mfg	BC
Honeywell, Inc.	APQC	(1980)	1942	38	4 divisions	10,222	Mfg/Srv	BC/WC
TRW Semiconductors	APQC	(1980)	1979	1	1 worksite	65	Mfg	BC
Electrical Co.	APQC	(1980)	1968	12	1 worksite	480	Mfg	BC/WC
Champion Int'l	APQC	(1980)	1977	3	companywide	800	Mfg	BC
Trans-Matic Mfg.	APQC	(1980)	1977	3	1 worksite	50	Mfg	BC/WC
Hinderliter Energy	APQC	(1981)	1978	3	1 worksite	285	Mfg	BC
Phillips Petroleum	APQC	(1981)	1932	48	companywide	24,135	Mfg	BC/WC
Tektreonix, Inc.	APQC	(1981)	1979	1	1 worksite	2,700	Mfg	BC
Potlatch Corp.	APQC	(1981)	1977	3	1 worksite	75	Mfg	BC
Northrop Corp.	APQC	(1982)	1978	4	1 division	1,000	Mfg/Svc	BC/WC
Herman Miller, Inc.	Frost	(1982)	1977	4	1 worksite	1,000	Mfg	BC/WC

B.1 Summary of Case Studies (*continued*)

Name of firm	Source	(Pub. date)	Program started	# Years	Location	# Workers	Sector	Occupation
Pacific NW Bell	Peterfreund	(1982)	1977	4	multisites	24,000	Srv	BC/WC
General Foods, Topeka	Walton	(1982)	1970	13	1 worksite	100	Mfg	BC
GM, Tarrytown	Guest	(1982a)	1970	13	1 worksite	4,000	Mfg	BC
Rushton Coal Mine	Goodman	(1982)	1973	6	1 worksite	200	Mng	BC
Harman, Bolivar plant	Macy	(1982)	1972	10	1 worksite		Mfg	BC
Ford, Sharonville, Ohio	Guest	(1982b)	1979	2	1 worksite	2,500	Mfg	BC/WC
Delco-Remy, Fitzgerald, Ga.	Cherry	(1982)	1975	7	1 worksite		Mfg	BC/WC
Martin Marietta	Thompson	(1982)	1979	3	1 worksite	3,300	Mfg	BC
Citibank	Walters	(1982)	1975	7	1 worksite		Srv	WC
Continental Insurance	APQC	(1983)	1981	1	36 worksites	5,500	Srv	WC
BEA Associates	APQC	(1983)	1978	5	1 worksite	45	Srv	WC
A-dec, Inc.	APQC	(1983)	1981	2	1 worksite	560	Mfg	BC/WC
Honeywell, Inc.	APQC	(1983)	1977	5	55 worksites	250	Srv	WC
Memorial Hospital	APQC	(1983)	1981	2	1 worksite	11	Srv	WC
Nucor Corp.	APQC	(1983)	1965	17	companywide	3,000	Mfg	BC/WC
Reynolds Aluminum	APQC	(1983)	1981	2	20 bus. units	1,450	Mfg	BC/WC
Norwest Bank St. Paul	APQC	(1983)	1983	1	1 worksite	347	Srv	WC
Southern Co. Services	APQC	(1984)	1979	5	1 division	3,000	Srv	WC
National Supply Co., Armco	APQC	(1984)	1982	2	1 worksite	310	Mfg	BC/WC
Honeywell Aerospace	APQC	(1984)	1981	3	1 division	20,000	Mfg	BC/WC
National Semiconductor	APQC	(1984)	1980	4	companywide	40,000	Mfg	BC/WC
Monsanto Textiles	APQC	(1984)	1980	4	1 worksite	1,200	Mfg	BC/WC

ZEBCO, Inc.	APQC	(1984)	2	1982	2 worksites	500	Mfg	BC/WC
City of Phoenix	APQC	(1984)	10	1979	city-wide	9,000	Srv	BC/WC
Florida Power & Light	APQC	(1984)	3	1981	companywide	13,000	Srv	BC/WC
U.S. Copyright Office	APQC	(1984)	4	1980	1 worksite	500	Srv	WC
Paul Revere Life Insurance	APQC	(1984)	1	1984	118 worksites	2,450	Srv	WC
Northrop Corp.	APQC	(1985)	6	1978	1 division	13,500	Mfg	BC/WC
Maxwell House	APQC	(1985)	4	1981	1 worksite	500	Mfg	BC
Maxwell House	APQC	(1985)	4	1981	1 worksite	500	Mfg	BC
U.S. Customs Service	APQC	(1985)	4	1981	10 worksites	1,580	Srv	WC
Cutter Labs	APQC	(1985)	6	1979	1 worksite	450	Mfg	BC/WC
Lincoln Electric	APQC	(1985)	50	1934	2 worksites	2,375	Mfg	BC/WC
Averitt Express	APQC	(1985)	14	1971	companywide	500	Srv	BC
Rohm & Haas Bayport	APQC	(1985)	4	1981	2 worksites	82	Mfg	BC
Steelcase	Rutigliano	(1985)	41	1944	companywide		Mfg	BC
Allegheny Ludlum Steel	APQC	(1986)	4	1982	companywide	5,000	Mfg	BC/WC
Naval Air Rework Facility	APQC	(1986)	2	1984	1 worksite	5,200	Srv	BC/WC
Ethyl Corp.	APQC	(1986)	5	1981	companywide	10,500	Mfg	WC
Lord Corp, Aerospace Div.	APQC	(1986)	2	1984	1 worksite	975	Mfg	BC/WC
Ford Louisville Plant	USDOL	(1986)	7	1979	1 worksite	3,000	Mfg	BC
InfoCorp*	Montgomery	(1986)	3	1982	1 worksite	170	Mfg	WC
Houston Lighting & Power	APQC	(1987)	3	1984	companywide	11,673	Srv	BC/WC
McDonnell Douglas, Mo.	APQC	(1987)	3	1984	companywide	1,400	Mfg	BC/WC
Polysar Gulf Coast	APQC	(1987)	9	1978	1 worksite	335	Mfg	BC/WC
Sewell Village Cadillac	APQC	(1987)	13	1974	companywide	235	Srv	WC
Sabine River Works	APQC	(1987)	5	1982	1 worksite	2,400	Mfg	BC/WC
First National Bank of Chicago	APQC	(1987)	6	1981	1 worksite	3,200	Srv	WC

B.1   Summary of Case Studies (continued)

Name of firm	Source	(Pub. date)	Program started	# Years	Location	# Workers	Sector	Occupation
McDonnell Douglas Astro.	APQC	(1987)	1985	2	1 division	4,500	Mfg	WC
Baxter Health Care	APQC	(1988)	1985	3	companywide	60,000	Mfg/Svc	BC/WC
Tenneco	APQC	(1988)	1985	3	2 divisions	700	Mfg	BC/WC
Scottsdale, Ariz.	APQC	(1988)	1981	7	citywide	1,007	Srv	WC
American Express	APQC	(1988)	1978	10	companywide	90,000	Srv	WC
N. Telecom/Santa Clara	APQC	(1988)	1985	3	1 worksite	250	Mfg	BC/WC
Preston Trucking	USDOL	(1988)	1978	10	multisites	5,300	Srv	BC
Harley Davidson	USDOL	(1988)	1983	5	3 worksites	1,800	Mfg	BC
Corning, RD&E	Seward	(1988)	1983	5	1 worksite	750	Srv	BC/WC
Ford-UAW EI Program	Banas	(1938)	1979	8	companywide		Mfg	BC
Maxwell House, GF*	APQC	(1989)	1985	4	1 worksite	600	Mfg	BC/WC
Beaumont Newspaper	APQC	(1989)	1986	3	1 worksite	320	Srv	WC
Lake Superior Paper	APQC	(1989)	1987	2	1 worksite	330	Mfg	BC/WC
Levi Strauss	APQC	(1939)	1985	5	1 division	19,000	Mfg	BC/WC
U.S. Shoe	APQC	(1939)	1984	5	11 worksites	4,000	Mfg	BC/WC
Motorola	Bhote	(1939)	1981	8	companywide		Mfg	BC/WC
Naval Pub. Center	Whitten	(1939)	1988	1	5 worksites	400	Srv	BC/WC
Seattle First National Bank	Murray/Marks	(1939)	1984	4	multisites	765	Srv	WC
Western Airlines	Wever	(1939)	1983	4	multisites	10,500	Srv	BC
Epic Health Care	APQC	(1990)	1988	2	38 worksites	10,000	Srv	BC/WC
Baxter	APQC	(1990)	1987	3	1 worksite	300	Srv	WC
Ethyl Corp.	APQC	(1990)	1984	6	companywide	5,000	Mfg	BC/WC

Company	Source	(Year)	Year	No.	Scope	Size	Type	BC/WC
First National Bank/Chicago	APQC	(1990)	1981	9	– division	3,700	Srv	WC
St. Luke's Episcopal Hospital	APQC	(1990)	1987	3	1 work unit	379	Srv	WC
Corning, SCC plant	Sheridan	(1990)	1989	1	1 worksite		Mfg	BC
Hearing Technology	Ross/Ormsby	(1990)	1985	4	1 worksite	100	Mfg	BC/WC
Dana Corp., Minn.	Sheridan	(1990)	1986	5	1 worksite	330	Mfg	BC
Toledo Scale, Ohio	Sheridan	(1990)	1985	6	1 worksite		Mfg	BC
Rolscreen, Carroll plant	Sheridan	(1990)	1982	9	1 worksite	250	Mfg	BC
Ford, Wixom plant	Sheridan	(1990)	1980	10	1 worksite	3,900	Mfg	BC
HP, Roseville, Calif.	Sheridan	(1990)	1980	10	1 worksite	800	Mfg	
Milliken & Co.	Corcoran	(1990)	1981	9	1 worksite		Mfg	BC/WC
Weaver's Popcorn	Hyatt	(1990)	1988	3	1 worksite	130	Mfg	BC/WC
IBM, Rochester, Minn.	Haavind	(1990)			1 worksite	8,100	Mfg	BC/WC
Duracell, Cleveland, Tenn.	Jones	(1990-91)		1	1 worksite		Mfg	BC
Capsugel	APQC	(1991)	1982	9	1 worksite	450	Mfg	BC/WC
LTV Aerospace	APQC	(1991)	1988	3	1 worksite	950	Mfg	BC/WC
Moore Response Marketing	APQC	(1991)	1982	9	2 worksites	700	Srv	WC
Zurich-American Insurance	APQC	(1991)	1988	3	6 worksites	2,700	Srv	WC
Rohm & Haas Louisville	USDOL	(1991)	1982	10	1 worksite	650	Mfg	BC/WC
Magma Copper	APQC	(1991)	1989	2	4 worksites	4,200	Mng	BC
Wohlert Corp.	USDOL	(1991)	1981	10	1 worksite	340	Mfg	BC
Warner Lambert	USDOL	(1991)	1982	4	1 worksite	1,200	Mfg	BC
US West	USDOL	(1991)	1980	11	multisites	56,000	Srv	BC/WC
TRW, Value Div.	USDOL	(1991)	1984	7	1 worksite	304	Mfg	BC
TRW, Software Systems	USDOL	(1991)	1984	7	1 worksite	1,260	Srv	WC
Thomas Lipton Co.	USDOL	(1991)	1988	3	1 worksite	400	Mfg	BC
Standard Oil Engineering Materials	USDOL	(1991)	1974	17	1 worksite	330	Mfg	BC

B.1 Summary of Case Studies (*continued*)

Name of firm	Source	(Pub. date)	Program started	# Years	Location	# Workers	Sector	Occupation
Shenandoah Life Insurance	USDOL	(1991)	1983	8	1 worksite	220	Srv	WC
ROHR Industries	USDOL	(1991)	1988	3	1 worksite	600	Mfg	BC
Rohm & Haas Knoxville	USDOL	(1991)	1980	11	1 worksite	350	Mfg	BC/WC
Rohm & Haas Kentucky	USDOL	(1991)	1984	7	1 worksite	800	Mfg	BC
Rohm & Haas Delaware	USDOL	(1991)	1982	9	1 worksite	900	Mfg	BC
Pillsbury	USDOL	(1991)	1980	11	1 worksite	400	Mfg	BC
ProTech Respirators	USDOL	(1991)	1972	20	1 worksite	70	Mfg	BC
Philip Morris	USDOL	(1991)	1979	12	1 worksite	4,500	Mfg	BC
Ohio Bell, Ameritech	USDOL	(1991)	1980	11	multisites	12,600	Srv	BC/WC
National Steel Corp.	USDOL	(1991)	1989	2	1 worksite	1,632	Mfg	BC
National Spinning Co.	USDOL	(1991)	1980	11	multisites	3,500	Mfg	BC
Motor Wheel Corp.	USDOL	(1991)	1979	12	1 worksite	333	Mfg	BC
Mobay Corp.	USDOL	(1991)	1984	7	1 worksite	1,100	Mfg	BC
McDonnell Douglas	USDOL	(1991)	1989	2	1 worksite	2,300	Mfg	BC
Logan Aluminum	USDOL	(1991)	1984	7	1 worksite	750	Mfg	BC
Johnsonville Sausage	USDOL	(1991)	1982	9	3 worksites	650	Mfg	BC
Johnson & Johnson	USDOL	(1991)	1983	8	1 worksite	700	Mfg	BC
Granville-Phillips	USDOL	(1991)	1980	11	1 worksite	78	Mfg	BC/WC
GM-UAW National Program	USDOL	(1991)	1973	18	multisites	330,000	Mfg	BC
GE, St. Louis	USDOL	(1991)	1982	9	2 worksites	74	Mfg	BC/WC
Ford, Dearborn Engine	USDOL	(1991)	1982	9	1 worksite	1,300	Mfg	BC
FMC Corp.	USDOL	(1991)	1984	7	1 worksite	288	Mfg	BC

Company	Source		Year		Scope	Employees	Type	Collar
FMC, Phosphorous Chemicals	USDOL	(1991)	1986	5	1 worksite	585	Mfg	BC
Duluth Public Schools	USDOL	(1991)	1984	7	multisites	2,000	Srv	BC/WC
Digital, Enfield, Conn.	USDOL	(1991)	1981	10	1 worksite	200	Mfg	BC/WC
Delco Chassis Div.	USDOL	(1991)	1989	2	1 worksite	3,000	Mfg	BC/WC
Delco-Remy, Albany	USDOL	(1991)	1978	13	1 worksite	510	Mfg	BC
Chrysler, Indianapolis	USDOL	(1991)	1983	8	1 worksite	1,150	Mfg	BC/WC
Best Foods	USDOL	(1991)	1978	13	1 worksite	135	Mfg	BC/WC
Bridgestone-Firestone	USDOL	(1991)	1990	2	multisites	19,900	Mfg	BC
AT&T Credit Corp.	USDOL	(1991)	1986	5	1 worksite	560	Srv	BC/WC
American Brass	USDOL	(1991)	1990	1	1 worksite	625	Mfg	BC
American Brass	USDOL	(1991)	1990	1	1 worksite	150	Mfg	WC
A. E. Staley	USDOL	(1991)	1986	5	1 worksite	1,200	Mfg	BC/WC
A. O. Smith	USDOL	(1991)	1984	7	8 worksites	2,700	Mfg	BC/WC
US West, Seattle	USDOL	(1991)	1990	1	1 worksite	130	Srv	BC/WC
Monsanto Co.	USDOL	(1991)	1985	6	1 worksite	1,030	Mfg	BC/WC
Monsanto Co.	USDOL	(1991)	1987	4	4 worksites	5,000	Mfg	BC/WC
L. E. Jones	USDOL	(1991)	1990	1	1 worksite	150	Mfg	BC
J. I. Case Co.	USDOL	(1991)	1986	5	4 worksites	3,500	Mfg	BC
Inland Steel Bar	USDOL	(1991)	1988	3	1 worksite	1,400	Mfg	BC
GM, Janesville	USDOL	(1991)	1988	3	1 worksite	5,500	Mfg	BC
GM, Fisher Guide Div.	USDOL	(1991)	1982	10	1 worksite	5,000	Mfg	BC
Con Ed, New York	USDOL	(1991)	1985	6	multisites	20,000	Srv	BC
Corning, Blacksburg	USDOL	(1991)	1989	2	1 worksite	190	Mfg	BC
Sherwin-Williams, Richmond	USDOL	(1991)	1976	15	1 worksite	220	Mfg	BC/WC
Xerox, Webster Plant	USDOL	(1991)	1980	11	1 worksite	850	Mfg	BC
Wallace Co.	APQC	(1991)	1985	6	companywide	280	Srv	BC/WC

B.1 Summary of Case Studies (*continued*)

Name of firm	Source	(Pub. date)	Program started	# Years	Location	# Workers	Sector	Occupation
Cadillac Motor	Braham	(1991)	1984	7	1 division	10,000	Mfg	BC/WC
Marlow Industries	NIST	(1991)	1987	4	companywide	160	Mfg	BC/WC
Zytec Corp.	NIST	(1991)	1984	7	companywide	748	Mfg	BC/WC
Solectron Corp.	NIST	(1991)	1977	13	companywide	2,100	Mfg	BC/WC
AT&T Shreveport Works	APQC	(1991)	1985	6	1 worksite	4,000	Mfg	BC/WC
Douglas Air/Long Beach, Calif.	Phillips	(1991)						
Midwestern Mfg.*	Havlovic	(1991)	1980	6	1 worksite	830	Mfg	BC
NW Airlines, Atlanta	Midas/Devine	(1991)	1987	3	1 worksite	636	Srv	BC/WC
Federal Express	Commission**	(1991)			companywide	72,000	Srv	BC
GM, NUMMI plant	Adler	(1992)	1984	9	1 worksite	3,000	Mfg	BC
Boeing Defense & Space	APQC	(1992)	1987	4	1 worksite	440	Mfg	BC
Globe Metallurgical	Rayner	(1992)	1984	8	1 worksite	250	Mfg	BC/WC
Gore Associates	Shipper	(1992)	1978	14	44 worksites	5,300	Mfg	BC/WC
GM, Saturn	LeFauve	(1992)	1985	8	1 worksite	5,000	Mfg	BC/WC
Exxon Research & Engineering	Eidt	(1992)			1 worksite		Srv	WC
Dun & Bradstreet Software	Kane	(1991)	1987	4	1 worksite	3,500	Srv	WC
Southern Paper Co.*	Meng	(1992)			1 worksite	500	Mfg	BC
Corning RD&E Div.	Seward	(1992)	1983	9	1 division	750	Mfg	BC/WC

*Pseudonym.

**Commission on the Skills of the American Workforce.

B.2 Summary of Management Methods

	Approach				Techniques			Structure	
Name of firm	STS	TQ	JIT	SPC	Performance measure-	Cost of Quality	Downsize	Delayer management	Integrate suppliers
Solar Turbines Int'l							x		
Columbus Auto Parts									
Shell Oil Co.									
Texas Am. Bancshares									
Control Data Corp.									
Beech Aircraft Corp.									
Allen-Bradley Co.									
Waters Associates									
Morse Borg-Warner									
Babcock & Wilcox									
Arcata Redwood									
Honeywell, Inc.									
TRW Semiconductors					x				
Electrical Co.									
Champion Int'l									
Trans-Matic Mfg.									
Hinderliter Energy									
Phillips Petroleum									
Tektreonix, Inc.					x				
Potlatch Corp.									
Northrop Corp.									
Herman Miller, Inc.					x				
Pacific NW Bell									
General Foods, Topeka	x							x	
GM, Tarrytown	x								
Rushton Coal Mine	x								
Harman, Bolivar plant									
Ford, Sharonville, Ohio							x		
Delco-Remy, Fitzgerald, Ga.	x							x	
Martin Marietta									
Citibank							x	x	
Continental Insurance					x		x		
BEA Associates					x				
A-dec, Inc.								x	
Honeywell, Inc.									
Memorial Hospital					x				
Nucor Corp.								x	
Reynolds Aluminum		x		x					

Name of firm	STS	TQ	JIT	SPC	Performance measure-	Cost of Quality	Downsize	Delayer management	Integrate suppliers
Norwest Bank St. Paul					x				
Southern Co. Services					x				
National Supply Co., Armco		x			x	x			
Honeywell Aerospace		x	x		x				
National Semiconductor		x			x				
Monsanto Textiles									
ZEBCO, Inc.		x	x	x	x	x			x
City of Phoenix					x		x		
Florida Power & Light		x			x	x			
U.S. Copyright Office	x								
Paul Revere Life Insurance	x	x		x	x	x			
Northrop Corp.					x				
Maxwell House							x		
Maxwell House							x		
U.S. Customs Service									
Cutter Labs				x	x				x
Lincoln Electric							x	x	
Averitt Express								x	
Rohm & Haas Bayport							x	x	
Steelcase									
Allegheny Ludlum Steel		x			x	x	x		
Naval Air Rework Facility		x			x	x			
Ethyl Corp.				x	x				
Lord Corp, Aerospace Div.		x			x				
Ford Louisville Plant	x								
InfoCorp*	x	x		x	x			x	
Houston Lighting & Power					x				
McDonnell Douglas, Mo.		x							x
Polysar Gulf Coast		x		x					x
Sewell Village Cadillac					x				
Sabine River Works		x			x	x	x	x	x
First National Bank of Chicago					x				
McDonnell Douglas Astro.					x				
Baxter Health Care	x	x	x		x	x			x
Tenneco									
Scottsdale, Ariz.									
American Express					x				
N. Telecom/Santa Clara		x	x	x	x				

B.2 Summary of Management Methods *(continued)*

Name of firm	STS	TQ	JIT	SPC	Performance measure-	Cost of Quality	Downsize	Delayer management	Integrate suppliers
Preston Trucking					x				
Harley Davidson			x	x			x	x	x
Corning, RD&E		x				x			
Ford-UAW EI Program									
Maxwell House, GF*		x					x		
Beaumont Newspaper									
Lake Superior Paper	x				x				
Levi Strauss		x							
U.S. Shoe		x	x	x					
Motorola		x	x	x	x			x	x
Naval Pub. Center		x		x	x				
Seattle First National Bank					x				
Western Airlines									
Epic Health Care		x							
Baxter		x			x				x
Ethyl Corp.		x		x	x	x			
First National Bank/Chicago		x			x				x
St. Luke's Episcopal Hospital					x				
Corning, SCC plant		x	x	x				x	
Hearing Technology									
Dana Corp., Minn.			x						
Toledo Scale, Ohio			x						
Rolscreen, Carroll plant			x						
Ford, Wixom plant		x							x
HP, Roseville, Calif.		x			x	x			
Milliken & Co.		x	x					x	x
Weaver's Popcorn		x			x				x
IBM, Rochester, Minn.		x	x	x	x	x			x
Duracell, Cleveland, Tenn.					x				
Capsugel		x	x	x	x				x
LTV Aerospace									
Moore Response Marketing	x							x	
Zurich-American Insurance					x				
Rohm & Haas Louisville	x	x	x	x				x	
Magma Copper									
Wohlert Corp.									
Warner Lambert									
US West		x							

B.2 Summary of Management Methods *(continued)*

Name of firm	STS	TQ	JIT	SPC	Performance measure	Cost of Quality	Downsize	Delayer management	Integrate suppliers
			Approach			Techniques		Structure	
TRW, Value Div.			x						
TRW, Software Systems									
Thomas Lipton Co.									
Standard Oil Engineering Materials									
Shenandoah Life Insurance								x	
ROHR Industries									
Rohm & Haas Knoxville	x							x	
Rohm & Haas Kentucky	x							x	
Rohm & Haas Delaware									
Pillsbury								x	
ProTech Respirators								x	
Philip Morris									
Ohio Bell, Ameritech		x							
National Steel Corp.									
National Spinning Co.									
Motor Wheel Corp.							x		
Mobay Corp.									
McDonnell Douglas		x							
Logan Aluminum									
Johnsonville Sausage									
Johnson & Johnson		x							
Granville-Phillips									
GM-UAW National Program									
GE, St. Louis				x				x	
Ford, Dearborn Engine									
FMC Corp.									
FMC, Phosphorous Chemicals									
Duluth Public Schools									
Digital, Enfield, Conn.	x		x					x	
Delco Chassis Div.									
Delco-Remy, Albany									
Chrysler, Indianapolis				x				x	
Best Foods	x			x				x	
Bridgestone-Firestone									
AT&T Credit Corp.	x				x				
American Brass									
American Brass									
A. E. Staley	x								

Name of firm	STS	TQ	JIT	SPC	Performance measure	Cost of Quality	Downsize	Delayer management	Integrate suppliers
	Approach				**Techniques**			**Structure**	
A. O. Smith									
US West, Seattle									
Monsanto Co.									
Monsanto Co.									
L. E. Jones									
J. I. Case Co.									
Inland Steel Bar									
GM, Janesville	x								
GM, Fisher Guide Div.									
Con Ed, New York									
Corning, Blacksburg		x	x	x				x	
Sherwin-Williams, Richmond	x	x		x					
Xerox, Webster Plant			x						
Wallace Co.		x		x	x		**x**		
Cadillac Motor		x							x
Marlow Industries		x			x			x	x
Zytec Corp.		x	x		x				x
Solectron Corp.		x		x	x				x
AT&T Shreveport Works		x	x	x		x			
Douglas Air/Long Beach, Calif.									
Midwestern Mfg.*			x						
NW Airlines, Atlanta		x			x				
Federal Express									
GM, NUMMI plant			x	x					
Boeing Defense & Space		x						x	
Globe Metallurgical		x		x	x				
Gore Associates								x	
GM, Saturn			x					x	x
Exxon Research & Engineering		x			x			x	
Dun & Bradstreet Software		x			x				
Southern Paper Co.*		x			x				
Corning RD&E Division		x			x	x			

*Pseudonym

B.3 Summary of Work Organization and Worker Participation

Name of firm	New technology	Broad jobs	Job rotation	SS	QWL	QC/PS	Supervised	Self-directed	Autonomous
		Job design			EI		Teams		
Solar Turbines Int'l						x			
Columbus Auto Parts				x					
Shell Oil Co.						x			
Texas Am. Bancshares									
Control Data Corp.						x			
Beech Aircraft Corp.				x					
Allen-Bradley Co.				x					
Waters Associates						x			
Morse Borg-Warner				x	·	x			
Babcock & Wilcox						x			
Arcata Redwood									
Honeywell, Inc.				x					
TRW Semiconductors						x			
Electrical Co.				x					
Champion Int'l						x			
Trans-Matic Mfg.				x		x			
Hinderliter Energy									
Phillips Petroleum				x					
Tektreonix, Inc.						x			
Potlatch Corp.									
Northrop Corp.						x			
Herman Miller, Inc.				x		x			
Pacific NW Bell				x		x			
General Foods, Topeka		x			x				x
GM, Tarrytown					x				
Rushton Coal Mine		x	x		x				x
Harman, Bolivar plant		x			x		x		
Ford, Sharonville, Ohio					x	x			
Delco-Remy, Fitzgerald, Ga.	x	x						x	
Martin Marietta				x		x			
Citibank	x	x				x			
Continental Insurance									
BEA Associates	x					x			
A-dec, Inc.		x				x	x		
Honeywell, Inc.	x								
Memorial Hospital	x			x					
Nucor Corp.									
Reynolds Aluminum						x			

Name of firm	New technology	Broad jobs	Job rotation	SS	QWL	QC/PS	Supervised	Self-directed	Autonomous
	Job design				**EI**		**Teams**		
Norwest Bank St. Paul						x			
Southern Co. Services	x					x			
National Supply Co., Armco	x			x		x			
Honeywell Aerospace	x				x	x			
National Semiconductor						x			
Monsanto Textiles	x					x			
ZEBCO, Inc.						x			
City of Phoenix				x		x			
Florida Power & Light						x			
U.S. Copyright Office	x	x			x	x	x		
Paul Revere Life Insurance				x		x			
Northrop Corp.				x		x			
Maxwell House	x	x						x	
Maxwell House	x					x			
U.S. Customs Service						x			
Cutter Labs	x					x			
Lincoln Electric		x	x						
Averitt Express									
Rohm & Haas Bayport	x	x	x			x			x
Steelcase						x			
Allegheny Ludlum Steel	x					x			
Naval Air Rework Facility				x		x	x		
Ethyl Corp.				x		x			
Lord Corp, Aerospace Div.						x	x	x	
Ford Louisville Plant						x			
InfoCorp*		x				x		x	
Houston Lighting & Power						x			
McDonnell Douglas, Mo.			x	x		x			
Polysar Gulf Coast						x			
Sewell Village Cadillac				x		x			
Sabine River Works		x				x			
First National Bank of Chicago						x			
McDonnell Douglas Astro.	x					x	x		
Baxter Health Care						x			
Tenneco						x			
Scottsdale, Ariz.	x	x							
American Express				x		x			
N. Telecom/Santa Clara	x					x		x	

B.3 Summary of Work Organization and Worker Participation *(continued)*

Name of firm	Job design				EI		Teams		
	New technology	Broad jobs	Job rotation	SS	QWL	QC/PS	Supervised	Self-directed	Autonomous
Preston Trucking				x		x			
Harley Davidson		x				x			
Corning, RD&E				x		x	x		
Ford-UAW EI Program					x	x			
Maxwell House, GF*							x		
Beaumont Newspaper						x			
Lake Superior Paper	x								x
Levi Strauss						x			
U.S. Shoe	x	x	x			x	x		
Motorola		x				x			
Naval Pub. Center						x			
Seattle First National Bank									
Western Airlines						x			
Epic Health Care						x			
Baxter	x					x			
Ethyl Corp.									
First National Bank/Chicago				x		x			
St. Luke's Episcopal Hospital						x			
Corning, SCC plant		x	x						x
Hearing Technology					x	x			
Dana Corp., Minn.						x	x		
Toledo Scale, Ohio							x		
Rolscreen, Carroll plant	x					x			
Ford, Wixom plant	x				x				
HP, Roseville, Calif.	x					x			
Milliken & Co.	x					x			
Weaver's Popcorn	x				x	x			
IBM, Rochester, Minn.	x					x			
Duracell, Cleveland, Tenn.						x			
Capsugel	x					x		x	
LTV Aerospace				x				x	
Moore Response Marketing		x						x	
Zurich-American Insurance						x			
Rohm & Haas Louisville			x		x	x		x	
Magma Copper	x		x					x	
Wohlert Corp.						x			
Warner Lambert						x			
US West						x			

B.3 Summary of Work Organization and Worker Participation *(continued)*

Name of firm	Job design				EI		Teams		
	New technology	Broad jobs	Job rotation	SS	QWL	QC/PS	Supervised	Self-directed	Autonomous
TRW, Value Div.						x	x		
TRW, Software Systems						x	x		
Thomas Lipton Co.						x	x		
Standard Oil Engineering Materials									
Shenandoah Life Insurance							x		
ROHR Industries		x				x	x		
Rohm & Haas Knoxville	x	x	x				x		
Rohm & Haas Kentucky	x	x	x				x		
Rohm & Haas Delaware						x			
Pillsbury		x					x		
ProTech Respirators		x				x	x		
Philip Morris					x	x			
Ohio Bell, Ameritech					x	x	x		
National Steel Corp.						x	x		
National Spinning Co.						x	x		
Motor Wheel Corp.						x			
Mobay Corp.						x	x		
McDonnell Douglas							x		
Logan Aluminum			x				x		
Johnsonville Sausage						x			x
Johnson & Johnson						x			
Granville-Phillips		x					x		
GM-UAW National Program					x	x			
GE, St. Louis		x							x
Ford, Dearborn Engine						x			
FMC Corp.							x		
FMC, Phosphorous Chemicals						x			
Duluth Public Schools					x	x			
Digital, Enfield, Conn.	x	x	x			x			x
Delco Chassis Div.						x			
Delco-Remy, Albany							x		
Chrysler, Indianapolis						x	x		
Best Foods							x		
Bridgestone-Firestone						x			
AT&T Credit Corp.							x		
American Brass						x			
American Brass							x		
A. E. Staley							x		

B.3 Summary of Work Organization and Worker Participation *(continued)*

Name of firm	New technology	Broad jobs	Job rotation	SS	QWL	QC/PS	Supervised	Self-directed	Autonomous
	Job design				**EI**		**Teams**		
A. O. Smith						x	x		
US West, Seattle							x		
Monsanto Co.						x	x		
Monsanto Co.						x			
L. E. Jones						x			
J. I. Case Co.						x			
Inland Steel Bar	x	x					x		
GM, Janesville						x			
GM, Fisher Guide Div.						x			
Con Ed, New York						x			
Corning, Blacksburg	x	x							x
Sherwin-Williams, Richmond	x		x	x		x		x	
Xerox, Webster Plant	x	x			x			x	
Wallace Co.	x					x			
Cadillac Motor						x			
Marlow Industries		x	x			x	x		
Zytec Corp.	x	x				x		x	
Solectron Corp.	x	x				x		x	
AT&T Shreveport Works	x					x			
Douglas Air/Long Beach, Calif.									
Midwestern Mfg.*					x				
NW Airlines, Atlanta						x			
Federal Express	x	x						x	
GM, NUMMI plant		x	x			x	x		
Boeing Defense & Space	x	x	x					x	
Globe Metallurgical	x	x	x			x		x	
Gore Associates						x		x	
GM, Saturn	x	x	x			x			x
Exxon Research & Engineering		x				x			
Dun & Bradstreet Software						x			
Southern Paper Co.*									
Corning RD&E Div.				x		x		x	

*Pseudonym

B.4 Summary of Types and Levels of Participation

Name of firm	Voluntary	Mandatory	Within depts.	Across depts.	Organization wide
Solar Turbines Int'l	x		x		
Columbus Auto Parts	x				
Shell Oil Co.	x		x		
Texas Am. Bancshares		x			
Control Data Corp.	x		x		
Beech Aircraft Corp.	x				
Allen-Bradley Co.	x				
Waters Associates		x	x		
Morse Borg-Warner	x		x		
Babcock & Wilcox	x		x		
Arcata Redwood					
Honeywell, Inc.	x				
TRW Semiconductors		x	x		
Electrical Co.	x				
Champion Int'l	x		x		
Trans-Matic Mfg.		x	x		
Hinderliter Energy		x			
Phillips Petroleum	x				
Tektreonix, Inc.	x		x		
Potlatch Corp.		x			
Northrop Corp.	x		x		
Herman Miller, Inc.	x		x		
Pacific NW Bell	x		x	x	
General Foods, Topeka	x		x		
GM, Tarrytown	x		x		
Rushton Coal Mine	x		x		
Harman, Bolivar plant	x		x		
Ford, Sharonville, Ohio	x		x		
Delco-Remy, Fitzgerald, Ga.		x	x		
Martin Marietta	x		x	x	
Citibank			x		
Continental Insurance		x			
BEA Associates			x	x	x
A-dec, Inc.		x	x	x	
Honeywell, Inc.					
Memorial Hospital	x		x		
Nucor Corp.					
Reynolds Aluminum	x		x	x	

Name of firm	Type of participation		Level of participation		
	Voluntary	Mandatory	Within depts.	Across depts.	Organization wide
Norwest Bank St. Paul	x		x		
Southern Co. Services			x		
National Supply Co., Armco	x		x	x	
Honeywell Aerospace			x	x	
National Semiconductor		x	x		
Monsanto Textiles	x		x		
ZEBCO, Inc.		x	x		
City of Phoenix			x		
Florida Power & Light		x	x	x	x
U.S. Copyright Office	x		x		x
Paul Revere Life Insurance		x	x		
Northrop Corp.	x		x	x	
Maxwell House	x		x		
Maxwell House	x		x		
U.S. Customs Service	x		x		
Cutter Labs	x		x	x	x
Lincoln Electric		x			
Averitt Express					
Rohm & Haas Bayport		x	x	x	
Steelcase	x		x		
Allegheny Ludlum Street	x		x	x	
Naval Air Rework Facility		x	x	x	x
Ethyl Corp.			x		
Lord Corp, Aerospace Div.	x		x	x	
Ford Louisville Plant	x		x		
InfoCorp*		x	x		
Houston Lighting & Power		x	x		
McDonnell Douglas, Mo.		x	x		
Polysar Gulf Coast	x		x		
Sewell Village Cadillac	x		x		
Sabine River Works		x	x	x	
First National Bank of Chicago	x		x		
McDonnell Douglas Astro.	x		x		
Baxter Health Care		x	x	x	x
Tenneco				x	
Scottsdale, Ariz.					
American Express		x	x		
N. Telecom/Santa Clara		x	x	x	

B.4 Summary of Types and Levels of Participation *(continued)*

Name of firm	Voluntary	Mandatory	Within depts.	Across depts.	Organization wide
Preston Trucking	x		x		
Harley Davidson	x		x		
Corning, RD&E	x		x		
Ford-UAW EI Program	x		x	x	
Maxwell House, GF*	x		x		
Beaumont Newspaper	x		x		
Lake Superior Paper		x	x		
Levi Strauss		x	x	x	x
U.S. Shoe		x	x	x	x
Motorola			x		
Naval Pub. Center	x		x	x	
Seattle First National Bank					
Western Airlines	x		x		
Epic Health Care	x		x	x	
Baxter	x		x	x	
Ethyl Corp.					
First National Bank/Chicago	x		x	x	
St. Luke's Episcopal Hospital	x		x		
Corning, SCC plant		x	x		x
Hearing Technology		x	x		
Dana Corp., Minn.			x		
Toledo Scale, Ohio	x		x		
Rolscreen, Carroll plant	x		x		
Ford, Wixom plant	x		x		
HP, Roseville, Calif.			x	x	
Milliken & Co.			x		
Weaver's Popcorn		x	x		
IBM, Rochester, Minn.			x	x	
Duracell, Cleveland, Tenn.			x		
Capsugel		x	x	x	
LTV Aerospace		x	x		
Moore Response Marketing		x	x	x	x
Zurich-American Insurance		x	x	x	
Rohm & Haas Louisville		x	x	x	
Magma Copper		x	x	x	
Wohlert Corp.	x		x	x	
Warner Lambert	x		x		
US West	x		x	x	x

B.4 Summary of Types and Levels of Participation *(continued)*

Name of firm	Type of participation — Voluntary	Mandatory	Level of participation — Within depts.	Across depts.	Organization wide
TRW, Value Div.	x		x		
TRW, Software Systems	x		x	x	
Thomas Lipton Co.	x		x		
Standard Oil Engineering Materials	x				x
Shenandoah Life Insurance			x		
ROHR Industries		x	x	x	
Rohm & Haas Knoxville		x	x		
Rohm & Haas Kentucky		x	x		
Rohm & Haas Delaware	x		x		x
Pillsbury		x	x		
ProTech Respirators		x	x		
Philip Morris	x		x		
Ohio Bell, Ameritech	x		x		
National Steel Corp.		x	x		
National Spinning Co.		x	x		
Motor Wheel Corp.					x
Mobay Corp	x		x		x
McDonnell Douglas		x	x		x
Logan Aluminum		x	x		
Johnsonville Sausage		x	x		
Johnson & Johnson	x		x		x
Granville-Phillips		x	x		
GM-UAW National Program	x		x		x
GE, St. Louis		x	x	x	x
Ford, Dearborn Engine	x		x		x
FMC Corp.		x	x	x	
FMC, Phosphorous Chemicals	x		x		x
Duluth Public Schools	x		x		x
Digital, Enfield, Conn.		x	x		
Delco Chassis Div.	x		x	x	x
Delco-Remy, Albany		x	x		x
Chrysler, Indianapolis		x	x		x
Best Foods		x	x		x
Bridgestone-Firestone	x				
AT&T Credit Corp.		x	x		
American Brass	x		x		
American Brass	x			x	
A. E. Staley		x	x	x	

B.4 Summary of Types and Levels of Participation *(continued)*

Name of firm	Voluntary	Mandatory	Within depts.	Across depts.	Organization wide
A. O. Smith	x		x		x
US West, Seattle	x		x		
Monsanto Co.		x	x		
Monsanto Co.		x	x	x	
L. E. Jones	x		x		x
J. I. Case Co.			x		x
Inland Steel Bar	x		x	x	x
GM, Janesville	x		x	x	x
GM, Fisher Guide Div.	x		x		
Con Ed, New York	x		x		
Corning, Blacksburg		x	x		x
Sherwin-Williams, Richmond		x	x	x	
Xerox, Webster Plant	x		x	x	
Wallace Co.		x	x	x	x
Cadillac Motor	x		x	x	
Marlow Industries	x		x		x
Zytec Corp.			x	x	x
Solectron Corp.			x	x	
AT&T Shreveport Works		x	x		
Douglas Air/Long Beach, Calif.					
Midwestern Mfg.*	x		x		
NW Airlines, Atlanta	x		x	x	
Federal Express		x	x		
GM, NUMMI plant			x	x	
Boeing Defense & Space		x	x	x	x
Globe Metallurgical		x		x	
Gore Associates	x		x	x	x
GM, Saturn		x	x	x	x
Exxon Research & Engineering	x		x	x	
Dun & Bradstreet Software		x	x	x	
Southern Paper Co.*					
Corning RD&E Div.	x		x	x	

*Pseudonym

B.5 Summary of the Domains of Participation

Name of firm	Tech/job design	Work process	Admin./sched.	Strategic planning
Solar Turbines Int'l		x		
Columbus Auto Parts				
Shell Oil Co.		x		
Texas Am. Bancshares				
Control Data Corp.		x		
Beech Aircraft Corp.		x		
Allen-Bradley Co.		x		
Waters Associates		x		
Morse Borg-Warner		x		
Babcock & Wilcox		x		
Arcata Redwood				
Honeywell, Inc.				
TRW Semiconductors		x		
Electrical Co.				
Champion Int'l		x		
Trans-Matic Mfg.		x		
Hinderliter Energy				
Phillips Petroleum				
Tektreonix, Inc.		x		
Potlatch Corp.				
Northrop Corp.		x		
Herman Miller, Inc.		x		
Pacific NW Bell		x	x	
General Foods, Topeka	x	x	x	
GM, Tarrytown	x	x		
Rushton Coal Mine	x	x		
Harman, Bolivar plant	x	x		
Ford, Sharonville, Ohio	x	x		
Delco-Remy, Fitzgerald, Ga.		x	x	
Martin Marietta		x		
Citibank	x			
Continental Insurance				
BEA Associates	x	x	x	
A-dec, Inc.		x		
Honeywell, Inc.				
Memorial Hospital		x		
Nucor Corp.				
Reynolds Aluminum		x		

Name of firm	Tech/job design	Work process	Admin./ sched.	Strategic planning
Norwest Bank St. Paul		x		
Southern Co. Services		x		
National Supply Co., Armco		x		
Honeywell Aerospace		x		
National Semiconductor		x		
Monsanto Textiles		x	x	
ZEBCO, Inc.		x		
City of Phoenix		x		
Florida Power & Light		x		
U.S. Copyright Office	x	x		
Paul Revere Life Insurance		x		
Northrop Corp.		x		
Maxwell House	x	x	x	
Maxwell House	x	x		
U.S. Customs Service	x	x		
Cutter Labs	x	x	x	
Lincoln Electric				
Averitt Express				
Rohm & Haas Bayport	x	x	x	
Steelcase	x	x		
Allegheny Ludlum Steel		x		
Naval Air Rework Facility		x		
Ethyl Corp.		x		
Lord Corp, Aerospace Div.		x		
Ford Louisville Plant	x	x		
InfoCorp*	x	x	x	
Houston Lighting & Power		x		
McDonnell Douglas, Mo.		x		
Polysar Gulf Coast		x		
Sewell Village Cadillac		x		
Sabine River Works		x		
First National Bank of Chicago		x		
McDonnell Douglas Astro.	x	x	x	
Baxter Health Care		x		
Tenneco		x		
Scottsdale, Ariz.				
American Express		x		
N. Telecom/Santa Clara	x	x	x	

Name of firm	Tech/job design	Work process	Admin./sched.	Strategic planning
Preston Trucking		x		
Harley Davidson	x	x		
Corning, RD&E	x	x		
Ford-UAW EI Program	x	x	x	
Maxwell House, GF*	x	x	x	
Beaumont Newspaper		x		
Lake Superior Paper	x	x	x	
Levi Strauss		x		
U.S. Shoe		x		
Motorola		x		
Naval Pub. Center		x		
Seattle First National Bank				
Western Airlines		x		
Epic Health Care		x	x	
Baxter		x		
Ethyl Corp.				
First National Bank/Chicago		x	x	
St. Luke's Episcopal Hospital		x	x	
Corning, SCC plant	x	x	x	
Hearing Technology		x		
Dana Corp., Minn.	x	x	x	
Toledo Scale, Ohio		x	x	
Rolscreen, Carroll plant		x		
Ford, Wixom plant		x		
HP, Roseville, Calif.		x		
Milliken & Co.		x		
Weaver's Popcorn		x		
IBM, Rochester, Minn.		x		
Duracell, Cleveland, Tenn.		x		
Capsugel		x		
LTV Aerospace		x		
Moore Response Marketing	x	x		
Zurich-American Insurance		x	x	
Rohm & Haas Louisville	x	x	x	
Magma Copper	x	x	x	
Wohlert Corp.		x		
Warner Lambert		x	x	
US West		x	x	

B.5 Summary of the Domains of Participation *(continued)*

Name of firm	Tech/job design	Work process	Admin./sched.	Strategic planning
TRW, Value Div.		x	x	
TRW, Software Systems		x	x	
Thomas Lipton Co.		x	x	
Standard Oil Engineering Materials	x	x		
Shenandoah Life Insurance	x	x	x	
ROHR Industries	x	x	x	
Rohm & Haas Knoxville	x	x	x	
Rohm & Haas Kentucky	x	x	x	
Rohm & Haas Delaware	x	x	x	
Pillsbury		x	x	
ProTech Respirators		x	x	
Philip Morris		x		
Ohio Bell, Ameritech	x	x		
National Steel Corp.	x	x	x	
National Spinning Co.	x	x	x	
Motor Wheel Corp.	x	x	x	
Mobay Corp.		x	x	
McDonnell Douglas	x	x	x	
Logan Aluminum	x	x	x	
Johnsonville Sausage		x	x	
Johnson & Johnson		x		
Granville-Phillips		x		
GM-UAW National Program		x	x	
GE, St. Louis	x	x	x	
Ford, Dearborn Engine		x		
FMC Corp.		x	x	
FMC, Phosphorous Chemicals		x	x	
Duluth Public Schools		x	x	x
Digital, Enfield, Conn.	x	x	x	
Delco Chassis Div.		x	x	
Delco-Remy, Albany		x	x	
Chrysler, Indianapolis	x	x	x	
Best Foods	x	x	x	
Bridgestone-Firestone				
AT&T Credit Corp.	x	x	x	
American Brass		x		
American Brass		x		
A. E. Staley	x			

Name of firm	Domain of participation Tech/job design	Work process	Admin./ sched.	Strategic planning
A. O. Smith	x	x	x	
US West, Seattle	x	x	x	
Monsanto Co.		x	x	
Monsanto Co.		x	x	
L. E. Jones		x	x	
J. I. Case Co.		x	x	
Inland Steel Bar	x			
GM, Janesville	x			
GM, Fisher Guide Div.	x	x		
Con Ed, New York	x	x		
Corning, Blacksburg	x	x	x	
Sherwin-Williams, Richmond	x	x	x	
Xerox, Webster Plant	x	x	x	x
Wallace Co.		x	x	
Cadillac Motor		x		
Marlow Industries		x		x
Zytec Corp.		x		x
Solectron Corp.		x		
AT&T Shreveport Works		x		
Douglas Air/Long Beach, Calif.				
Midwestern Mfg.*		x		
NW Airlines, Atlanta	x	x		
Federal Express		x		
GM, NUMMI plant		x		
Boeing Defense & Space		x	x	
Globe Metallurgical	x	x		
Gore Associates		x	x	
GM, Saturn	x	x	x	x
Exxon Research & Engineering	x	x		
Dun & Bradstreet Software	x	x		
Southern Paper Co.*				
Corning RD&E Div.	x	x	x	

*Pseudonym

B.6 Summary of Human Resource Policies

Name of firm	Education and training						Incentives	
	Info. share	Behavioral	TQ	Skills	Cross	SPC	Recognition	Job security
Solar Turbines Int'l		x						
Columbus Auto Parts								
Shell Oil Co.		x						
Texas Am. Bancshares		m						
Control Data Corp.		m						
Beech Aircraft Corp.								
Allen-Bradley Co.								
Waters Associates		x						
Morse Borg-Warner								
Babcock & Wilcox		x						
Arcata Redwood		m						
Honeywell, Inc.								
TRW Semiconductors		m						
Electrical Co.								
Champion Int'l		x						
Trans-Matic Mfg.								
Hinderliter Energy								
Phillips Petroleum								
Tektreonix, Inc.	x	x					x	
Potlatch Corp.								
Northrop Corp.		x						
Herman Miller, Inc.								x
Pacific NW Bell								
General Foods, Topeka		x			x			
GM, Tarrytown	x	x			x			
Rushton Coal Mine		x			x			
Harman, Bolivar plant	x				x			x
Ford, Sharonville, Ohio	x	x						
Delco-Remy, Fitzgerald, Ga.		x			x			
Martin Marietta	x	x					x	
Citibank				x	x			
Continental Insurance								
BEA Associates								
A-dec, Inc.		x						
Honeywell, Inc.								
Memorial Hospital		x			x		x	
Nucor Corp.								
Reynolds Aluminum	x	x			x	x		

Name of firm	Education and training						Incentives	
	Info. share	Behavioral	TQ	Skills	Cross	SPC	Recognition	Job security
Norwest Bank St. Paul		x						
Southern Co. Services		x						
National Supply Co., Armco		x	x	x				
Honeywell Aerospace		x	x	m				
National Semiconductor	x	x		x				
Monsanto Textiles		x						
ZEBCO, Inc.	x	x					x	
City of Phoenix		x		x				
Florida Power & Light		x	x				x	
U.S. Copyright Office	x	x		x				
Paul Revere Life Insurance		x	x					x
Northrop Corp.	x	x		x			x	
Maxwell House	x			x	x			x
Maxwell House	x			x				x
U.S. Customs Service		x					x	
Cutter Labs		x		x	x	m		x
Lincoln Electric				x	x			x
Averitt Express				x				
Rohm & Haas Bayport				x	x			x
Steelcase								
Allegheny Ludlum Steel	x	x				x	x	
Naval Air Rework Facility		m				x		
Ethyl Corp.						x		
Lord Corp, Aerospace Div.	x	x			x		x	
Ford Louisville Plant	x	x						
InfoCorp*	x	x	x	x		x	x	
Houston Lighting & Power		x		x			x	
McDonnell Douglas, Mo.								x
Polysar Gulf Coast	x	x		x	x	x		
Sewell Village Cadillac		x						
Sabine River Works		x	x					
First National Bank of Chicago							x	
McDonnell Douglas Astro.		x		x				
Baxter Health Care	x			x			x	
Tenneco		m						
Scottsdale, Ariz.				x				
American Express	x		x				x	
N. Telecom/Santa Clara	x	x	x	x	x	x		

226

Name of firm	Info. share	Behavioral	TQ	Skills	Cross	SPC	Recognition	Job security
	Education and training						Incentives	
Preston Trucking	x						x	
Harley Davidson	x	x				x		
Corning, RD&E		x	x	x	x	x	x	
Ford-UAW EI Program	x	x		x				
Maxwell House, GF*	x			x	x			x
Beaumont Newspaper		x					x	
Lake Superior Paper	x	x		x	x			
Levi Strauss		x	x				x	
U.S. Shoe		x	x		x	x		
Motorola		x	x	x		x		
Naval Pub. Center		x	x			x	x	
Seattle First National Bank		x		x				
Western Airlines	x							
Epic Health Care	x	m					x	
Baxter	x		x	x			x	
Ethyl Corp.							x	
First National Bank/Chicago			x				x	
St. Luke's Episcopal Hospital		x					x	
Corning, SCC plant	x	x		x	x	x		x
Hearing Technology								
Dana Corp., Minn.		x		x	x		x	
Toledo Scale, Ohio				x	x			
Rolscreen, Carroll plant								
Ford, Wixom plant								
HP, Roseville, Calif.								
Milliken & Co.							x	
Weaver's Popcorn	x							
IBM, Rochester, Minn.		x		x	x	x		
Duracell, Cleveland, Tenn.								
Capsugel						x		
LTV Aerospace				x	x			
Moore Response Marketing	x	x		x				
Zurich-American Insurance		x						
Rohm & Haas Louisville	x	x	x	x	x	x		
Magma Copper	x	x						
Wohlert Corp.	x	x				x		
Warner Lambert		x						
US West		x						

B.6 Summary of Human Resource Policies *(continued)*

Name of firm	Info. share	Behavioral	TQ	Skills	Cross	SPC	Recognition	Job security
TRW, Value Div.				x				
TRW, Software Systems		x	x					
Thomas Lipton Co.		x		x				
Standard Oil Engineering Materials								
Shenandoah Life Insurance				x	x			
ROHR Industries								
Rohm & Haas Knoxville		x						x
Rohm & Haas Kentucky		x		x	x	x		
Rohm & Haas Delaware	x	x						
Pillsbury				x				
ProTech Respirators				x	x			
Philip Morris								
Ohio Bell, Ameritech		x	x	x				
National Steel Corp.	x	x		x				
National Spinning Co.		x		x				
Motor Wheel Corp.								
Mobay Corp.		x		x				
McDonnell Douglas	x	x	x	x				
Logan Aluminum		x	x	x	x			
Johnsonville Sausage		x		x				
Johnson & Johnson		x	x	x				
Granville-Phillips		x		x	x			
GM-UAW National Program		x		x				
GE, St. Louis	x	x		x		x		
Ford, Dearborn Engine		x						
FMC Corp.		x						
FMC, Phosphorous Chemicals								
Duluth Public Schools								
Digital, Enfield, Conn.		x		x	x			
Delco Chassis Div.								
Delco-Remy, Albany	x	x						
Chrysler, Indianapolis								x
Best Foods		x		x				
Bridgestone-Firestone								
AT&T Credit Corp.	x	x		x				
American Brass		x						
American Brass		x						
A. E. Staley								

B.6   Summary of Human Resource Policies *(continued)*

Name of firm	Info. share	Behavioral	TQ	Skills	Cross	SPC	Recognition	Job security
		Education and training						Incentives
A. O. Smith		x						
US West, Seattle		x						
Monsanto Co.		x						x
Monsanto Co.		x						
L. E. Jones		x						
J. I. Case Co.								
Inland Steel Bar		x		x				
GM, Janesville								
GM, Fisher Guide Div.		x		x				
Con Ed, New York		x						
Corning, Blacksburg	x	x		x	x	x		x
Sherwin-Williams, Richmond	x	x		x	x	x		
Xerox, Webster Plant	x	x		x				
Wallace Co.	x	x	x		x	x	x	
Cadillac Motor				x	x			
Marlow Industries	x	x	x	x	x	x	x	
Zytec Corp.	x		x	x				
Solectron Corp.		x	x			x		
AT&T Shreveport Works		x	x		x			
Douglas Air/Long Beach, Calif.								
Midwestern Mfg.*		x		x		x		
NW Airlines, Atlanta		x		x				
Federal Express	x			x	x			
GM, NUMMI plant	x	x		x	x			x
Boeing Defense & Space	x			x	x			
Globe Metallurgical	x			x		x		x
Gore Associates		x		x				x
GM, Saturn	x	x		x	x			x
Exxon Research & Engineering		x	x	x			x	
Dun & Bradstreet Software			x					
Southern Paper Co.*				x				
Corning RD&E Div.		x	x	x	x	x	x	

*Pseudonym

B.7 Summary of Compensation Systems

Name of firm	Monetary incentives						Pay unit	
	Gainsharing	Profit sharing	ESOP	Pay/skill	Award	Bonus	Individual	Group
Solar Turbines Int'l								
Columbus Auto Parts	x							x
Shell Oil Co.								
Texas Am. Bancshares								
Control Data Corp.								
Beech Aircraft Corp.					x	x		
Allen-Bradley Co.					x	x		
Waters Associates						x		
Morse Borg-Warner	x							x
Babcock & Wilcox								
Arcata Redwood								
Honeywell, Inc.					x	x		
TRW Semiconductors								
Electrical Co.								
Champion Int'l								
Trans-Matic Mfg.		x				x		x
Hinderliter Energy	x							x
Phillips Petroleum					x	x		
Tektreonix, Inc.								
Potlatch Corp.	x					x		x
Northrop Corp.								
Herman Miller, Inc.	x					x		x
Pacific NW Bell								
General Foods, Topeka				x				
GM, Tarrytown								
Rushton Coal Mine								
Harman, Bolivar plant	x						x	
Ford, Sharonville, Ohio								
Delco-Remy, Fitzgerald, Ga.				x			x	
Martin Marietta					x		x	x
Citibank							x	
Continental Insurance								
BEA Associates						x	x	
A-dec, Inc.								
Honeywell, Inc.								
Memorial Hospital								
Nucor Corp.	x	x	x		x	x		x
Reynolds Aluminum								

Name of firm	Monetary incentives						Pay unit	
	Gainsharing	Profit	ESOP	Pay/skill	Award	Bonus	Individual	Group
Norwest Bank St. Paul					x		x	
Southern Co. Services								
National Supply Co., Armco	x							
Honeywell Aerospace								
National Semiconductor								
Monsanto Textiles								
ZEBCO, Inc.								
City of Phoenix					x	x	x	
Florida Power & Light								
U.S. Copyright Office					x		x	
Paul Revere Life Insurance					x		x	x
Northrop Corp.								
Maxwell House							x	
Maxwell House				x			x	
U.S. Customs Service								
Cutter Labs								
Lincoln Electric		x	x		x	x	x	
Averitt Express		x					x	
Rohm & Haas Bayport				x			x	
Steelcase		x	x			x	x	
Allegheny Ludlum Steel								x
Naval Air Rework Facility								
Ethyl Corp.								
Lord Corp, Aerospace Div.								
Ford Louisville Plant								
InfoCorp*	x							x
Houston Lighting & Power								
McDonnell Douglas, Mo.	x			x		x	x	x
Polysar Gulf Coast						x	x	x
Sewell Village Cadillac					x			
Sabine River Works								
First National Bank of Chicago						x		x
McDonnell Douglas Astro.								
Baxter Health Care							x	
Tenneco								
Scottsdale, Ariz.								
American Express					x		x	
N. Telecom/Santa Clara				x			x	

Name of firm	Monetary incentives						Pay unit	
	Gainsharing	Profit sharing	ESOP	Pay/skill	Award	Bonus	Individual	Group
Preston Trucking	x				x		x	x
Harley Davidson								
Corning, RD&E								
Ford-UAW EI Program								
Maxwell House, GF*				x			x	
Beaumont Newspaper					x		x	
Lake Superior Paper				x			x	
Levi Strauss								
U.S. Shoe	x			x			x	
Motorola		x						
Naval Pub. Center								
Seattle First National Bank					x		x	
Western Airlines		x	x					x
Epic Health Care			x			x		x
Baxter					x		x	
Ethyl Corp.							x	
First National Bank/Chicago							x	x
St. Luke's Episcopal Hospital								
Corning, SCC plant				x		x	x	x
Hearing Technology								
Dana Corp., Minn.				x			x	
Toledo Scale, Ohio				x			x	
Rolscreen, Carroll plant								
Ford, Wixom plant								
HP, Roseville, Calif.								
Milliken & Co.								
Weaver's Popcorn		x				x	x	x
IBM, Rochester, Minn.								
Duracell, Cleveland, Tenn.								
Capsugel								
LTV Aerospace	x			x			x	x
Moore Response Marketing								
Zurich-American Insurance								
Rohm & Haas Louisville				x			x	
Magma Copper								
Wohlert Corp.								
Warner Lambert								
US West								

Name of firm	Gainsharing	Profit	ESOP	Pay/skill	Award	Bonus	Individual	Group
TRW, Value Div.	x			x			x	x
TRW, Software Systems								
Thomas Lipton Co.		x	x					
Standard Oil Engineering Materials								
Shenandoah Life Insurance								
ROHR Industries	x							x
Rohm & Haas Knoxville								
Rohm & Haas Kentucky								
Rohm & Haas Delaware								
Pillsbury				x			x	
ProTech Respirators	x							x
Philip Morris								
Ohio Bell, Ameritech								
National Steel Corp.	x	x						x
National Spinning Co.		x						x
Motor Wheel Corp.								
Mobay Corp.	x							x
McDonnell Douglas	x							x
Logan Aluminum				x			x	
Johnsonville Sausage		x				x	x	
Johnson & Johnson				x			x	
Granville-Phillips		x			x			
GM-UAW National Programs								
GE, St. Louis		x				x	x	
Ford, Dearborn Engine								
FMC Corp.								
FMC, Phosphorous Chemicals								
Duluth Public Schools								
Digital, Enfield, Conn.				x			x	
Delco Chassis Div.								
Delco-Remy, Albany		x						
Chrysler, Indianapolis								
Best Foods				x			x	
Bridgestone-Firestone								
AT&T Credit Corp.	x			x			x	x
American Brass				x			x	
American Brass				x			x	
A. E. Staley								

233

Name of firm	Gainsharing	Profit sharing	ESOP	Pay/skill	Award	Bonus	Individual	Group
	Monetary incentives						Pay unit	
A. O. Smith		x						x
US West, Seattle								
Monsanto Co.								
Monsanto Co.				x			x	
L. E. Jones	x							x
J. I. Case Co.								
Inland Steel Bar				x			x	
GM, Janesville								
GM, Fisher Guide Div.								
Con Ed, New York								
Corning, Blacksburg				x	x	x		x
Sherwin-Williams, Richmond	x	x		x			x	x
Xerox, Webster Plant								
Wallace Co.							x	
Cadillac Motor								
Marlow Industries								
Zytec Corp.				x			x	
Solectron Corp.								
AT&T Shreveport Works								
Douglas Air/Long Beach, Calif.								
Midwestern Mfg.*	x							x
NW Airlines, Atlanta								
Federal Express								
GM, NUMMI plant								
Boeing Defense & Space				x			x	
Globe Metallurgical	x							x
Gore Associates	x	x					x	x
GM, Saturn					x			x
Exxon Research & Engineering								
Dun & Bradstreet Software								
Southern Paper Co.*				x		x	x	
Corning RD&E Div.								

*Pseudonym

B.8 Summary of Industrial Relations Systems

Name of firm	Institutionalization				System		
	Union present	LM committees	Union contract	Company policy	Consultative	Substantive	Representative
Solar Turbines Int'l	x			x	x		
Columbus Auto Parts	x			x	x		
Shell Oil Co.				x	x		
Texas Am. Bancshares				x	x		
Control Data Corp.				x	x		
Beech Aircraft Corp.	x			x	x		
Allen-Bradley Co.	x			x	x		
Waters Associates				x	x		
Morse Borg-Warner	x			x	x		
Babcock & Wilcox	x			x	x		
Arcata Redwood				x	x		
Honeywell, Inc.				x	x		
TRW Semiconductors				x	x		
Electrical Co.				x	x		
Champion Int'l	x			x	x		
Trans-Matic Mfg.				x	x		
Hinderliter Energy				x			
Phillips Petroleum	x			x	x		
Tektreonix, Inc.				x	x		
Potlatch Corp.	x			x	x		
Northrop Corp.				x	x		
Herman Miller, Inc.		x				x	x
Pacific NW Bell	x			x	x		
General Foods, Topeka				x		x	
GM, Tarrytown	x	x	x		x	x	x
Rushton Coal Mine	x	x	x		x	x	x
Harman, Bolivar plant	x	x	x		x	x	x
Ford, Sharonville, Ohio	x	x	x		x		x
Delco-Remy, Fitzgerald, Ga.	x			x		x	
Martin Marietta	x	x			x		x
Citibank				x			
Continental Insurance				x			
BEA Associates				x	x		
A-dec, Inc.				x	x	x	
Honeywell, Inc.							
Memorial Hospital				x	x		
Nucor Corp.				x			
Reynolds Aluminum	x			x	x		

Name of firm	Institutionalization				System		
	Union present	LM committees	Union contract	Company policy	Consultative	Substantive	Representative
Norwest Bank St. Paul				x	x		
Southern Co. Services				x	x		
National Supply Co., Armco	x	x		x	x		x
Honeywell Aerospace	x			x	x		
National Semiconductor				x	x		
Monsanto Textiles				x	x		
ZEBCO, Inc.	x			x	x		
City of Phoenix	x			x	x		
Florida Power & Light	x			x	x		
U.S. Copyright Office	x	x	x		x	x	x
Paul Revere Life Insurance				x	x		
Northrop Corp.				x	x		
Maxwell House	x	x	x			x	x
Maxwell House	x	x	x			x	x
U.S. Customs Service	x	x	x		x		x
Cutter Labs				x	x	x	
Lincoln Electric				x			
Averitt Express							
Rohm & Haas Bayport				x	x		
Steelcase					x	x	
Allegheny Ludlum Steel	x			x	x		
Naval Air Rework Facility	x			x			
Ethyl Corp.	x			x	x		
Lord Corp, Aerospace Div.	x			x	x	x	
Ford Louisville Plant	x		x		x		x
InfoCorp*				x		x	
Houston Lighting & Power	x			x	x		
McDonnell Douglas, Mo.	x		x		x	x	x
Polysar Gulf Coast				x			
Sewell Village Cadillac				x	x		
Sabine River Works				x	x		
First National Bank of Chicago				x	x		
McDonnell Douglas Astro.				x		x	
Baxter Health Care				x	x		
Tenneco				x	x	x	
Scottsdale, Ariz.				x			
American Express				x	x		
N. Telecom/Santa Clara				x	x	x	

B.8 Summary of Industrial Relations Systems *(continued)*

Name of firm	Union present	LM committees	Union contract	Company policy	Consultative	Substantive	Representative
	Institutionalization					System	
Preston Trucking	x	x		x	x	x	x
Harley Davidson	x	x		x	x	x	x
Corning, RD&E							
Ford-UAW EI Program	x	x	x		x		x
Maxwell House, GF*	x	x	x			x	x
Beaumont Newspaper				x	x		
Lake Superior Paper				x		x	
Levi Strauss	x			x	x		
U.S. Shoe				x		x	
Motorola				x	x		
Naval Pub. Center				x	x		
Seattle First National Bank				x			
Western Airlines	x	x	x		x		x
Epic Health Care				x	x		
Baxter				x	x		
Ethyl Corp.	x			x			
First National Bank/Chicago				x	x		
St. Luke's Episcopal Hospital				x	x		
Corning, SCC plant	x	x	x			x	x
Hearing Technology				x	x		
Dana Corp., Minn.	x			x	x	x	
Toledo Scale, Ohio				x		x	
Rolscreen, Carroll plant				x	x		
Ford, Wixom plant	x	x	x		x		x
HP, Roseville, Calif.				x	x		
Milliken & Co.				x	x		
Weaver's Popcorn				x	x	x	
IBM, Rochester, Minn.				x	x		
Duracell, Cleveland, Tenn.				x	x		
Capsugel				x		x	
LTV Aerospace				x		x	
Moore Response Marketing				x		x	
Zurich-American Insurance				x	x		
Rohm & Haas Louisville	x			x	x	x	
Magma Copper	x		x			x	
Wohlert Corp.	x	x		x	x		x
Warner Lambert	x			x	x		
US West	x	x	x		x		x

Name of firm	Institutionalization				System		
	Union present	LM committees	Union contract	Company policy	Consultative	Substantive	Representative
TRW, Value Div.	x	x		x	x	x	x
TRW, Software Systems							
Thomas Lipton Co.	x	x		x	x		x
Standard Oil Engineering Materials	x	x				x	
Shenandoah Life Insurance				x		x	
ROHR Industries	x	x		x		x	x
Rohm & Haas Knoxville	x	x	x			x	x
Rohm & Haas Kentucky	x	x		x		x	x
Rohm & Haas Delaware	x	x		x		x	x
Pillsbury				x		x	
ProTech Respirators				x		x	
Philip Morris	x	x		x	x		x
Ohio Bell, Ameritech	x	x	x		x	x	x
National Steel Corp.	x	x	x		x	x	x
National Spinning Co.				x	x	x	
Motor Wheel Corp.	x	x		x		x	x
Mobay Corp.	x	x	x		x		x
McDonnell Douglas	x	x	x			x	x
Logan Aluminum				x		x	
Johnsonville Sausage				x		x	
Johnson & Johnson	x	x		x	x		x
Granville-Phillips				x		x	
GM-UAW National Program	x	x	x		x		x
GE, St. Louis				x		x	
Ford, Dearborn Engine	x	x	x		x	x	x
FMC Corp.				x		x	
FMC, Phosphorous Chemicals	x	x	x			x	x
Duluth Public Schools	x	x	x			x	x
Digital, Enfield, Conn.				x		x	
Delco Chassis Div.	x	x	x		x		x
Delco-Remy, Albany	x	x	x			x	x
Chrysler, Indianapolis	x	x	x			x	x
Best Foods				x		x	
Bridgestone-Firestone	x	x	x				x
AT&T Credit Corp.				x		x	
American Brass	x	x	x		x		x
American Brass						x	
A. E. Staley	x	x				x	x

B.8   Summary of Industrial Relations Systems *(continued)*

Name of firm	Institutionalization				System		
	Union present	LM committees	Union contract	Company policy	Consultative	Substantive	Representative
A. O. Smith	x	x	x		x	x	x
US West, Seattle	x					x	
Monsanto Co.				x		x	
Monsanto Co.				x	x		
L. E. Jones	x	x			x		
J. I. Case Co.	x	x			x		x
Inland Steel Bar	x	x	x		x		x
GM, Janesville	x	x	x			x	x
GM, Fisher Guide Div.	x	x	x		x		x
Con Ed, New York	x	x			x		x
Corning, Blacksburg	x	x	x			x	x
Sherwin-Williams, Richmond				x		x	
Xerox, Webster Plant	x	x	x		x	x	x
Wallace Co.				x		x	
Cadillac Motor	x				x	x	
Marlow Industries				x	x	x	x
Zytec Corp.				x	x	x	x
Solectron Corp.				x	x	x	
AT&T Shreveport Works				x		x	
Douglas Air/Long Beach, Calif.							
Midwestern Mfg.*	x	x	x		x		x
NW Airlines, Atlanta	x					x	
Federal Express				x		x	
GM, NUMMI plant	x	x	x		x	x	x
Boeing Defense & Space	x		x			x	
Globe Metallurgical				x	x	x	
Gore Associates				x	x	x	
GM, Saturn	x	x	x		x	x	x
Exxon Research & Engineering				x	x		
Dun & Bradstreet Software				x	x		
Southern Paper Co.*				x			
Corning RD&E Div.				x		x	

*Pseudonym

B.9 Summary of Performance Outcomes

Name of firm	Profits	Savings	Productivity	Quality	Cost of quality	Cycle time	Customer service	Reduced inventory	Reduced ratio: empl./sup.	Reduced grievances	Improved cooperation	Improved morale	Improved QWL	Reduced turnover	Reduced absentees	Improved base pay	Bonus
Solar Turbines Int'l	x											x	x				
Columbus Auto Parts	x	x										x					x
Shell Oil Co.											x						
Texas Am. Bancshares														x			
Control Data Corp.											x						
Beech Aircraft Corp.	x										x						
Allen-Bradley Co.	x										x						
Waters Associates		x	x								x						
Morse Borg-Warner		x								x		x		x	x		x
Babcock & Wilcox		x									x						
Arcata Redwood		x	x								x						
Honeywell, Inc.	x						x										
TRW Semiconductors		x										x	x				
Electrical Co.											x		x				
Champion Int'l	x	x									x						
Trans-Matic Mfg.	x	x									x			x	x		x
Hinderliter Energy		x										x		x			x
Phillips Petroleum	x																
Tektreonix, Inc.	x											x					
Potlatch Corp.		x															x
Northrop Corp.	x	x	x														
Herman Miller, Inc.	x	x									x						

Company												
Pacific NW Bell			x									
General Foods, Topeka	x	x	x					x	x	x		x
GM, Tarrytown		x					x	x				
Rushton Coal Mine		x						x		x		x
Harman, Bolivar plant		x	x				x	x			x	
Ford, Sharonville, Ohio	x	x	x					x				
Delco-Remy, Fitzgerald, Ga.		x	x					x	x	x		
Martin Marietta		x	x				x	x				
Citibank	x	x			x						x	
Continental Insurance		x	x									
BEA Associates	x					x						x
A-dec, Inc.		x	x		x							
Honeywell, Inc.		x										
Memorial Hospital		x	x		x							x
Nucor Corp.		x				x						
Reynolds Aluminum		x	x				x	x				
Norwest Bank St. Paul		x					x	x				
Southern Co. Services		x		x								
National Supply Co., Armco		x						x				
Honeywell Aerospace		x						x				
National Semiconductor		x	x						x		x	
Monsanto Textiles	x	x					x	x				
ZEBCO, Inc.	x	x						x	x	x		
City of Phoenix	x								x			x
Florida Power & Light	x	x									x	
U.S. Copyright Office	x											

B.9 Summary of Performance Outcomes (*continued*)

Name of firm	Profits	Savings	Productivity	Quality	Cost of quality	Cycle time	Customer service	Reduced inventory	Reduced ratio: empl./sup.	Reduced grievances	Improved cooperation	Improved morale	Improved QWL	Reduced turnover	Reduced absentees	Improved base pay	Bonus
Paul Revere Life Insurance	x				x												x
Northrop Corp.		x	x														
Maxwell House	x															x	
Maxwell House	x	x	x	x						x	x					x	
U.S. Customs Service		x	x	x			x				x		x				
Cutter Labs	x	x	x	x													
Lincoln Electric	x	x	x						x		x			x	x		x
Averitt Express									x					x			
Rohm & Haas Bayport	x		x						x					x	x		
Steelcase	x	x												x			x
Allegheny Ludlum Steel	x	x	x		x												
Naval Air Rework Facility	x	x	x														
Ethyl Corp.	x	x															
Lord Corp, Aerospace Div.			x	x			x						x				
Ford Louisville Plant							x			x					x		
InfoCorp*							x				x	x					x
Houston Lighting & Power	x						x						x				
McDonnell Douglas, Mo.			x				x				x	x	x	x	x		x
Polysar Gulf Coast	x	x	x				x				x	x		x	x		x
Sewell Village Cadillac							x										x
Sabine River Works	x							x									
First National Bank of Chicago	x						x										

B.9 Summary of Performance Outcomes (continued)

Name of firm	Profits	Savings	Productivity	Quality	Cost of quality	Cycle time	Customer service	Reduced inventory	Reduced ratio: empl./sup.	Reduced grievances	Improved cooperation	Improved morale	Improved QWL	Reduced turnover	Reduced absentees	Improved base pay	Bonus
Dana Corp., Minn.		x	x	x		x	x	x					x			x	
Toledo Scale, Ohio		x	x	x		x	x	x								x	
Rolscreen, Carroll plant		x	x	x		x		x									
Ford, Wixom plant		x	x	x		x											
HP, Roseville, Calif.		x	x	x	x				x								
Milliken & Co.		x	x	x	x	x	x	x									
Weaver's Popcorn			x														x
IBM, Rochester, Minn.		x	x	x	x			x									
Duracell, Cleveland, Tenn.		x	x								x		x				
Capsugel	x	x	x	x	x	x		x									
LTV Aerospace	x	x	x	x					x				x				x
Moore Response Marketing	x																
Zurich-American Insurance													x				
Rohm & Haas Louisville							x		x	x							
Magma Copper		x	x								x	x					
Wohlert Corp.	x									x							
Warner Lambert		x	x	x								x					
US West				x													x
TRW, Value Div.	x	x	x							x	x						
TRW, Software Systems													x				
Thomas Lipton Co.	x	x											x				
Standard Oil Engineering Materials	x	x	x	x							x		x				

Shenandoah Life Insurance

ROHR Industries

Rohm & Haas Knoxville

Rohm & Haas Kentucky

Rohm & Haas Delaware

Pillsbury

ProTech Respirators

Philip Morris

Ohio Bell, Ameritech

National Steel Corp.

National Spinning Co.

Motor Wheel Corp.

Mobay Corp.

McDonnell Douglas

Logan Aluminum

Johnsonville Sausage

Johnson & Johnson

Granville-Phillips

GM-UAW National Programs

GE, St. Louis

Ford, Dearborn Engine

FMC Corp.

FMC, Phosphorous Chemicals

Duluth Public Schools

Digital, Enfield, Conn.

Delco Chassis Div.

B.9 Summary of Performance Outcomes (*continued*)

Name of firm	Profits	Savings	Productivity	Quality	Cost of quality	Cycle time	Customer service	Reduced inventory	Reduced ratio: empl./sup.	Reduced grievances	Improved cooperation	Improved morale	Improved QWL	Reduced turnover	Reduced absentees	Improved base pay	Bonus
Delco-Remy, Albany									x								
Chrysler, Indianapolis									x								
Best Foods																	
Bridgestone-Firestone											x						
AT&T Credit Corp.	x	x										x			x		x
American Brass																	
American Brass																	
A. E. Staley																	
A. O. Smith	x	x										x					x
US West, Seattle	x	x	x														
Monsanto Co.		x	x									x					
Monsanto Co.		x															
L. E. Jones		x	x	x													
J. I. Case Co.								x		x			x				x
Inland Steel Bar																	
GM, Janesville																	
GM, Fisher Guide Div.		x	x														
Con Ed, New York			x				x										
Corning, Blacksburg		x	x						x								
Sherwin-Williams, Richmond	x	x	x			x											x
Xerox, Webster Plant	x	x	x	x						x							x
Wallace Co.	x	x	x	x		x	x										

Cadillac Motor		x		x							
Marlow Industries	x	x	x	x		x		x	x	x	
Zytec Corp.	x	x	x		x			x	x	x	
Solectron Corp.		x	x	x							
AT&T Shreveport Works	x	x	x								
Douglas Air/LB, Calif.	x										
Midwestern Mfg.*						x		x	x	x	x
NW Airlines, Atlanta											
Federal Express			x								
GM, NUMMI plant	x	x	x		x	x	x	x	x	x	
Boeing Defense & Space	x			x		x	x		x	x	
Globe Metallurgical	x	x			x						x
Gore Associates	x	x			x	x					
GM, Saturn	x	x	x	x	x	x	x	x	x	x	
Exxon Research & Engineering	x	x	x								
Dun & Bradstreet Software		x	x								
Southern Paper Co.*	x						x		x	x	
Corning RD&E Div.	x	x	x		x	x	x				x

*Pseudonym

NOTES

CHAPTER 1

1. Throughout this book, we use the terms *work system* and *production system* interchangeably to refer to the system of work at the firm or organization level. Work systems include four components: management methods, work organization, human resource practices, and industrial relations. (See also chapter 4.) We distinguish this level of organization from the institutional or socioeconomic framework in which firms are embedded.

2. The Malcolm Baldrige National Quality Award, created by public law, is the highest level of national recognition for quality that a U.S. company can receive. The award is managed by the U.S. Department of Commerce, National Institute of Standards and Technology, and is administered by the American Society for Quality Control. The first awards were made in 1988.

CHAPTER 2

1. Following Frederick Taylor's scientific management techniques, Taylorism refers to an organization of work based on the separation of conception and execution, the use of large-scale dedicated equipment, and a detailed division of labor into routinized tasks to produce large volumes of standardized products.

2. Levine and Tyson distinguish three types of participation: consultative, giving workers a voice or input into management decisions; substantive, allowing workers the power to make decisions over certain production issues; and representative, providing workers with a role in decision making through their unions.

CHAPTER 3

1. Codetermination refers to legally mandated rights of employees to participate in management decision making. Since 1982, 40 "exemplary" firms and 148 organizations—mostly small and medium-sized firms and public sector agencies—have taken part in government-sponsored organizational development programs (Naschhold 1992).

CHAPTER 5

1. William Freund and Eugene Epstein (1984) summarize the New York Stock Exchange survey (1982); Edward E. Lawler III, Gerald Ledford, and Susan A. Mohrman (1989) as well as Adrienne Eaton and Paula Voos (1992) review the U.S. GAO survey (1987).

2. Detailed and representative survey data are central to policy making. We believe it is essential that the Bureau of Labor Statistics incorporate more detailed questions on workplace innovations into its regular national surveys of establishments.

3. This approach differs from meta-analyses that seek to conduct a rigorous scientific test of hypotheses (see Bullock and Tubbs 1987).

4. Although 465 business units of firms responded (with an average employment of 7,884 each), the response rate for the survey was only 6.5 percent.

5. An establishment is defined as a plant or other facility at a business address. It is distinct from a company. For example, each General Motors plant is a separate establishment.

CHAPTER 6

1. Appendix B lists the cases and their detailed characteristics. The cases include U.S. corporations only. We do not include worker-owned firms because we believe they represent a unique set of circumstances. The chart lists cases chronologically, by date of the case write-up. This strategy enables us to see patterns of change over time in the programs that firms implemented in various industries. Some companies are listed more than once; in this case, each item represents a snapshot at a different point in time—allowing us to see the evolution or change in the company's program. We categorized the elements of the programs according to the conceptual famework developed in part II of this book: technology and work organization, management coordination, human resource policies, and labor relations. The introduction to appendix B lists and defines the detailed categories we used.

2. We refer to case studies by the name of the company and the date of the study. This corresponds to the chronological listing of the cases in appendix B. Cases are in the form Honeywell, 1980, with a comma before the date; citations to items in the reference section at the back of the book are in the form Ledford, Lawler, and Mohrman 1988, without a comma.

3. We draw here on Levine and Tyson's distinction between consultative, substantive, and representative structures (1990). In the first instance, management consults with employees about production-related (the design of jobs, the work process, the product strategy) and other issues (administrative, personnel); in the second, employees have decision-making rights in the areas identified above; in the third, unions represent the interests of employees through joint bodies or committees or in collective bargaining negotiations. These three structures may exist separately or in conjunction with one another.

4. For a good history and discussion of quality circles in the United States, see Ledford, Lawler, and Mohrman 1988.

5. As is apparent from the prior discussion on alternative models, most of these alternative pay systems did not originate abroad but rather among American industrial relations, human resource, and compensation specialists. In addition to profit sharing and gainsharing, other forms of pay for performance are based on the application of theories of organizational behavior and economics to management. Most recently, the "new economics of personnel" combines psychology and economics to develop guidelines for compensation policies (Mitchell and Zaidi 1990; Mitchell, Lewin, and Lawler 1990; Lazear 1992).

6. The empirical research demonstrating the peformance effects of various pay strategies is not particularly helpful in providing guidance as to which alternatives "work best." Some research shows that individual incentive plans (e.g., piece rates or commissions) can motivate individuals to improve their performance, but there is virtually no evidence on the consequences of merit pay (Milkovich and Wigdor 1991) or pay for skill. Some studies show that gainsharing has a positive effect on performance (Schuster 1984; Kaufman 1992) and that a participation component makes a difference (Gowen and Rynes 1991). Studies find weak evidence that pay linking executive and managerial performance to firm performance improves the financial performance of the firm (Leonard 1990; Gibbons and Murphy 1990; Kahn and Sherer 1990). By contrast, Daniel Mitchell, David Lewin, and Edward Lawler III (1990) found that taken together, economic participation strategies (profit sharing, gainsharing, stock options, employee stock ownership plans, bonuses, or incentive plans) were not related to productivity or profitability, although profit sharing alone was. Noneconomic participation (employee-involvement programs), however, positively affected both productivity and profits. A central problem of interpretation is that the effects of compensation strategies depend intimately on the organizational and labor market context (Milkovich and Wigdor 1991:151–58). For comprehensive reviews, see Ehrenberg 1990 and Gerhart, Milkovich, and Murray 1992.

7. Lawler, Mohrman, and Ledford (1992) found that a small percentage (7 percent) of firms in their sample used rewards as a central strategy to improve performance.

8. The coal miners whom Eric Trist first studied improved their productivity by reorganizing mining from individualized tasks along a long wall to group work along a short wall. This study began the sociotechnical systems movement at Tav-

istock and led to a series of studies elsewhere that refined sociotechnical systems theory (Trist, 1981; Trist and Bamforth 1951; David and Cherns 1975).

9. The plant boasts impressive results: defect rates dropped from 1,800 parts per million (ppm) to 9 ppm between 1987 and 1990; customer lead times fell from five weeks to days; and process losses were halved (Sheridan 1990; on-site visit to Corning, Oct. 7–8, 1992).

10. The emphasis is captured in a statement made by Irving Bluestone when he was vice-president of the UAW General Motors Department: "Traditionally management has called upon labor to cooperate in increasing productivity and improving the quality of the product. My view of the other side of the coin is more appropriate; namely, that management should cooperate with the workers to find ways to enhance the dignity of labor and to tap the creative resources in each human being in developing a more satisfying work life, with emphasis on worker participation in the decision-making process" (quoted in Guest 1982a:92).

11. The UAW and General Motors created the first QWL program in a letter of understanding in contract negotiations in 1973.

12. George Strauss and Tove Hammer argue that, in contrast to European unions, American unions did not see the need for industrial democracy, which they understood to mean more union control of the workplace: American unions already had the right to bargain over a wider range of working conditions at the plant level (what became known as job control unionism) than did European unions, which tended to focus more narrowly on wage negotiations at industry and/or national levels (Strauss and Hammer 1987:16).

CHAPTER 7

1. These include transportation, communication, and public utilities (SIC 40); wholesale and retail trade (SIC 50); finance, insurance, and real estate (SIC 60); other services (hotel and lodging, personal services, business services, repair services, entertainment, health services, legal services, educational services, and social, membership, and miscellaneous services) (SIC 70–80); and government.

2. Between 1950 and 1973, annual productivity growth averaged 2.2 percent in manufacturing and 1.4 percent in services; for the 1973–87 period, the rates were 1.1 percent and 0.2 percent respectively (McKinsey Global Institute 1992).

3. See U.S. Congress, Office of Technology Assessment 1987 for a good overview of the internationalization of services.

4. The application of Taylorism to the service sector created a market segmented between a majority of services that were low cost and of poor quality and luxury services at the high end—a segmentation that paralleled segmentation in goods production.

5. See, for example, the discussion by Paul Starr (1987) on the limits of privatization and the report of the federal Office of Management and Budget that billions of dollars of public money have been wasted by private companies to which government work has been transferred in the last decade (Schindler 1992).

6. This trend may be changing. Accounts in the popular press say that the use of self-managed teams in white-collar settings has grown dramatically in the last year or two (Krass 1991). The survey by Osterman (1993) also supports this view; he finds significantly more self-managed teams in services than in manufacturing.

7. Thanks to David Levine for making this point as well as for other comments in this section.

8. Juran's quality handbook provides a detailed guide to applying quality concepts such as "fitness for use" to services as well as developing service performance standards and conformance measures, appropriate quality "parameters," and data requirements (Zimmerman and Enell 1988).

9. This percentage is probably an overstatement, given the low response rate of about 25 percent.

10. Schlesinger and Heskett cite several examples of service firms that have achieved success with this high-performance route, including Taco Bell, Dayton Hudson department store, ServiceMaster janitorial services, Au Bon Pain, Fidelity Bank of Philadelphia, and Marriott's Fairfield Inns (1991a, 1991b).

11. See Keefe and Boroff (1994) for a detailed review of the uneven AT&T/CWA relationship.

12. For a more detailed case study of the joint CWA/BellSouth quality program, see Batt (1993).

CHAPTER 8

1. We describe a wide range of management methods, types of work organization, and human resource and industrial relations practices in the glossary of terms in the appendix.

2. Since 1988, the National Institute of Standards and Technology of the Department of Commerce and the American Society for Quality Control have administered the Malcolm Baldrige National Quality Award. It is modeled after Japan's Deming Award for quality. Since then, many states, industry associations, and publications have begun similar though less comprehensive quality awards so that even more firms have become involved in or influenced by "the quality movement."

3. By self-directed teams we mean groups of workers who have substantial discretion over the work process, make changes in production methods as needed, and take on many of the tasks traditionally carried out by front-line supervisors, such as allocating and coordinating work between different employees and scheduling. Clearly, there is a range of variation in the optimal degree of autonomy that groups have, and this is likely to depend on the nature of the work as well as the preferences of the particular group of employees. In the extreme, such teams are truly autonomous and have no supervisors, as in the Volvo plant at Uddevalla, Sweden, where the ratio of managers to employees is approximately 1:60 (Hancke 1993). In most U.S. cases, the ratio is considerably larger, supervisors act as "coaches," and teams are more accurately described as "semi-autonomous." In this book, we use

the term *self-directed* or *self-managed* to include this range of variation in the autonomy of groups.

4. "Lean production," write Womack, Jones, and Roos (1990: 225), "is a superior way for humans to make things. . . . It follows that the whole world should adopt lean production, and as quickly as possible."

5. Since 1988, seventeen companies have won awards in three categories: manufacturing (Motorola, Westinghouse Commercial Nuclear Fuel Division, Milliken and Company, Xerox Business Products, Cadillac Motor Company, IBM Rochester, Solectron, Zytec, AT&T Network Systems Group/Transmission Systems Business Unit, and Texas Instruments' Defense Systems & Electronics Group); services (Federal Express, AT&T Universal Card, and the Ritz-Carlton Hotel in Atlanta); and small business (Globe Metallurgical, Wallace, Marlow Industries, and Granite Rock).

6. One company described the Baldrige feedback process as "the best consulting bargain around" (Gomez del Campo 1993).

7. The seven categories are customer focus and satisfaction (300 points), leadership (90 points), information and analysis (80 points), strategic quality planning (60 points), management of process quality (140 points), quality and operational results (180 points), and human resource development and management (150 points).

8. In reality, there are many different versions of TQM, some emphasizing the link to customers and robust product design, some the importance of a strong managerial role and leadership (Juran and Gyrna 1988), some the cost of nonconformance (Crosby 1979), and some the importance of employee involvement (Deming 1984).

9. In a footnote to the section on employee involvement and empowerment of front-line workers, the Baldrige criteria state, "Different involvement goals and indicators may be set for different categories of employees, depending on company needs and on the types of responsibilities of each employee category."

10. For example, Solectron Corporation has taken a "team-focused" approach to employee involvement and has trained most workers in problem-solving methods and statistical process control. Motorola uses problem-solving teams throughout the company to establish quality goals. The Wallace Company uses teams and has empowered "associates" to make decisions not exceeding $1,000 without consulting a supervisor. Zytec Corporation uses cross-functional design teams, and several departments are self-managed.

11. Information on the Baldrige winners here and below comes from case studies conducted by the bureau administering the Baldrige Award in the U.S. Department of Commerce, by the U.S. Department of Labor, by the American Productivity and Quality Center, and by Gomez del Campo (1993).

12. We draw heavily on the case studies of Gomez del Campo (1993) for these profiles.

13. For the following analysis of these cases, we draw on a combination of case materials and interviews with participants. For Xerox, we rely largely on March 1993 interviews with Xerox manager Nick Argona and ACTWU union representa-

tive Tony Costanza, co-managers of the "Joint Process Architecture," which initiated organizational changes at Xerox, and on interviews with Peter Lazes, consultant on the transformation process at Xerox in the 1980s. For Saturn, we rely on September 1992 interviews with Dick Tracey, former GM and Saturn manager, currently at the Industrial Technology Institute; also LeFauve and Hax 1992; Fraser 1992; and Rubinstein, Bennett, and Kochan 1993). Information on Corning comes from an on-site visit and interviews in October 1992.

14. Work units at Saturn "are self-directed and empowered with the authority, responsibility, and resources necessary to meet their day to day assignments and goals including producing to budget, quality, housekeeping, safety and health, maintenance, material and inventory control, training, job assignments, repairs, scrap control, vacation approvals, absenteeism, supplies, record keeping, personnel selection and hiring, work planning, and work scheduling" (Rubinstein, Bennett, and Kochan 1993).

15. Among the autonomous work groups at Xerox are the "mod squads"—autonomous groups of electricians, painters, and carpenters who have cut costs by 30 percent by eliminating three or four steps and layers of employees as the teams took over advising, engineering, drafting of blueprints, and supplier relationships.

CHAPTER 9

1. As Smith (1991) argues, this provides the economic rationale for legally mandated codetermination.

2. This decision came in the 1980 *NLRB v. Yeshiva University* case. Although that case applied specifically to academic faculties, it is uncertain whether it applies as well to blue-collar or other hourly workers performing managerial functions.

3. In December 1992, the NLRB found that the "action committees" set up by Electromation, Inc., a nonunion company in Elkhart, Indiana, to deal with issues ranging from bonuses to the treatment of employee absenteeism, violated the 1935 National Labor Relations Act, which bars companies from setting up management-dominated committees. At Electromation, managers determined the purposes and goals of the committees, fixed their size and membership from a list of volunteers, and included a management representative (Victor 1993).

CHAPTER 10

1. Countries such as France that have imposed a pay-or-play system based on a straight training tax have found that small firms usually end up subsidizing larger firms. Small firms without the resources to do the training end up paying the tax, which goes into a public fund; small firms also lack the slack time on production lines to train workers and the administrative capability to access the public fund.

GLOSSARY

PERSONNEL POLICIES/PRACTICES

Employment security: Company policy designed to prevent layoffs.

Hiring based partly on employee input: Management consults with and obtains employee input about hiring new employees.

Realistic job preview or portrayal to potential job hires: Instead of attempting to persuade potential new hires of the desirability of a job, both the undesirable and the desirable parts of the job are emphasized in the hiring process. Giving potential new employees a realistic portrayal of the job increases self-selection and prepares new hires for unpleasant conditions.

Suggestion system: A program that elicits individual employee suggestions on improving work or the work environment.

PAY/REWARD SYSTEMS

All-salaried pay system: A system in which all employees are salaried, thus eliminating the distinction between hourly and salaried employees.

Knowledge/skill-based pay: An alternative to traditional job-based pay that sets pay levels based on how many skills employees have or how many jobs they potentially can do, not on the job they are currently holding. Also called pay for skills, pay for knowledge, and competency-based pay.

Profit sharing: A bonus plan that shares some portion of company profits with employees. It does not include dividend sharing.

Gainsharing: Gainsharing plans are based on a formula whereby some portion of gains in productivity, quality, cost effectiveness, or other performance indicators is shared with all employees in an organization (such as a plant) in the form of bonuses. Gainsharing plans typically include a system of employee suggestion committees. Gainsharing differs from profit sharing or an employee stock ownership plan in that the basis of the formula is some set of local performance measures, not company profits. Examples include the Scanlon Plan, the Improshare Plan, the Rucker Plan, and various custom-designed plans.

Individual incentives: Bonuses or other financial compensation are tied to short-term or long-term individual performance.

Work group or team incentives: Bonuses or other financial compensation are tied to short-term or long-term work group, permanent team, or temporary team performance.

Nonmonetary recognition awards for performance: Any nonmonetary reward (including gifts, publicity, dinners, and so-on) for individual or group performance.

Employee stock ownership plan (ESOP): A credit mechanism that enables employees to buy their employer's stock, thus giving them an ownership stake in the company; the stock is held in trust until employees quit or retire.

EMPLOYEE INVOLVEMENT INNOVATIONS/PROGRAMS

Survey feedback: Use of employee attitude survey results not simply as part of an employee opinion poll but as part of a larger problem-solving process in which survey data are used to encourage, structure, and measure the effectiveness of employee participation.

Job enrichment or redesign: Design of work that is intended to increase worker performance and job satisfaction by increasing skill variety, autonomy, significance and identity of the task, and performance feedback.

Quality circles or problem-solving teams: Structured employee participation groups in which groups of volunteers from particular work areas meet regularly to identify and suggest improvements for work-related problems. Management provides group problem-solving training to facilitate this process. The goals of QCs are improved quality and productivity; there are no direct rewards for participation. The groups' only power is to suggest changes to management.

Employee participation groups other than quality circles: Any employee participation groups, such as task teams or cross-functional teams, that do not fall within the definitions of either self-managing work teams or quality circles. These groups typically involve employees from different work, department, or functional areas.

Union-management quality of worklife (QWL): Joint union-management committees, usually existing at multiple organizational levels, alongside the established union and management relationships and collective bargaining committees. QWL committes usually are prohibited from directly addressing contractual issues such as pay. Rather, they are charged with developing changes that will improve both organizational performance and employee quality of work life.

Joint partnership processes (structures, architectures): Joint labor-management committees that address broad issues at the plant, enterprise, corporate, or organizational level that affect the viability of the firm or organization. The focus is on strategic goals and on policy and planning to meet those goals.

Self-managing work teams: Also termed autonomous work groups, semi-autonomous work groups, self-regulating work teams, or simply work teams. The work group (in some cases, acting without a supervisor) is responsible for a whole product or service and makes decisions about task assignments and work methods. The team may be responsible for its own support services, such as maintenance, purchasing, and quality control, and may perform certain personnel functions, such as hiring and firing team members and determining pay increases.

Employee councils: Also termed works councils. Elected bodies of employees, with representatives from every occupational grouping, that receive information and engage in joint decision making with management on operational issues at the plant or work-site level. Issues addressed may include training, occupational safety and health, deployment of technology, and operating procedures.

Adapted from Lawler, Mohrman, and Ledford 1992: 145–46.

REFERENCES

Abernathy, William J., Kenneth Wayne. 1974. "Limits of the Learning Curve." *Harvard Business Review* 52 (Sept.–Oct.): 109–19.

Adler, Paul. 1992. "The 'Learning Bureaucracy': New United Motors Manufacturing, Inc." In *Research in Organizational Behavior*, edited by Barry Shaw and Larry Cummings, 15:111–94. Greenwich, Conn.: JAI Press.

American Management Association (AMA). 1992. *Downsizing and Assistance to Displaced Workers*. New York: AMA.

Andress, Frank J. 1954. "The Learning Curve as a Production Tool." *Harvard Business Review* 32 (Jan.–Feb.): 87–96.

Appelbaum, Eileen. 1989. "The Growth of the U.S. Contingent Labor Force." In *Microeconomic Issues in Labor Economics*, edited by Robert Drago and Richard Perlman, 62–82. New York: Harvester Wheatsheaf.

———. 1992. "Structural Change and the Growth of Part-Time and Contingent Employment." In *New Policies for the Part-Time and Contingent Workforce*, edited by Virginia L. DuRivage, 1–14. Armonk, N.Y.: M. E. Sharpe.

Argona, Nick. 1992. *Employee Involvement and Leadership through Quality: The Journey of Choice, 1980–2000*. Webster, N.Y.: Xerox.

Arthur D. Little. 1992. *Executive Caravan TQM Survey*. March 24.

Arthur, Jeffrey. 1990. "Industrial Relations and Business Strategies in American Steel Minimills." Ph.D. diss. Cornell University.

Auer, Peter, and Claudius Riegler. 1990. *Post-Taylorism: The Enterprise as a Place of Learning Organizational Change*. Stockholm: Swedish Work Environment Fund, and Berlin: Wissenschaftszentrum Berlin.

Bahr, Morton, and William Ketchum. 1993. "Workplace of the Future." *Human Resource Management Journal* 32. In press.

Bailey, Thomas. 1992. "Discretionary Effort and the Organization of Work: Employee Participation and Work Reform since Hawthorne." Paper prepared for the Sloan Foundation, New York. Aug.

Banas, Paul. 1988. "Employee Involvement: A Sustained Labor/Management Initiative at the Ford Motor Company." In *Productivity in Organizations*, edited by John Campbell, Richard Campbell, and Associates, 388–416. San Francisco: Jossey-Bass.

Bassie, Laurie. 1992. *Smart Workers, Smart Work: A Survey of Small Businesses on Workplace Education and Reorganization of Work*. Washington, D.C.: Southport Institute for Policy Analysis.

Batt, Rosemary. 1993. "Work Reorganization and Labor Relations in Telecommunications Services: A Case Study of BellSouth Corporation," MIT Industrial Performance Center. Working Paper no. 004-93WP. Aug.

Batt, Rosemary, and Paul Osterman. 1993a. *A National Policy for Workplace Training*. Washington, D.C.: Economic Policy Institute.

———. 1993b. *Workplace Training Policy: Case Studies from State and Local Experience*. Washington, D.C.: Economic Policy Institute.

Beaumont, P. B., L. C. Hunter, and R. Phayre. 1993. "Human Resources and Total Quality Management: Some Case Study Evidence." Paper presented at meeting of the Canadian Industrial Relations Association, Ottawa, June 3–5.

Belzer, Michael. 1992. "Gain Sharing and Collective Bargaining." Institute of Collective Bargaining, New York State School of Industrial and Labor Relations, Cornell University. Typescript.

Berg, Peter. 1993. "Training Institutions and Industrial Relations in Germany and the United States: The Importance of Inter-Institutional Linkages for Understanding Labor Adjustment." Paper presented at conference, The Shifting Boundaries of Labor Politics: New Directions for Comparative Research and Theory, Center for European Studies, Harvard University, March 12–14.

Berggren, Christian. 1993. "Volvo Uddevalla—A Dream Plant for Dealers?" Department of Work Science, Royal Institute of Technology, Stockholm. Feb.

Bhote, Keki R. 1989. "Motorola's Long March to the Malcolm Baldrige National Quality Award." *National Productivity Review* 8:365–76.

Bishop, John. 1991. "Employer Training and Skill Shortages: A Review of the State of Knowledge." Working Paper No. 91-32. Center for Advanced Human Resource Studies, New York State School of Industrial and Labor Relations, Cornell University.

Blinder, Alan. 1990. *Paying for Productivity*. Washington, D.C.: Brookings Institution.

Bluestone, Barry, and Irving Bluestone. 1992. *Negotiating the Future: A Labor Perspective on American Business*. New York: Basic Books.

Boston Consulting Group. 1972. *Perspectives on Experience*. Ann Arbor, Mich.: UMI Out of Print Books on Demand.

Bosworth, Brian. 1992. *State Strategies for Manufacturing Modernization*. Washington, D.C.: National Governors' Association.

Boyer, Robert. 1989. "New Directions in Management Practices and Work Organization: General Principles and National Trajectories." Paper presented at OECD conference, Technical Change as a Social Process: Society, Enterprise, and Individual, Helsinki, Dec. 11–13.

Boyer, Robert, and Pascal Petit. 1989. *Kaldor's Growth Theories: Past, Present, and Prospects.* Paris: CEPREMAP.

Boyett, Joseph H., A. T. Kearney, and Henry P. Conn. 1992. "What's Wrong with Total Quality Management?" *Tapping the World Journal* 3 (Spring): 10–14.

Bradley, Keith, and Stephen Hill. 1983. "After Japan: The Quality Circle Transplant and Productivity Efficiency." *British Journal of Industrial Relations* 21 (3):291–311.

Braham, James. 1991. "Bible or Babble." *Machine Design* 63 (14):34–39.

Brown, Clair, and Michael Reich. 1989. "When Does Cooperation Work? A Look at NUMMI and Van Nuys." *California Management Review* 31 (Summer): 26–44.

Brown, Clair, Michael Reich, and David Stern. 1991. "Skills and Security in Evolving Employment Systems: Observations from Case Studies." Typescript.

Brown, Clair, Michael Reich, David Stern, and Lloyd Ulman. 1993. "Conflict and Cooperation in Labor-Management Relations in Japan and the United States." In *Proceedings of the Forty-fifth Annual Industrial Relations Research Association*, 426–36. Madison, Wis.: Industrial Relations Research Association.

Brown-Humes, Christopher. 1992. "Volvo to Close Two Plants with the Loss of 4,500 Jobs." *Financial Times*, Nov. 5, 1.

Bullock, R. J., and Mark Tubbs. 1987. "The Case Meta-Analysis Method." *Research in Organizational Change and Development* 1:171–228.

Bureau of National Affairs (BNA). 1984. *Productivity Improvement Programs.* Personnel Policies Forum Survey no. 138. Washington, D.C.: BNA.

———. 1988. *Changing Pay Practices: New Developments in Employee Compensation.* BNA Special Report. Washington, D.C.: BNA. July.

———. 1991. *Non-Traditional Incentive Pay Programs.* Personnel Policies Forum Survey no. 148. Washington, D.C.: BNA. May.

Business Week. 1992. "Saturn: GM Finally Has a Real Winner." Aug. 17, 86–91.

Camlin, Scott P., Kathleen R. Scharf, and Richard E. Walton. 1993. "Union-Management Partnerships: A Context for Joint Decision-Making." Paper presented at conference, Innovations in Negotiation and Grievance Handling in the New Industrial Relations Order, Harvard University, May 20–21.

Campbell, Duncan. 1992. "Is the Single Firm Vanishing?" In *Is the Single Firm Vanishing? Inter-Enterprise Networks, Labour and Labour Institutions*, edited by Werner Sengenberger and Duncan Campbell, 1–7. Geneva: International Institute for Labour Studies.

Capelli, Peter. 1993. "What Employers Want in a Workforce* (*And What They Are Doing to Get It)." Paper presented at the annual national meetings of the Industrial Relations Research Association, Anaheim, Calif., Jan. 6.

Carnevale, Anthony. 1992. "What Training Means in an Election Year." *Training and Development* 46 (Oct.): 45–53.

Carnevale, Anthony, and Harold Goldstein. 1990. "Schooling and Training for Work in America: An Overview." In *New Developments in Worker Training: A Legacy for the 1990s*, edited by Louis A. Ferman, Michele Hoyman, Joel Cutcher-Gershenfeld, and Ernest J. Savoie, 25–54. Madison, Wis.: Industrial Relations Research Association.

Carre, Françoise. 1992. "Temporary Employment in the Eighties." In *New Policies for the Part-Time and Contingent Workforce*, edited by Virginia L. DuRivage, 45–88. Armonk, N.Y.: M. E. Sharpe.

Chandler, Alfred D., Jr. 1990. *Scale and Scope: The Dynamics of Industrial Capitalism*. Cambridge: Harvard University Press/Belknap Press.

———. 1992. "Organizational Capabilities and the Economic History of the Industrial Enterprise." *Journal of Economic Perspectives* (Summer): 79–100.

Cherry, Richard. 1982. "The Development of General Motors' Team-Based Plants." In *The Innovative Organization: Productivity Programs in Action*, edited by Robert Zager and Michael Rosow, 125–48. Elmsford, N.Y.: Pergamon Press.

Clark, Kim B., and Takahiro Fujimoto. 1991. *Product Development Performance: Strategy, Organization, and Management in the World Auto Industry*. Boston: Harvard Business School Press.

Cohen, Susan, and Gerald Ledford. 1991. "The Effectiveness of Self-Managing Teams: A Quasi-Experiment." CEO Publication No. G91-6. Center for Effective Organizations, School of Business Administration, University of Southern California. March.

Cole, Robert E. 1980. "Learning from the Japanese: Prospects and Pitfalls." *Management Review* 69 (Sept.): 22–42.

———. 1982. "Diffusion of Participatory Work Structures in Japan, Sweden, and the United States." In *Changes in Organizations: New Perspectives on Theory, Research, and Practice*, edited by Paul S. Goodman, 166–225. San Francisco: Jossey-Bass.

———. 1989. *Strategies for Learning: Small Group Activities in American, Japanese, and Swedish Industry*. Berkeley: University of California Press.

Commission on the Skills of the American Workforce. 1990. *America's Choice: High Skills or Low Wages!* Rochester, N.Y.: National Center on Education and the Economy.

———. 1991. *America's Choice: High Skills or Low Wages!* Vol. 2, *Supporting Materials*. Rochester, N.Y.: National Center on Education and the Economy.

Cooke, William N. 1990. *Labor-Management Cooperation: New Partnerships or Going in Circles?* Kalamazoo, Mich.: W. E. Upjohn Institute for Employment Research.

———. 1991. "Joint Labor-Management Decision Making: Choices, Outcomes, and Problems." *Workplace Topics* (Dec.): 48–84.

———. 1992. "Employee Participation, Group-Based Pay Incentives, and Company Performance: A Union-Nonunion Comparison." College of Urban, Labor, and Metropolitan Affairs, Wayne State University. Typescript.

Corcoran, Elizabeth. 1990. "Milliken & Co.: Managing the Quality of a Textile Revolution." *Scientific American*, April, 74–75.

Creticos, Peter, Steve Duscha, and Robert Sheets. 1990. "State-Financed, Customized Training Programs: A Comparative State Survey." Report submitted to the Office of Technology Assessment (OTA), U.S. Congress. Sept. 30.

Creticos, Peter, and Robert Sheets. 1990. *Evaluating State-Financed Workplace-Based Retraining Programs: A Report on the Feasibility of a Business Screening and Performance Outcome Evaluation System.* A joint study of the National Commission for Employment Policy and the National Governors' Association. Research Report No. 89-08. Washington, D.C.: National Commission for Employment Policy. May.

———. 1991. *Evaluating State-Financed Workplace-Based Retraining Programs: Case Studies of Retraining Projects.* A joint study of the National Commission for Employment Policy and the National Governors' Association. Washington, D.C.: National Commission for Employment Policy.

Crosby, Philip. 1979. *Quality Is Free.* New York: Mentor Books.

Crotty, James R., and Don Goldstein. 1993. "Do U.S. Financial Markets Allocate Credit Efficiently? The Case of Corporate Restructuring in the 1980s." In *Transforming the U.S. Financial System: Equity and Efficiency for the 21st Century,* edited by Bob Pollin, Gary Dymski, and Gerald Epstein. Washington, D.C.: Economic Policy Institute. In press.

Cutcher-Gershenfeld, Joel. 1991. "The Impact on Economic Performance of a Transformation in Workplace Relations." *Industrial and Labor Relations Review* 44 (2):241–60.

David, L. E., A. B. Cherns, and Associates. 1975. *The Quality of Working Life,* Vols. 1 and 2. New York: Free Press.

Delaney, John Thomas, David Lewin, and Casey Ichniowski. 1989. *Human Resource Policies and Practices in American Firms.* Report for the Bureau of Labor-Management Relations and Cooperative Programs (BLMR). BLMR no. 137. Washington, D.C.: Government Printing Office.

Deming, W. Edwards. 1984. *Out of the Crisis.* Cambridge: MIT Press.

Dertouzos, Michael, Richard Lester, and Robert Solow. 1988. *Made in America.* Cambridge: MIT Press.

Development Dimensions International. 1990. *Self-Directed Teams: A Study of Current Practice.* Development Dimensions International, Association for Quality and Participation, and *Industry Week.*

Drago, Robert. 1988. "Quality Circle Survival: An Exploratory Analysis." *Industrial Relations* 27 (Fall): 336–51.

Eaton, Adrienne E., and Paula B. Voos. 1992. "Union and Contemporary Innovations in Work Organization, Compensation, and Employee Participation." In *Unions and Economic Competitiveness,* edited by Lawrence Mishel and Paula B. Voos, 175–215. Armonk, N.Y.: M. E. Sharpe.

Edwards, Richard. 1993. *Rights at Work: Employment Relations in the Post-Union Era.* Washington, D.C.: Brookings Institution.

Ehrenberg, Ronald, ed. 1990. "Do Compensation Policies Matter?" *Industrial and Labor Relations Review* 43 (3) (special issue on compensation policies).

Eidt, Clarence. 1992. "Applying Quality to R&D Means 'Learn-as-You-Go.'" *Research-Technology Management* 35 (July–Aug.): 24–31.

Employee Benefits Research Institute (EBRI). 1990. *An Overview of Employee Benefits, 1990*. Washington, D.C.: EBRI.

Ernst and Young and the American Quality Foundation. 1991. *The International Quality Study: Top-Line Findings*. Cleveland: Ernst and Young and American Quality Foundation.

———. 1992. *The International Quality Study: Best Practices Report*. Cleveland: Ernst and Young and American Quality Foundation.

Fargher, John. 1992. "Managing Process Improvement at the Cherry Point Naval Aviation Depot." *National Productivity Review* 11:533–47.

Ferman, Louis A., Michele Hoyman, Joel Cutcher-Gershenfeld, and Ernest J. Savoie, eds. 1991. *Joint Training Programs: A Union-Management Approach to Preparing Workers for the Future*. Ithaca, N.Y.: ILR Press.

Fine, Charles. 1991. "Quality Improvement and Learning in Productive Systems." *Management Science* 32 (Oct.): 1301–15.

FitzRoy, Felix, and Kornelius Kraft. 1987. "Cooperation, Productivity, and Profit Sharing." *Quarterly Journal of Economics* 102 (Feb.): 23–35.

Florida, Richard, and Martin Kenney. 1991. "Transplanted Organizations: The Transfer of Japanese Industrial Organization to the U.S." *American Sociological Review* 56 (3):381–98.

Fraser, Douglas. 1992. *Restructuring the Workplace: A Union Perspective*. LERC Monograph Series, no. 11. Eugene: Labor Education and Research Center, University of Oregon.

Freeman, Richard B. 1991. "Employee Councils, Worker Participation, and Other Squishy Stuff." In *Proceedings of the Forty-Third Annual Meeting of the Industrial Relations Research Association*, 328–37. Madison, Wis.: Industrial Relations Research Association.

Freeman, Richard B., and James L. Medoff. 1984. *What Do Unions Do?* New York: Basic Books.

Freeman, Richard B., and Joel Rogers. 1993. "Who Speaks for Us? Employee Representation in a Non-Union Labor Market." In *Employee Representation Alternatives and Future Directions*, edited by Bruce Kaufman and Morris Kleiner, Madison, Wis.: Industrial Relations Research Association. In press.

Freund, William, and Eugene Epstein. 1984. *People and Productivity: New York Stock Exchange Guide to Financial Incentives and the Quality of Work Life*. Homewood, Ill.: Dow Jones-Irwin.

Frost, Carl. 1982. "The Scanlon Plan at Herman Miller, Inc.: Managing an Organization by Innovation." In *The Innovative Organization: Productivity Programs in Action*, edited by Robert Zager and Michael Rosow, 63–87. Elmsford, N.Y.: Pergamon Press.

Garvin, David. 1991. "How the Baldrige Award Really Works." *Harvard Business Review* 69 (Nov.–Dec.): 80.

Gerhart, Barry, George Milkovich, and Brian Murray. 1992. "Pay, Performance, and Participation." In *Research Frontiers in Industrial Relations and Human Resources*, 193–238. Madison, Wis.: Industrial Relations Research Association.

Gibbons, Robert, and Kevin Murphy. 1990. "Relative Performance Evaluation for Chief Executive Officers." *Industrial and Labor Relations Review* 43 (3):30S–51S.

Gilbert, James D. 1992. "TQM Flops—A Chance to Learn from the Mistakes of Others." *National Productivity Review* 11:491–99.

Golden, Lonnie, and Eileen Appelbaum. 1992. "What Was Driving the Boom in Temporary Employment?" *American Journal of Economics and Sociology* 51 (July): 473–93.

Gomez del Campo, Guillermo. 1993. "TQM Implementation in the U.S. and Japan: Lessons from Baldrige and Deming Winners." Master's thesis, Sloan School of Management, MIT.

Goodman, Paul. 1982. "The Rushton Quality of Work Life Experiments: Lessons to Be Learned." In *The Innovative Organization: Productivity Programs in Action*, edited by Robert Zager and Michael Rosow, 222–59. Elmsford, N.Y.: Pergamon Press.

Goodman, Paul, and Associates. 1979. *Assessing Organizational Change: The Rushton Quality of Work Experiment.* New York: Wiley.

Gowen, Charles, and Sara Rynes. 1991. "The Effects of Changes in Participation and Group Size on Gainsharing Success: A Case Study." *Journal of Organizational Behavior Management* 11:147–69.

Grabher, Gernot. 1991. "Rebuilding Cathedrals in the Desert: New Patterns of Cooperation between Large and Small Firms in the Coal, Iron, and Steel Complex of the German Ruhr Area." In *Regions Reconsidered: Economic Networks, Innovation and Local Development*, edited by E. M. Bergman et al., 59–75. London: Mansell.

Grant Thornton Accountants and Management Consultants. 1991. *Grant Thornton Survey of American Manufacturers: A National Study of Executives' Attitudes and Opinions towards Quality and Global Competition.* New York: Grant Thornton.

Guest, Robert. 1982a. "Tarrytown: Quality of Work Life at a General Motors Plant." In *The Innovative Organization: Productivity Programs in Action*, edited by Robert Zager and Michael Rosow, 88–108. Elmsford, N.Y.: Pergamon Press.

———. 1982b. "The Sharonville Story: Worker Involvement at a Ford Motor Company Plant." In *The Innovative Organization: Productivity Programs in Action*, edited by Robert Zager and Michael Rosow, 44–62. Elmsford, N.Y.: Pergamon Press.

Haavind, Robert. 1990. "IBM's Rochester Facility Strives for a Perfect 10." *Electronic Business* 16 (19):74–77.

Hahn, Jeffrey, and Kevin Smith. 1990. "Wrongful Discharge: The Search for a Legislative Compromise." *Employee Relations Law Journal* 15 (4):515–39.

Hammer, Michael. 1990. "Reengineering Work: Don't Automate, Obliterate." *Harvard Business Review* 68 (July–Aug.): 104–12.

Hammer, Michael, and James Champy. 1992. *Reengineering Work: A Manifesto for Business Revolution.* New York: Warner Books.

Hammer, Tove Helland. 1988. "New Developments in Profit Sharing, Gainsharing, and Employee Ownership." In *Productivity in Organizations: New Perspectives from Industrial and Organizational Psychology,* edited by John Campbell, Richard Campbell, and Associates, 328–66. San Francisco: Jossey-Bass.

Hancke, Bob. 1993. "The Volvo Plant in Uddevalla." Paper presented for the Harman Program in Technology, Public Policy, and Human Development, Center for Science and International Affairs, John F. Kennedy School of Government, Harvard University, April 29.

Harrison, Bennett. 1993. "Big Firms, Small Firms, Network Firms: Dualism and Development in the Age of Flexibility." Carnegie Mellon University. Typescript.

Havlovic, Stephen. 1991. "Quality of Work Life and Human Resource Outcomes." *Industrial Relations* 30 (Fall): 469–79.

Hayes, Robert H., and Steven C. Wheelwright. 1984. *Restoring Our Competitive Edge: Competing through Manufacturing.* New York: Wiley.

Helper, Susan. 1991. "How Much Has Really Changed between U.S. Automakers and Their Suppliers?" *Sloan Management Review* 32 (Summer): 15–28.

Helper, Susan, and David I. Levine. 1992. "Long-Term Supplier Relations and Product Market Structure." *Journal of Law, Economics, and Organization* 8 (Oct.): 561–81.

Hemp, Paul. 1992. "Preaching the Gospel: 'Reengineering' Is the Hottest Word in Consulting: But Is It Just Another Gimmick for Hire?" *Boston Globe,* June 30, 35.

Herzberg, Frederick. 1968. "One More Time: How Do You Motivate Employees?" *Harvard Business Review* 46 (Jan.–Feb.): 53–62.

Heskett, James L., W. Earl Sasser, Jr., and Christopher W. L. Hart. 1990. *Service Breakthroughs: Changing the Rules of the Game.* New York: Free Press.

Hill, Stephen. 1991. "Why Quality Circles Failed But Total Quality Management Might Succeed." *British Journal of Industrial Relations* 29 (4):541–68.

Hochner, Arthur, Cherlyn Granrose, Judith Goode, Elaine Simon, and Eileen Appelbaum. 1988. *Job-Saving Strategies: Worker Buyouts and QWL.* Kalamazoo, Mich.: W. E. Upjohn Institute for Employment Research.

Holley, June, and Roger Wilkens. n.d. *Creating Flexible Manufacturing Networks in North America: The Co-Evolution of Technology and Industrial Organization.* Athens, Ohio: Acenet.

Holusha, John. 1992. "Global Yardsticks Are Set to Measure 'Quality.'" *New York Times,* Dec. 23, D6.

Hopkins, Shirley A. 1989. "Have U.S. Financial Institutions Really Embraced Quality Control?" *National Productivity Review* 8:407–21.

Hyatt, Joshua. 1990. "Surviving on Chaos." *Inc.,* May, 60–71.

Ichniowski, Casey, Kathryn Shaw, and Giovanna Prennushi. 1993. "The Effects of Human Resource Management Practice on Productivity." Typescript. June.

Ishikawa, Kaoru. 1985. *Total Quality Control: The Japanese Way.* Englewood Cliffs, N.J.: Prentice Hall.

Japan Labor Bulletin. 1991. "Recent Debate over Just-in-Time System." Nov. 1., 37–41.

Jasper, Herbert. 1992. "Down the Quality Road." *Government Executive* 24 (April): 37–41.

Jones, Steven, Randy Powell, and Scott Roberts. 1990–91. "Comprehensive Measurement to Improve Assembly Line Work Group Effectiveness." *National Productivity Review* 10:45–55.

Juran, J. M., and Frank Gyrna. 1988. *Juran's Quality Control Handbook.* 4th ed. New York: McGraw-Hill.

Kahn, Lawrence, and Peter Sherer. 1990. "Contingent Pay and Managerial Performance." *Industrial and Labor Relations Review* 43 (3):107S–20S.

Kaldor, Nicholas. 1966. *Causes of the Slow Rate of Growth in the United Kingdom.* Cambridge, U.K.: Cambridge University Press.

———. 1972. "The Irrelevance of Equilibrium Economics." *Economic Journal* 82 (Dec.): 373–98.

Kane, Edward. 1991. "Implementing TQM at Dun & Bradstreet Software." *National Productivity Review* 10:405–16.

Katz, Harry. 1985. *Shifting Gears: Changing Labor Relations in the U.S. Auto Industry.* Cambridge: MIT Press.

———. 1988. "Policy Debates over Work Reorganization in North American Unions." In *New Technology and Industrial Relations,* edited by Richard Hyman and Wolfgang Streeck, 220–32. London: Basil Blackwell.

Katz, Harry, and Jeffrey Keefe. 1993. "Report on a Study of Training, Adjustment Policies, and the Restructuring of Work in Large Unionized Firms." Paper presented at the annual national meetings of the Industrial Relations Research Association, Anaheim, Calif., Jan. 6.

Katz, Harry, Thomas A. Kochan, and Kenneth Gobeille. 1983. "Industrial Relations Performance, Economic Performance, and Quality of Working Life Efforts." *Industrial and Labor Relations Review* 37 (1):3–17.

Katzell, Raymond, and Daniel Yankelovich. 1975. *Work Productivity and Job Satisfaction: An Evaluation of Policy-Related Research.* New York: Harcourt Brace.

Kaufman, Roger. 1992. "The Effects of IMPROSHARE on Productivity." *Industrial and Labor Relations Review* 45 (2): 311–22.

Keefe, Jeffrey, and Karen Boroff. 1994. "Telecommunications Labor Management Relations after Divestiture." In *Contemporary Collective Bargaining in the Private Sector,* edited by Paula Voos. Forthcoming. Madison, Wis.: Industrial Relations Research Association.

Keefe, Jeffrey, and Harry Katz. 1990. "Job Classifications and Plant Performance." *Industrial Relations* 1 (Spring): 111–18.

Kelley, Maryellen R. 1990. "New Process Technology, Job Design, and Work Organization: A Contingency Model." *American Sociological Review* 55 (April):191–208.

Klein, Janice. 1991. "A Reexamination of Autonomy in Light of New Manufacturing Practices." *Human Relations* 44 (1): 21–33.

———. 1993. "Teams." In *The American Edge: Leveraging Manufacturing's Hidden Assets,* edited by Janice Klein and Jeffrey Miller. New York: McGraw-Hill.

Klingel, Sally, and Ann Martin. 1988. *A Fighting Chance: New Strategies to Save Jobs and Reduce Costs.* Ithaca, N.Y.: ILR Press.

Knuth, Matthias. 1991. "Trade Union Strategy, Co-Determination and the Quality of Work in West Germany." Paper presented at the Twelfth Conference of the International Working Party on Labour Market Segmentation, Vaneze, Italy.

Kochan, Thomas, Harry Katz, and Robert McKersie. 1986. *The Transformation of American Industrial Relations.* New York: Basic; Ithaca: ILR Press, 1994.

Kochan, Thomas, Harry Katz, and Nancy Mower. 1984. *Worker Participation and American Unions: Threat or Opportunity?* Kalamazoo, Mich.: W. E. Upjohn Institute for Employment Research.

Kochan, Thomas, Robert McKersie, and John Chalykoff. 1986. "The Effects of Corporate Strategy and Workplace Innovations on Union Representation." *Industrial and Labor Relations Review* 39 (4):487–501.

Kochan, Thomas, and Paul Osterman. 1991. "Human Resource Development and Utilization: Is There Too Little in the U.S.?" MIT. Typescript.

Kochan, Thomas, and Michael Useem, eds. 1992. *Transforming Organizations.* New York: Oxford University Press.

Kopelman, Richard. 1985. "Job Redesign and Productivity: A Review of the Evidence." *National Productivity Review* 4:237–55.

Krass, Peter. 1991. "Managing without Managers—Self-Managed Teams Improve IT Productivity But Challenge CIO's Traditional Role." *Information Week*, Nov. 11, 44–49.

Krueger, Alan. 1991. "The Evolution of Unjust Dismissal Legislation in the United States." *Industrial and Labor Relations Review* 44 (4):644–60.

Lawler, Edward E., III, Gerald Ledford, and Susan A. Mohrman. 1989. *Employee Involvement in America: A Study of Contemporary Practice.* Houston: American Productivity and Quality Center.

Lawler, Edward E., III, and Susan A. Mohrman. 1987. "Quality Circles: After the Honeymoon." *Organizational Dynamics* 15 (Spring): 42–54.

Lawler, Edward E., III, Susan A. Mohrman, and Gerald Ledford. 1992. *Employee Involvement and TQM: Practice and Results in Fortune 5000 Companies.* San Francisco: Jossey-Bass.

Lazear, Edward. 1992. "Compensation, Productivity, and the New Economics of Personnel." In *Research Frontiers in Industrial Relations and Human Resources,* edited by David Lewin, Olivia Mitchell, and Peter Sherer, 341–80. Madison, Wis.: Industrial Relations Research Association.

Lazes, Peter, and Tony Costanza. 1984. "Xerox Cuts Costs without Layoffs through Union-Management Collaboration." Labor-Management Cooperation Brief no 1. Bureau of Labor-Management Relations and Cooperative Programs, U.S. Department of Labor. July.

Lazes, Peter, Leslie Rumpeltes, Ann Hoffner, Larry Pace, and Anthony Costanza. 1991. "Xerox and the ACTWU: Using Labor-Management Teams to Remain Competitive." *National Productivity Review* 10:339–49.

Lazonick, William. 1992. "Controlling the Market for Corporate Control: The Historical Significance of Managerial Capitalism." *Industrial and Corporate Change* 1 (3):445–88.

Leana, Carrie, and Gary Florkowski. 1992. "Employee Involvement Programs: Integrating Psychological Theory and Management Practice." *Research in Personnel and Human Resources Management* 10:233–70.

Ledford, Gerald, Edward E. Lawler III, and Susan A. Mohrman. 1988. "The Quality Circle and Its Variations." In *Productivity in Organizations*, edited by John Campbell, Richard Campbell, and Associates, 255–94. San Francisco: Jossey-Bass.

LeFauve, Richard G., and Arnoldo C. Hax. 1992. "Managerial and Technological Innovations at Saturn Corporation." *MIT Management* (Spring):8–19.

Leonard, Jonathan. 1990. "Executive Pay and Firm Performance." *Industrial and Labor Relations Review* 43 (3):13S–29S.

Lesieur, F. G., ed., 1958. *The Scanlon Plan: A Frontier in Labor-Management Cooperation.* Cambridge: MIT Press.

Levering, Robert, Milton Moskowitz, and Michael Katz. 1984. *The One Hundred Best Companies to Work for in America.* Reading, Mass.: Addison-Wesley.

Levine, David I. 1992. "Public Policy Implications of Imperfections in the Market for Worker Participation." *Economic and Industrial Democracy* 13 (May):183–206.

Levine, David I., and Laura D'Andrea Tyson. 1990. "Participation, Productivity, and the Firm's Environment." In *Paying for Productivity*, edited by Alan Blinder, 183–243. Washington, D.C.: Brookings Institution.

Lincoln, James, and Arne Kalleberg. 1990. *Culture, Control, and Commitment: A Study of Work Organization and Work Attitudes in the United States and Japan.* Cambridge: Cambridge University Press.

Locke, E. A., and D. M. Schweiger. 1979. "Participation in Decision Making: One More Look." *Research in Organizational Behavior* 1 (10):265–339.

Locke, Richard. 1992. "The Demise of the National Union in Italy: Lessons for Comparative Industrial Ratings Theory." *Industrial and Labor Relations Review* 45 (2): 229–49.

Luria, Dan. 1992. "Identifying High-Performance Work Organizations: Initial Observations." Industrial Technology Institute, Ann Arbor, Mich. Typescript.

Lynch, Lisa. 1989. "Private Sector Training and Its Impact on the Earnings of Young Workers." National Bureau of Economic Research (NBER) Working Paper no. 2872. Cambridge: NBER.

———. 1993. *A National Training Agenda: Lessons from Abroad.* Washington, D.C.: Economic Policy Institute.

Maccoby, Michael. 1992. "Transforming R&D Services at Bell Labs." *Research-Technology Management* 38 (Jan.–Feb.): 46–49.

MacDuffie, John Paul. 1991. "Beyond Mass Production: Flexible Production Systems and Manufacturing Performance in the World Auto Industry." Ph.D. diss., Sloan School of Management, MIT.

MacDuffie, John Paul, and John F. Krafcik. 1990. *Integrating Technology and Hu-*

man *Resources for High Performance Manufacturing: Evidence from the International Auto Industry.* Cambridge: International Motor Vehicle Program, MIT.

McKinsey Global Institute. 1992. *Service Sector Productivity.* Washington, D.C.: McKinsey and Company.

McLagan, Patricia. 1991. "The Dark Side of Quality." *Training* 28 (Nov.): 31–33.

Macy, Barry A. 1982. "The Bolivar Quality of Work Life Program: Success or Failure?" In *The Innovative Organization: Productivity Programs in Action,* edited by Robert Zager and Michael Rosow, 184–221. Elmsford, N.Y.: Pergamon Press.

Main, Jeremy. 1990. "How to Win the Baldrige Award." *Fortune,* April 23, 119–28.

————. 1991. "Is the Baldrige Overblown?" *Fortune,* July 1, 63–66.

Manji, James F. 1992. "Manufacturing Excellence Awards: Our Six Winners." *Controls and Systems* 39 (Jan.): 28–44.

Marsh, Robert M. 1992. "The Difference between Participation and Power in Japanese Factories." *Industrial and Labor Relations Review* 45 (2):250–57.

Marshall, Ray, and Marc Tucker. 1992. "The Demand for Excellence: Can and Will Employers and Labor Lead the Way?" In *Thinking for a Living: Work, Skills, and the Future of the American Economy,* edited by Ray Marshall and Marc Tucker, 91–108. New York: Basic Books.

Martin, James. 1990. *Two Tier Compensation Structures: Their Impact on Unions, Employers, and Employees.* Kalamazoo, Mich.: W. E. Upjohn Institute for Employment Research.

Mathews, Jay. 1992. "The Cost of Quality: Faced with Hard Times, Business Soars on Total Quality Management." *Newsweek,* Sept. 7, 48–49.

Matteis, Richard. 1979. "The New Back Office Focuses on Customer Service." *Harvard Business Review* 57 (March–April): 146–59.

Meng, G. Jonathan. 1992. "Using Job Descriptions, Performance, and Pay Innovations to Support Quality: A Paper Company's Experience." *National Productivity Review* 11:247–55.

Michl, T. 1985. "International Comparisons of Productivity Growth: Verdoorn's Law Revisited." *Journal of Post Keynesian Economics* 7 (Summer): 474–92.

Midas, Michael, and Thomas Devine. 1991. "A Look at Continuous Improvement at Northwest Airlines." *National Productivity Review* 10:379–93.

Milakovich, Michael. 1991. "Total Quality Management in the Public Sector." *National Productivity Review* 10:195–213.

Milkman, Ruth. 1991. *Japan's California Factories: Labor Relations and Economic Globalization.* Los Angeles: Institute of Industrial Relations, University of California.

Milkovich, George, and Alexandra Wignor, eds. 1991. *Pay for Performance: Evaluating Performance Appraisal and Merit Pay.* Washington, D.C.: National Academy Press.

Miller, Cyndee. 1992. "Baldrige Award under Fire; Overhaul Pledged." *Marketing News,* May 11, 1–3.

Miller, Katherine, and Peter Monge. 1986. "Participation, Satisfaction, and Productivity: A Meta-Analytic Review." *Academy of Management Journal* 29:727–53.

Mishel, Lawrence, and Jared Bernstein. 1993. *Declining Wages for High School and College Graduates: Pay and Benefits Trends by Education, Gender, Occupation, and State, 1979–1991.* Washington, D.C.: Economic Policy Institute.

Mishel, Lawrence, and Paula Voos, eds. 1992. *Unions and Economic Competitiveness.* Armonk, N.Y.: M. E. Sharpe.

Mitchell, Daniel. 1991. "Pay Systems and Labor Market Flexibility in the U.S.A." *Work Flexibility Review* 1 (Feb.): 61–96.

Mitchell, Daniel, David Lewin, and Edward Lawler III. 1990. "Alternative Pay Systems, Firm Performance, and Productivity." In *Paying for Productivity*, edited by Alan Blinder, 15–94. Washington, D.C.: Brookings Institution.

Mitchell, Daniel, and Mahmood Zaidi, eds. 1990. "A Symposium: The Economics of Human Resource Management." *Industrial Relations* 29 (2) (special issue on human resource management).

Montgomery, Leslie Lynn. 1986. "Improving Productivity and Quality of Work Life: An Impact Study of Work Redesign at INFOCORP." Ph.D. diss., Harvard University School of Education.

Murray, Cathy, and Nicki Mertes. 1989. "Swimming Upstream—Breakthrough Productivity Gains at Seattle First National Bank." *National Productivity Review* 8:261–71.

Nagel, Roger, and Rick Dove. 1991. *21st Century Manufacturing Enterprise Strategy: An Industry-Led View*, Vols. 1 and 2. Bethlehem, Penn.: Iacocca Institute, Lehigh University.

Naschold, Frieder. 1993. *Evaluation Report Commissioned by the Board of LOM Programme.* Berlin: Wissenschaftszentrum Berlin.

National Education Association (NEA). 1988. *Employee Participation Programs: Considerations for the School Site.* Washington, D.C.: NEA.

———. 1992. *Negotiating Change: Education Reform and Collective Bargaining.* Washington, D.C.: NEA.

New York Stock Exchange Office of Economic Research. 1982. *People and Productivity: A Challenge to Corporate America.* New York: New York Stock Exchange Office of Economic Research.

New York Times. 1993. "U.A.W. Keeps Saturn Pact." Jan. 18, D3.

O'Reilly, Charles. 1989. "Corporations, Culture, and Commitment: Motivation and Social Control in Organizations." *California Management Review* 31 (Summer): 9–26.

Osterman, Paul. 1988. *Employment Futures: Reorganization, Dislocation, and Public Policy.* New York and Oxford: Oxford University Press.

———. 1991. "The Productivity Consequences of Alternative Internal Labor Market Arrangements." Paper prepared for the Swedish Delegation on Productivity, Sloan School of Management, MIT. Feb.

———. 1993. "How Common Is Workplace Transformation and How Can We Explain Who Adopts It? Results from a National Survey." Paper presented at the meetings of the Allied Social Science Association, Anaheim, Calif., Jan.

Parker, Mike, and Jane Slaughter. 1988. *Choosing Sides: Unions and the Team Concept.* Boston: South End Press.

Pearlstein, Steven. 1992. "Job Losses Are Likely to Continue; Business Upheaval Hobbles Recovery." *Washington Post*, Nov. 6, A1.

Peterfreund, Stanley, 1982. " 'Face-to-Face' at Pacific Northwest Bell." In *The Innovative Organization: Productivity Programs in Action*, edited by Robert Zager and Michael Rosow, 21–43. Elmsford, N.Y.: Pergamon Press.

Phillips, Steven Lindsay. 1991. "Total Quality Management, Self-Managing Teams, and Organizational Change: A Longitudinal Field Study in an Aerospace Manufacturing Company." Ph.D. diss., University of Southern California.

Piore, Michael J. 1990. "Work, Labour and Action: Work Experience in a System of Flexible Production." In *Industrial Districts and Inter-Firm Co-Operation in Italy*, edited by F. Pyke, G. Becattini, and W. Sengenberger, 52–74. Geneva: International Labour Office.

Piore, Michael J., and Charles Sabel. 1984. *The Second Industrial Divide*. New York: Basic Books.

Porter, Michael. 1992. "Capital Choices: Changing the Way America Invests in Industry." Research report presented to the Council on Competitiveness and co-sponsored by the Harvard Business School.

Proctor, B. H. 1986. "A Sociotechnical Work Design System at Digital Enfield: Utilizing Untapped Resources." *National Productivity Review* 5:262–70.

Pyke, Frank. 1992. *Industrial Development through Small-Firm Cooperation: Theory and Practice*. Geneva: International Labour Office.

Rayner, Bruce. 1992. "Trial-by-Fire Transformation: An Interview with Globe Metallurgical's Arden C. Sims." *Harvard Business Review* 70 (May–June): 116–29.

Richardson, Charley. 1992. "Progress for Whom? New Technology, Unions, and Collective Bargaining." In *Software and Hardhats: Technology and Workers in the Twenty-first Century*, prepared by the Industrial Union Department, AFL-CIO, 151–74. Washington, D.C.: Labor Policy Institute.

Roach, Stephen. 1991. "Services under Siege—The Restructuring Imperative." *Harvard Business Review* 69 (Sept.–Oct.): 82–91.

Rogers, Joel, and Barbara Wootton. 1992. "Works Councils in the United States: Could We Get There from Here?" Typescript.

Roose, Diana. 1992. *High Performance Office Work: Improving Jobs and Productivity. An Overview with Case Studies of Clerical Job Redesign*. Cleveland: 9 to 5 Working Women Education Fund.

Ross, H. Terrance, and Marion M. Ormsby. 1990. "Teamwork Breeds Quality at Hearing Technology, Inc." *National Productivity Review* 9:321–27.

Rothstein, Richard. 1993. *Setting the Standard: International Labor Rights and U.S. Trade Policy*. Washington, D.C.: Economic Policy Institute.

Rubinstein, Saul, Michael Bennett, and Thomas Kochan. 1993. "The Saturn Partnership: Co-Management and the Reinvention of the Local Union." In *Employee Representation: Alternatives and Future Directions*, edited by Bruce Kaufman and Morris Kleiner, Madison, Wisc.: Industrial Relations Research Association. In press.

Rutigliano, Anthony. 1985. "Steelcase: Nice Guys Finish First." *Management Review* 74 (Nov.): 46–51.

Sabel, Charles F. 1992. "Studied Trust: Building New Forms of Co-operation in a Volatile Economy." In *Industrial Districts and Local Economic Regeneration*, edited by Frank Pyke and Werner Sengenberger, 215–50. Geneva: International Institute for Labour Studies, International Labour Organisation.

Schindler, Keith. 1992. "U.S. Admits Waste in Its Contracts." *New York Times*, Dec. 2, A1.

Schlesinger, Leonard, and James Heskett. 1991a. "Breaking the Cycle of Failure in Services." *Sloan Management Review* 32 (Spring): 17–28.

———. 1991b. "The Service-Driven Company." *Harvard Business Review* 69 (Sept.–Oct.): 73–81.

———. 1991c. "Enfranchisement of Service Workers." *California Management Review* 33 (Summer): 83–100.

Schuster, Michael. "The Scanlon Plan: A Longitudinal Analysis." 1984. *Journal of Applied Behavioral Science* 20 (1):23–28.

Seashore, Stanley. 1981. "Quality of Working Life Perspective. The Michigan Quality of Work Program: Issues of Measurement, Assessment, and Outcome Evaluation. In *Perspectives on Organization Design and Behavior*, edited by Andrew Van de Ven and William Joyce, 89–134. New York: Wiley.

Sengenberger, Werner. 1990. "The Role of Labour Standards in Industrial Restructuring: Participation, Protection, and Promotion." Discussion Paper No. 19. International Institute for Labour Studies, Geneva.

Sengenberger, Werner, and Frank Pyke. 1992. "Industrial Districts and Local Economic Regeneration: Research and Policy Issues." In *Industrial Districts and Local Economic Regeneration*, edited by Frank Pyke and Werner Sengenberger, 3–29. Geneva: International Institute for Labour Studies.

Service Employees' International Union (SEIU). 1992. "Creating Conditions for Excellence in the Public Sector." Typescript.

Seward, Eve. 1992. "Quality in R&D: It All Began with a Customer's Request." *Research-Technology Management* 35 (Sept.–Oct.): 28–34.

Sheridan, John. 1990. "America's Best Plants: IW Salutes 12 Facilities That Have Achieved True Manufacturing Excellence." *Industry Week*, Oct. 15, 27–64.

Shipper, Frank, and Charles Manz. 1992. "Employee Self-Management without Formally Designated Teams: An Alternative Road to Empowerment." *Organizational Dynamics* 20 (Winter): 48–61.

Shuster, Jay, and Patricia Zingheim. 1992. *The New Pay: Linking Employee and Organizational Performance*. Toronto: Maxwell Macmillan Canada.

Simmons, John, and William Mares. 1983. *Working Together*. New York: Knopf.

Smith, Michael. 1986. "Employee Involvement Finds Dramatic Turnaround at Ford's Louisville Assembly Plant." Labor-Management Cooperation Brief no. 9. Bureau of Labor-Management Relations and Cooperative Programs, U.S. Department of Labor. Nov.

Smith, Stephen. 1991. "On the Economic Rationale for Codetermination Law." *Journal of Economic Behavior and Organization* 16 (Dec.): 261–81.

Sonnenstuhl, William J., and Harrision M. Trice. 1990. *Strategies for Employee Assistance Programs: The Crucial Balance*. Ithaca, N.Y.: ILR Press.

Sorge, Arndt, and Wolfgang Streeck. 1987. "Industrial Relations and Technical Change: The Case for an Extended Perspective." Research Unit Labour Market and Employment (IIM) Discussion Paper IIM/LMP 87-1. Wissenschaftszentrum Berlin. March.

Soskice, David. 1991. "Institutional Infrastructure for International Competitiveness: A Comparative Analysis of the U.K. and Germany." In *Economics for the New Europe*, edited by Anthony Atkinson and Renato Brunetta, 45–66. Houndsmills, Basingstoke, Hampshire: Macmillan.

Starr, Paul. 1987. *The Limits of Privatization*. Washington, D.C.: Economic Policy Institute.

Stovicek, Don. 1991. "Manufacturing Excellence Awards: The Five Winners." *Automation* 38 (Jan.): 18–28.

Strauss, George, and Tove Hammer. 1987. *Worker Participation in the United States*. Geneva: International Labour Organisation.

Streeck, Wolfgang. 1991. "On the Institutional Conditions of Diversified Quality Production." In *Beyond Keynesianism: The Socio-Economics of Production and Full Employment*, edited by Egon Matzner and Wolfgang Streeck, 21–61. Brookfield, Vt.: Edward Elgar Publishing.

Teece, David J. 1993. "The Dynamics of Industrial Capitalism: Perspectives on Alfred Chandler's Scale and Scope." *Journal of Economic Literature* 31 (March): 199–225.

Templin, Neal. 1992. "A Decisive Response to Crisis Brought Ford Enhanced Productivity." *Wall Street Journal*, Dec. 15, A1.

Tennessee Valley Authority (TVA). 1976. *The Quality of Worklife Experiment*, Vol. 1, TVA.

Teresko, John, et al. 1991. "IW's Second Annual Salute." *Industry Week*, Oct. 21, 27–60.

Thelen, Kathleen. 1991. *Union of Parts: Labor Politics in Postwar Germany*. Ithaca, N.Y.: Cornell University Press.

Thompson, Philip. 1982. "Quality Circles at Martin Marietta Corporation, Denver Aerospace/Michoud Division." In *The Innovative Organization: Productivity Programs in Action*, edited by Robert Zager and Michael Rosow, 3–19. Elmsford, N.Y.: Pergamon Press.

Tilly, Chris. 1992. "Short Hours, Short Shrift: The Causes and Consequences of Part-Time Employment." In *New Policies for the Part-Time and Contingent Workforce*, edited by Virginia L. DuRivage, 15–44. Armonk, N.Y.: M. E. Sharpe.

Tomkins, Jonathan. 1988. "Legislating the Employment Relationship: Montana's Wrongful-Discharge Law." *Employee Relations Law Journal* 14 (3):387–98.

Towers Perrin. 1992. *Workforce 2000 Today: A Bottom-Line Concern*. Towers Perrin.

Trigilia, Carlo. 1990. "Work and Politics in the Third Italy's Industrial Districts." In *Industrial Districts and Inter-firm Co-operation in Italy*, edited by F. Pyke, G. Becattini, and W. Sengenberger, 160–84. International Institute for Labour Studies. Geneva: International Labour Organisation.

Trist, Eric. 1981. "The Sociotechnical Perspective: The Evolution of Sociotechnical Systems as a Conceptual Framework and as an Action Research Program." In *Perspectives on Organization Design and Behavior*, edited by Andrew Van de Ven and William Joyce, 19–75. New York: Wiley.

Trist, E., and K. W. Bamforth. 1951. "Some Social and Psychological Consequences of the Long Wall Method of Coal-Getting." *Human Relations* 4 (1):3–38.

Turner, Lowell. 1991. *Democracy at Work: Changing World Markets and the Future of Labor Unions*. Ithaca, N.Y.: Cornell University Press.

Turner, Lowell, and Peter Auer. 1992. "The Political Economy of New Work Organization: Different Roads, Different Outcomes." Research Area Labour Market and Employment discussion paper. Wissenschaftszentrum Berlin. June.

U.S. Congress. Office of Technology Assessment (OTA). 1987. *International Competition in Services*. Publication no. OTA-ITE-328. Washington, D.C.: Government Printing Office.

———. 1993. *Pulling Together for Productivity: A Union-Management Experiment at U.S. West*. Washington, D.C.: Government Printing Office. September.

U.S. Department of Commerce. Technology Administration. National Institute of Standards and Technology (NIST). 1992. *Malcolm Baldrige National Quality Award, 1992 Award Criteria*. Gaithersburg, Md.: NIST.

U.S. Department of Labor. Bureau of Labor-Management Relations and Cooperative Programs. 1985. *Quality of Work Life: AT&T and CWA Examine Process after Three Years*. Washington, D.C.: Government Printing Office.

U.S. General Accounting Office (GAO). 1987. *Survey of Corporate Employee Involvement Efforts*. Washington, D.C.: GAO.

———. 1990. *Quality Management: Scoping Study*. Washington, D.C.: GAO.

———. 1991a. *Management Practices: U.S. Companies Improve Performance through Quality Efforts*. Publication no. NSIAD-91-190. Washington, D.C.: GAO.

———. 1991b. *Continuous Improvement: The Quality Challenge*. Washington, D.C.: GAO.

Victor, Kirk. 1993. "In Round One, a Win for Labor." *National Journal*, Jan. 16, 161.

Waggoner, John. 1992. "AT&T Card Aimed High from Start." *USA Today*, Oct. 15, B-1.

Wall, Toby, Nigel Kemp, Paul Jackson, and Chris Clegg. 1986. "Outcomes of Autonomous Work Groups: A Long-Term Field Experiment." *Academy of Management Journal* 29:280–304.

Walters, Roy W. 1982. "The Citibank Project: Improving Productivity through Work Redesign." In *The Innovative Organization: Productivity Programs in Action*, edited by Robert Zager and Michael Rosow, 109–24. Elmsford, N.Y.: Pergamon Press.

Walton, Mary. 1986. *The Deming Management Method*. New York: Perigree Books, Putnam Publishing Group.

Walton, Richard. 1982. "The Topeka Work System: Optimistic Visions, Pessimistic

Hypotheses, and Reality." In *The Innovative Organization: Productivity Programs in Action*, edited by Robert Zager and Michael Rosow, 260–87. Elmsford, N.Y.: Pergamon Press.

Washington Post. 1992. "Cooperation Worth Copying? In N.Y., Xerox and Its Union Team to Keep U.S. Jobs from Moving to Mexico." Dec. 13, H-1.

Weitzman, L. Martin, and Douglas L. Kruse. 1990. "Profit-Sharing and Productivity." In *Paying for Productivity: A Look at the Evidence*, edited by Alan Blinder, 95–140. Washington, D.C.: Brookings Institution.

Welch, James. 1992. "Service Quality Measurement at American Express Travelers' Cheque Group." *National Productivity Review* 11:463–71.

Wever, Kirsten R. 1989. "Toward a Structural Account of Union Participation in Management: The Case of Western Airlines." *Industrial and Labor Relations Review* 42 (4):600–609.

Wever, Kirsten S., and Christopher S. Allen. 1992. "Is Germany a Model for Managers?" *Harvard Business Review* 70 (Sept.–Oct.): 36–43.

Wever, Kirsten S., Peter Berg, and Thomas Kochan. 1993. *Skill Training in the U.S. and Germany: The Importance of Participation*. Washington, D.C.: Economic Policy Institute.

Whitten, Shirley. 1989. "Award-Winning Total Quality at the Naval Publications and Forms Center." *National Productivity Review* 8:273–86.

Williams, Karel, Colin Haslam, John Williams, Tony Cutler, Andy Adcroft, and Sukhdev Johal. 1992. "Against Lean Production," *Economy and Society* 21 (Aug.): 321–54.

Womack, James P., Daniel T. Jones, and Daniel Roos. 1990. *The Machine That Changed the World*. New York: Rawson Associates.

Wyatt Data Services, Cole Surveys. 1991. *Restructuring—Cure or Cosmetic Surgery. Results of Corporate Change in the '80s with Rx's for the '90s*. Boston: Wyatt.

Zager, Robert, and Michael Rosow, eds. 1982. *The Innovative Organization: Productivity Programs in Action*. Elmsford, N.Y.: Pergamon Press.

Zimmerman, Charles, and John W. Enell. 1988. "Service Industries." In *Juran's Quality Control Handbook*, edited by J. M. Juran and Frank Gryna, 331–72. 4th ed. New York: McGraw-Hill.

Zipkin, Paul H. 1991. "Does Manufacturing Need a JIT Revolution?" *Harvard Business Review* 69 (Jan.–Feb.): 40–50.

Zuboff, Shoshana. 1988. *In the Age of the Smart Machine: The Future of Work and Power*. New York: Basic Books.

INDEX

ABOUT THE AUTHORS

Eileen Appelbaum is the associate research director of the Economic Policy Institute. She is the author of numerous articles and books on labor markets, including *Back to Work* (1981), an empirical analysis of the experiences of mature women returning to work; *Job Saving Strategies: Worker Ownership and QWL* (1988), a co-authored work that examines the effects of employee participation on outcomes for workers and on firm performance; and *Labor Market Adjustments to Structural Change and Technological Progress* (1990), a co-edited volume that examines adjustment processes in the United States and other developed economies. She is on leave as professor of economics at Temple University and has been a guest research fellow at the Wissenschaftszentrum Berlin. She received her Ph.D. in economics from the University of Pennsylvania.

Rosemary Batt is a doctoral candidate in labor relations and human resource policy at the Sloan School at MIT. She is co-author of "International Human Resource Studies: A Framework for Future Research," with Thomas Kochan and Lee Dyer, in *Research Frontiers in Industrial Relations and Human Resource Management* (1992); and the Economic Policy Institute report *A National Policy for Workplace Training* (1993) with Paul Osterman. She is completing dissertation research on work reorganization and employment policy in the telecommunications industry.

The Economic Policy Institute was founded in 1986 to widen the debate about policies to achieve healthy economic growth, prosperity, and opportunity in the difficult new era America has entered.

Today, America's economy is threatened by stagnant growth and increasing inequality. Expanding global competition, changes in the nature of work, and rapid technological advances are altering economic reality. Yet many of our policies, attitudes, and institutions are based on assumptions that no longer reflect real world conditions.

Central to the Economic Policy Institute's search for solutions is the exploration of the economics of teamwork—economic policies that encourage every segment of the American economy (business, labor, government, universities, voluntary organizations, etc.) to work cooperatively to raise productivity and living standards for all Americans. Such an undertaking involves a challenge to conventional views of market behavior and a revival of a cooperative relationship between the public and private sectors.

With the support of leaders from labor, business, and the foundation world, the Institute has sponsored research and public discussion of a wide variety of topics: trade and fiscal policies; trends in wages, incomes, and prices; the causes of the productivity slowdown; labor market problems; U.S. and Third World debt; rural and urban policies; inflation; state-level economic development strategies; comparative international economic performance; and studies of the overall health of the U.S. manufacturing sector and of specific key industries.

The Institute works with a growing network of innovative economists and other social science researchers in universities and research centers all over the country who are willing to go beyond the conventional wisdom in considering strategies for public policy.

Founding scholars of the Institute include: Jeff Faux, EPI President; Lester Thurow, Sloan School of Management, MIT; Ray Marshall, former U.S. Secretary of Labor, Professor at the LBJ School of Public Affairs, University of Texas; Barry Bluestone, University of Massachusetts–Boston; Robert Reich, U.S. Secretary of Labor; Robert Kuttner, author; editor, *The American Prospect*, columnist, *Business Week*; and Washington Post Writers Group.

For additional information about the Institute, contact EPI at 1730 Rhode Island Ave., NW, Suite 200 / Washington, D.C. 20036 / (202) 775-8810.